# Foucault's Seminars on Antiquity

Classical Receptions in Twentieth-Century Writings

**Series Editor: Laura Jansen**

Each book in this ground-breaking new series considers the influence of antiquity on a single writer from the twentieth century. From Woolf to Walcott and Fellini to Foucault, the modalities and texture of this modern encounter with antiquity are explored in the works of authors recognized for their global impact on modern fiction, poetry, art, philosophy, and socio-politics.

A distinctive feature of twentieth-century writing is the tendency to break with tradition and embrace the new sensibilities of the time. Yet the period continues to maintain a fluid dialogue with the Greco-Roman past, drawing on its rich cultural legacy and thought, even within the most radical movements that ostentatiously questioned and rejected that past. Classical Receptions in Twentieth-Century Writing approaches this dialogue from two interrelated perspectives: it asks how modern authors' appeal to the classical past opens up new readings of their oeuvres and contexts, and it considers how this process in turn renders new insights into the classical world. This two-way perspective offers dynamic and interdisciplinary discussions for readers of Classics and modern literary tradition.

Also new in this series:
*Fellini's Eternal Rome*, Alessandro Carrera
*James Joyce and Classical Modernism*, Leah Culligan Flack
*Tony Harrison: Poet of Radical Classicism*, Edith Hall
*Virginia Woolf's Greek Tragedy*, Nancy Worman

**Editorial Board**
Prof. Richard Armstrong (University of Houston)
Prof. Francisco Barrenechea (University of Maryland)
Prof. Shane Butler (Johns Hopkins University)
Prof. Paul A. Cartledge (University of Cambridge)
Prof. Moira Fradinger (Yale University)
Prof. Francisco García Jurado (Universidad Complutense de Madrid)
Prof. Barbara Goff (University of Reading)
Prof. Simon Goldhill (University of Cambridge)
Dr. Constanze Güthenke (University of Oxford)
Prof. Edith Hall (King's College London)
Prof. Judith Hallett (University of Maryland)
Dr. George Kazantzidis (University of Patras)
Prof. Andrew Laird (Brown University)
Prof. Vassilis Lambropoulos (University of Michigan)
Prof. Charles Martindale (University of Bristol/University of York)
Dr. Pantelis Michelakis (University of Bristol)
Prof. Neville Morley (University of Exeter)
Prof. James Porter (University of California, Berkeley)
Prof. Phiroze Vasunia (University College London)

# Foucault's Seminars on Antiquity

*Learning to Speak the Truth*

Paul Allen Miller

BLOOMSBURY ACADEMIC
LONDON • NEW YORK • OXFORD • NEW DELHI • SYDNEY

BLOOMSBURY ACADEMIC
Bloomsbury Publishing Plc
50 Bedford Square, London, WC1B 3DP, UK
1385 Broadway, New York, NY 10018, USA
29 Earlsfort Terrace, Dublin 2, Ireland

BLOOMSBURY, BLOOMSBURY ACADEMIC and the Diana logo are trademarks of
Bloomsbury Publishing Plc

First published in Great Britain 2022
This paperback edition published 2023

Copyright © Paul Allen Miller, 2022

Paul Allen Miller has asserted his right under the Copyright, Designs and
Patents Act, 1988, to be identified as Author of this work.

For legal purposes the Acknowledgments on pp. x–xi constitute an extension
of this copyright page.

Cover design: Terry Woodley
Cover image © Jean-Paul Sartre and Michel Foucault at a demonstration in Paris, France, in
1969. (Photo by GERARD-AIME / Gamma-Rapho via Getty Images)

All rights reserved. No part of this publication may be reproduced or transmitted
in any form or by any means, electronic or mechanical, including photocopying,
recording, or any information storage or retrieval system, without prior
permission in writing from the publishers.

Bloomsbury Publishing Plc does not have any control over, or responsibility for,
any third-party websites referred to or in this book. All internet addresses given in
this book were correct at the time of going to press. The author and publisher
regret any inconvenience caused if addresses have changed or sites have
ceased to exist, but can accept no responsibility for any such changes.

A catalogue record for this book is available from the British Library.

Library of Congress Cataloging-in-Publication Data

Names: Miller, Paul Allen, 1959– author.
Title: Foucault's seminars on antiquity : learning to speak the truth / Paul Allen Miller.
Other titles: Classical receptions in twentieth-century writing.
Description: New York : Bloomsbury Academic, 2021. | Series: Classical receptions in
twentieth-century writing | Includes bibliographical references and index.
Identifiers: LCCN 2021018868 (print) | LCCN 2021018869 (ebook) |
ISBN 9781474278669 (hardback) | ISBN 9781474278683 (ebook) |
ISBN 9781474278676 (epub)
Subjects: LCSH: Foucault, Michel, 1926–1984. | Philosophy, Ancient.
Classification: LCC B2430.F724 M5543 2021  (print) | LCC B2430.F724 (ebook) |
DDC 180—dc23
LC record available at https://lccn.loc.gov/2021018868
LC ebook record available at https://lccn.loc.gov/2021018869

ISBN: HB:    978-1-4742-7866-9
       PB:    978-1-3502-5259-2
       ePDF:  978-1-4742-7868-3
       eBook: 978-1-4742-7867-6

Series: Classical Receptions in Twentieth-Century Writing

Typeset by RefineCatch Limited, Bungay, Suffolk

To find out more about our authors and books visit www.bloomsbury.com
and sign up for our newsletters

*To Chuck and David, that was a lot of fun, wasn't it?*

# Contents

| | | |
|---|---|---|
| Acknowledgments | | viii |
| Series Editor's Preface | | x |
| Introduction | | 1 |
| 1 | The Government of the Living: Acts of Truth from *Oedipus* to the Primitive Church | 17 |
| 2 | Subjectivity and Truth: From the Interpretation of Dreams to the Philosophic Life | 51 |
| 3 | Hermeneutics of the Subject: Spirituality, *Parrhēsia*, and Truth | 83 |
| 4 | The Government of the Self and Others: Truth-Telling and the Real of Philosophy in Plato's *Seventh Letter* and Beyond | 123 |
| 5 | The Courage of Truth: Philosophical Life in the Face of Death | 155 |
| Notes | | 189 |
| References | | 197 |
| Index | | 213 |

# Acknowledgments

This book has many beginnings. One of its earliest can be found in a 1992 conference I organized with Charles Platter and David Larmour at Texas Tech University on Foucault's *History of Sexuality*. Thanks are owed first to Chuck and David as good friends and peerless collaborators. Texas Tech University was very supportive as was the University of Georgia, where Chuck was domiciled. Wonderful colleagues from across the country like Amy Richlin, Page Dubois, David Halperin, Jeff Carnes, Nigel Nicholson, and Ellen Greene helped make it a success. From this conference came our book, *Rethinking Sexuality: Foucault and Classical Antiquity* (1998). A few years after the conference, I had a chance meeting with the late Wolfgang Haase at Boston University, which led to a plenary address at a meeting in Tübingen of the Institute for the Study of the Classical Tradition on "The Classical Roots of Poststructuralism" and a later publication in his journal. There followed an NEH grant in 2004 that allowed me to spend time in Paris where the records of Foucault's lectures were deposited at the Institut Mémoires de l'édition contemporaine (since relocated to Normandy). There, I first discovered his late lectures, which had only just begun to be published. The grant also allowed me to write and publish *Postmodern Spiritual Practices* (2007), which led to an invitation from Miriam Leonard to contribute *Diotima at the Barricades* (2016) to a new series edited by her, Tim Whitmarsh, and Brooke Holmes at Oxford, Classics in Theory. So, when Laura Jansen then wrote and asked if I would like to write something on Cixous for her new series, Classical Receptions in Twentieth-Century Writing, intimidated by the prospect of tackling Cixous's more than seventy published books, I countered with Foucault's late lectures, *et voilà*.

Along the way, I have incurred too many debts to catalog in full. But I would be remiss if I did not thank Jill Frank with whom I have had a wonderful and illuminating dialogue on Plato for the last twenty years. She read and offered comments on Chapter 3. Charles Stocking, who I first met as the world's best postdoc, has been a valued interlocutor for many years. Charles read and offered comments on the Introduction and Chapter 1. Richard Armstrong and Alexandra Lianeri invited me to present in slightly altered form the contents of the Introduction at their virtual Translation and Classical Reception Studies Workshop, October 2020. Pierre Zoberman, who I first met many years ago in Tübingen, has hosted me more times than I can count in Paris, found me apartments, and generally made it possible and pleasant for me to pursue my research while in France. I also owe a debt to the University of South Carolina which generously provided me the sabbatical necessary to complete work on my manuscript. Lastly, thanks are owed to my reader, editors, and the entire superb team at Bloomsbury.

# Series Editor's Preface

The present volume marks the fifth innovative contribution to the series *Classical Receptions in Twentieth-Century Writing* (*CRTW*), a project that seeks to explore the modalities and textures of modern classicisms in the works of writers recognized for their global impact on modern philosophy, poetics, politics, and the arts. *CRTW* approaches this aim from two distinct yet interrelated perspectives: it asks how modern authors' appeals to the classical past open up new understandings of their oeuvres and contexts, and it considers how this process in turn renders new insights into the classical world and its sense of impact on our modernity. In plotting twentieth-century receptions of Greco-Roman antiquity from this two-way perspective, the series aims to promote dynamic, highly interdisciplinary discussions for readers of Classics and Literary and Classical Studies. Indeed, a key feature of the series is its extensive range and scope. It looks at both Anglophone and non-Anglophone writers from modernities around the globe, as well as writers still or until recently active in their field, such as Tony Harrison in the fourth volume of the series, or our forthcoming studies in Wole Soyinka and Simon Armitage. Each of these authors is considered primarily as a writer whose interest in antiquity has contributed to a significant revision of philosophical and political thought, aesthetics, identity studies, gender studies, translation studies, visual culture, performance studies, urban studies and cultural criticism, amongst other areas of knowledge. In this sense, *CRTW* aspires to promote a new intellectual space and critical direction for those producing research on Twentieth-Century Studies with a focus on Classics and vice versa.

The series furthermore aims to re-energize aspects of reception premises and practice. Over the last two decades, Classical Reception has developed broadly into four main fruitful areas of investigation: periods and/or movements (e.g. Humanism; the Enlightenment; the Victorians), media (e.g. film; sculpture; painting; the stage; musicology; comics), theory and criticism (e.g. psychoanalysis; gender studies; deconstruction; postcolonialism), and geopolitical regions (e.g. Africa; the Caribbean; Latin America; Eastern Europe; Australasia). These lines of enquiry have been instrumental in shaping methodological agendas and directions, as well as offering tremendous insights into discourses of Greco-Roman antiquity in space and time. Yet, within the histories of classical receptions focusing on periods and regions, the twentieth century has been underexamined as a thematic unit. On the one hand, there has been a preponderance of focus in studies in English on Anglophone, Francophone, and Germanophone receptions. This has been in part corrected by postcolonial reception studies with a focus on geopolitical regions outside of Western Europe. What has been missing is a perspective that combines not only an appreciation of Western and non-Western receptions, but also an understanding of these reception phenomena within a global, and not merely regional, framework. *CRTW* seeks to address this tangible gap, moving beyond isolated treatments and into full-scale investigations of authors recognized both for radical re-readings of the classical past and for challenging received ideas about the identity and cultural mobility of antiquity in the Western tradition. Interdisciplinarity is at the heart of such a reconsideration of reception in the series. Instead of treating reception as a sub-discipline of Classics, or as an expansion of the disciplinary boundaries of Classics, *CRTW* conceives it as a hub for interdisciplinary exchange amongst multiple subjects, disciplinary practices, and scholarly expertise. It addresses some of the most profound shifts in practices of reading, writing, and thinking in recent years within the arts and humanities, as well as in the poetics of reading the classics that one finds in twentieth-century writing itself.

Beyond reception, each individual study in the series draws attention to the specific quality of a modern author's classicism, as well as the ways in which that author negotiates classical ideals and values. Such is the case with French philosopher, political activist, and historian of ideas Michel Foucault (Poitiers 1926–Paris 1984), whose dialogue with the classics becomes more poignant during the last years of his life. In *Foucault's Seminars on Antiquity: Learning to Speak the Truth*, Paul Allen Miller offers a distinctive reading of how the classics, and especially the figure of Socrates, inform Foucault's ongoing preoccupation with the question of truth—its ontology, its relation to power, the ways we come to speak about it, and, ultimately, how we come to know our own. This line of questioning makes up the structure of Miller's five chapters, in which he closely examines the contents of Foucault's lectures delivered at the Collège de France between 1980 and 1984, when he was also completing volumes two and three of *The History of Sexuality*. Miller concentrates on four central topics in Foucault's classically informed lectures: (i) his neologism *alèthurgies*, or "acts of truth," in which truth is presented as an activity rather than a property of things; (ii) "the truth of the self," which Foucault interprets as the product of technologies forming a subject's own sense of what truth is; (iii) spiritual practices, in which the ability to know the truth relates to how subjects act and exercise that truth; and (iv) *parrhēsia*, which Miller defines as 'the courage to speak the truth whether to the assembled citizens, the prince, or oneself' (p. 15). In his exploration of these themes, Miller draws strategic attention to how Foucault carefully selects a wide range of classical authors, texts, and philosophies (from Sophocles, Plato, Aristotle, and Xenophon to Plutarch, the Stoics and Cynics, Cicero, Galen, and Dio Cassius, amongst others) both to substantiate his thinking about the "modalities through which power constitutes itself in relation to truth" (p. 8) and trace a genealogy of the Western subject as a speaker of truth. Here, Miller sheds light on an important aspect of Foucault's rethinking of the classical tradition. For Foucault, the classics do not serve as a fundamental, unquestionable source of wisdom for Western modernity. Instead, he plots them as parallel histories of truth and ontologies of the self, as he addresses conflicts between competing conceptions or regimes of truth in, for instance, Sophocles' *Oedipus Tyrannus* or the sociopolitical powers that construct the false truths leading to Socrates' death. From this perspective, Foucault's antiquity becomes yet another layer in the formulation of the Western subject as a speaker of truth, as well as how this truth is recurrently compromised and renegotiated through shifting forms of power, discourses, and levels of authority. Equally perceptive is Miller's application of Foucault's arguments about truth-telling to the academe's own reception of Foucault, especially in North America. In the closing pages of his study, he sheds intimate light on aspects of the late Foucault that gain the status of legendary truth in American Humanities during the 1980s and 1990s, including some quarters of the discipline of Classics, which has likewise produced and reproduced its own distinct truth-telling about Foucault, his engagement with antiquity and the history of sexuality. Miller's lucid exploration of late Foucault thus becomes timely when considering Classics and its epistemic systems in our new millennium. Whether our endeavours to speak the truth prompt us to resist or enact dramatic changes in the field and beyond it, it may be worthwhile to recall Foucault's—and Socrates'—warning that the truth is never an objective property one possesses. Instead, it is a discursive event, an "act" framed by our own circumstances, ambitions, and perceptions of reality. Foucault's late thought on the Classics and their tradition across his twentieth-century modernity is also, necessarily, an instantiation of this phenomenon.

Laura Jansen, University of Bristol

# Introduction

> One must write the whispering voices so "loudly" that the whole world and everyone goes into becoming, or more precisely, has the potential to become otherwise than how they are today. One must express the voices so clearly that everyone will be fearless in the expression of their freedom.
>
> Lawlor 2016: 270

Michel Foucault is one of the most radical voices in twentieth-century philosophy. He is the author of "histories" of marginal figures, of discourses, and of forms of life that stand beyond, opposed to, or outside the reason or *logos* that delimits philosophy's traditional domain—madness, the clinic, the prison, sexuality. He produced texts on Artaud, Bataille, Roussel, and Nietzsche. He wrote sympathetic descriptions of the Iranian revolution and published memoires of the intersex, Hercule Barbin, and the parricide, Pierre Rivière. His express mission was to overturn our certainties and our self-evident truths through the production of an "historical ontology of ourselves" (1994d: 618): an archeology, genealogy, or a radical historicization that would reveal the discourses constructing our present reality to be the sedimented and contingent practices of previous intentionalities, power struggles, and moments of resistance. Foucault's histories uncover a fossil record of our practices of truth, of our desires, pleasures, and intensities, which have been, *and therefore can be*, repurposed and re-elaborated from one struggle to the next.[1] This fundamental act of uncovering or unveiling has the purpose to allow us—readers, philosophers, and individuals, but also members of scientific and political institutions—to "think differently," to get outside ourselves, to get beyond the definitions, procedures, and discourses that define what it means to make a true statement, to form ourselves, to exercise power, and to resist (1984a: 14–15). It opens up the prospect of what he would call "a thought from the outside" (1986), what Nietzsche termed "the transvaluation of all values" (1972: 60).

And yet, what lies behind these questions are in many ways the most traditional of philosophical questions (Martin 1988: 15). What is truth? What does is it mean to make a true statement? Does it matter? How is truth determined? What is its object? Is there only one truth or multiple truths? How are criteria of verification and exclusion established? What is the truth of myself? How do I know it? What can or should I do with this knowledge? What can or should others do with this knowledge? These are very simple questions, very basic questions, and within them is encoded the whole of traditional philosophy (Foucault 2011: 33). Aesthetics, ethics, politics, epistemology, and metaphysics are all dependent on and subordinate to the ways we have and will answer these questions. The answers to these questions determine what reason is and what falls within or outside its norms. They decide how sciences are constituted and organized, how norms are established, and how subjects know and form themselves. These are the questions that preoccupied Foucault throughout his career and that he posed in terms of madness, criminality, and sexuality. They may seem abstract, but nothing could be further from the truth, as Foucault's histories make painfully, vividly clear. They are also the basic questions of the Western philosophical tradition.

When Socrates roamed the streets of Athens importuning his fellow citizens, his questions were designed to do nothing so much as produce the very "thought from the outside"—a fundamental rethinking of our understanding of the good, the just, and the true—that remained Foucault's lodestar. Socrates' questions were so disconcerting to his fellow Athenians they executed him: the first recorded instance in the West of someone dying for the Truth.[2] Nonetheless, it is easy to forget the radical nature of this Socratic stance. We, too, easily assimilate Socrates to a reading of the Platonic corpus that sees him as the mouthpiece for an established truth, if not a directly dogmatic Platonism, of the kind the early Foucault and his close interlocutor, Gilles Deleuze, positioned themselves against.[3]

In this regard, it may be illustrative to recall three significant Socratic moments, with the understanding that more could be offered. Our first example comes from shortly before the trial that would lead to his death. On his way to a preliminary hearing, Socrates runs into Euthyphro in the portico of the King Archon. Euthyphro is about to charge his father with manslaughter over the death of a slave. Socrates is struck by the certitude that would lead Euthyphro to indict his father for a serious crime. He assumes Euthyphro must be, or at least must believe himself to be, an expert in matters of a piety and justice: an expertise of which Socrates is sorely in need for his trial. In a pattern common to many of the Socratic dialogues, however, when Socrates interrogates Euthyphro on the meaning of these terms, the latter's ignorance of the matters on which he professed expertise is revealed, producing a moment of aporia that offers both him and us the opportunity to think anew: "we will have to start our inquiry about piety all over again from the beginning!" (15c; Tredennick 1969: 41, punctuation modified). The observation is less an admission of defeat than an admonition to continue the inquiry in the face of both necessary failure and Socrates' imminent trial and death. There is a sense in which the inquiry is its own end.

In the *Apology*, Socrates recounts the story of two times he risked his life for the truth and what it commanded of him (32a4–32e1).[4] In the first instance, Socrates tells how, when he served briefly in the executive arm of the Athenian Council (*Boulē*), during the Peloponnesian War, he resisted a popular but unlawful movement to execute several Athenian generals: they had been unable to recuperate the bodies of the dead after the naval victory at Arginusae. In the second instance, during the rule of the Thirty Tyrants after Athens's loss in the war, Socrates refused to be part of a group chosen to bring back Leon of Salamis for execution. This was a risky step. Socrates probably only escaped death because the regime collapsed shortly thereafter. In each case, he offered up his body for his understanding of what the truth demanded. He did so not in the name of an inherited or pre-established truth, but rather in the name of the question, in the name of the possibility of seeking after and speaking the truth. As he says, after the guilty verdict has been announced, but before he is sentenced to death:

> And so someone might say, "Oh Socrates, if only you were silent and would leave us in peace, you could depart us and live." And this is the most difficult of all things to persuade some of you: for if I say to you this is to disobey the god and therefore impossible, you will not believe me. If I say this is the greatest good for people, to spend each day making arguments about excellence and about the other things you hear me talking about, and questioning myself and others, and that the unquestioned life is not liveable for a human being, you will believe this even less.
>
> *Apology* 37e3–38a6[5]

Philosophy, literally the "love of wisdom," is defined by Socrates, not as something one possesses, certainly not as a set of universal values that are endlessly affirmed, but as the unceasing questioning that makes it possible to think and act differently, as the endless examination that makes life livable.

It is this radical Socratic questioning that will occupy Foucault for the last five years of his life, not as an object of antiquarian interest, but as a way of thinking in a sustained manner about how the subject comes to speak the truth, about the relationship between truth and power, and about the courage needed to speak the truth while risking marginalization, misunderstanding, or even death (Brion and Harcourt 2012: 287). Foucault will examine these topics not only in terms of Socrates and his project, but also in terms of Plato, Plutarch, the Stoics, and the early church fathers. He will close his final set of lectures in May of 1984, shortly before his death, with an evocation of the Cynics. The tradition tells us these were the dogs of philosophy (*cynes*): street-corner philosophers who left behind no body of work, no elaborated theory, but confronted their fellow citizens, unshod, poorly clothed, contemptuous of authority. They were naked in body and naked in their commitment to the truth as a form of unveiling, a form of stripping away the false pretenses, self-delusions, and comfortable hypocrisies that constituted the lived reality of their interlocutors. The Cynics were marginal figures who seemed mad to their fellow citizens, flouters of norms, indecent, and perverse. In their commitment to the truth of bare nature, they would masturbate in the streets. Their speech and their bodies performed philosophy even as they embodied the very marginality that the early Foucault chronicled in his histories of madness, prisons, and sexuality. They were self-consciously the heirs to the most disturbing parts of the Socratic legacy and every bit as committed to the proposition that a life that had not been severely and directly questioned was not livable. Diogenes, the most famed member of the Cynic movement, would roam the streets of Athens with a lamp, shining it in the face of his fellow citizens, looking for (and failing to find) an honest man, always at his post.[6]

Foucault's final lectures at the Collège de France were not, however, the sole time he engaged with the ancient tradition. His first course at the Collège, *La volonté de savoir*, was devoted to archaic and classical Greece. There, he examined how the concept of truth that we recognize today became established during the fifth and fourth centuries BCE. In doing so, he was following in the wake of Marcel Detienne's, *The Masters of Truth in Archaic Greece* (1996), which described the notion of "truth" operative in archaic Greece as one produced by divinely inspired poets, prophets, and kings. This archaic model imagined truth not as the correspondence between a proposition and its referent but as authoritative pronouncement and communal memory. Lurking behind Detienne's inquiry (and Foucault's as well) is Heidegger's investigation of the changing meaning of *alētheia* ("truth," or for Heidegger "unhiddenness") from the Homeric to the classical period. The implicit argument of all three thinkers (Foucault, Detienne, and Heidegger) is that our familiar correspondence theory of truth is only truly established with the advent of Platonic metaphysics, the fullest statement of which is found in the Myth of the Cave with its clear distinction between epistemic subjects and objects.[7]

The title of Foucault's course should be familiar to many: it was repurposed six years later for volume one of the *History of Sexuality*, *La volonté de savoir*, "the will to know." The echo of Nietzsche's *Will to Power* is hardly accidental.[8] The 1970–71 course included a lecture on Nietzsche that is now lost but of which we can judge the general tenor by one given at McGill in April of 1971 (Defert 2011: 276–7). What Foucault proposes to undertake in the course is a genealogy of knowledge, a history that opposes itself to the traditional philosophical concept of factual knowledge as the product of a natural human faculty. He argues instead for the emergence of truth as it is found in Plato and Aristotle—that is, as the correspondence between the perception of a subject and the reality of an independent object—as a discursive event, the product of social and political struggles in archaic Greece (Foucault 2011: 187–8; Defert 2011: 259). He does this not by simply accepting Nietzsche's theses or by commenting upon his text, but by tracing the nature and definition of truth, veridiction, and verification, from Homer through the social changes that produced the tyrannies that ruled archaic Greece, to the emergence of philosophy, the beginnings of science, and a definition of observed, factual knowledge (*connaissance*) as we would understand it in the fifth and fourth centuries (Foucault 2011: 191–2; Defert 2011: 269–70, 273).[9] Where in the classical Aristotelian model, which will later become canonical for Western epistemic practice, the "will to know" is nothing more than curiosity, in the Nietzschean model what lies behind factual knowledge is struggle and the will to power, the need to gain control of one's environment and circumstances (Foucault 2011: 190, 202–5).

The Aristotelian model's opposition to that of Nietzsche frames the course. Unlike in the lectures of the eighties, Socrates is largely absent, and the role of Plato is greatly reduced in *The Will to Know* (Defert 2011: 258). The first lecture discusses Aristotle's exclusion of the sophists and Platonic reminiscence from the realm of knowledge as defined in the *Metaphysics*. The second undertakes a more general problematization of observed factual knowledge in Spinoza, Kant, and Nietzsche (with most of the Nietzsche portion missing). Then, on January 6, Foucault devotes his entire lecture to Aristotle's exclusion of sophistic argument from philosophy, and hence from knowledge of the truth. While this is a detailed and quite fascinating argument, owing to the limits of a brief introduction, it will be necessary to schematize.

The essence of Aristotle's argument is that philosophy is a discourse that is characterized by its relation to the truth. The truth is defined by its participation in Being. Being in itself is eternal, and thus whatever portion of a philosophical discourse touches upon the true is also eternal. This means that philosophy is an affair of meaning or the signified as opposed to one of perishable material expression or the signifier. What is true in philosophy, therefore, is independent of any individual formulation or speech act. The truth is always translatable from one medium or language to another. A sophism, however, is an argument that depends not on the signified and its relation to Being, but on an ambiguity or ambivalence in the signifier that allows the meaning of a term or terms to shift within the argument. Thus, where philosophy is a discourse that effaces itself before the reality toward which it gestures, and thus factual knowledge is simply the product of the subject making accurate statements about observed realities, sophistry is invested in the materiality of discourse itself, and therefore the propositions it offers, rather than effacing themselves before an external truth, become a concrete reflection of the desires, passions, and interests of the speaker (Foucault 2011: 32–3, 43, 46–7, 60, 65–6).

For Nietzsche, it is precisely those desires and passions that produce knowledge as an expression of the will to power, of the need for humans to control and manipulate their environment. As Foucault summarizes at the beginning of the lecture on Nietzsche given at McGill that same academic year:

> The possibility of observed factual knowledge is not a formal law; it finds its possibility in a space of play where it is a question of other things: of the instincts and not of reason, formal knowledge, or experience . . . "There is not 'an instinct of knowledge'; the intellect is in the service of diverse instincts."
> Foucault 2011: 196, citing the *Will to Power*, aphorism 274

By tracing the genealogy of our concept of truth and revealing it to be a materially dependent and hence time-bound notion, Foucault not only denaturalizes the Aristotelian concept of truth, he also opens it up to an examination of the passions that produced it. The "will to know" is shown not to be an innate and unchanging human faculty but a contingent set of acts, discourses, and institutions, whether we are speaking of the origins of the fifth-century Greek *polis* or the emerging *scientia sexualis* of eighteenth- and nineteenth-century Europe.

Thus, there is a line of continuity that runs from Foucault's earliest work to his final lectures on the Cynics. Whether the question is the relationship of madness to the discourses of reason that seek to understand, sequester, and "cure" it, or the archeology of the clinical gaze, the human sciences, and the discourse of sexuality, or how the Socratic "care of the self" became our own endless therapeutic patter, the problem of who gets to speak what truths and for what purposes remains central:

> The problem that I have always tried to pursue is globally to know how the truth comes to things and how it happens that there may be a certain number of domains that little by little are integrated into the problematic of and the search for truth.
> Foucault 2012a: 247

One example of this continuity, to which we shall return, is Foucault's interest in *Oedipus Tyrannus* as a staging of the simultaneous interplay of different games of truth operative in fifth-century Athens: prophetic and divine truth; the truth of kings; and the truth of common perception. This reading of Sophocles is first advanced in the *Will to Know*, but it is refined and rearticulated many times over the years. *Oedipus* moves from being a prime exhibit in Foucault's Nietzschean genealogy of truth, through providing a counternarrative to Freud's universalization of Oedipal desire, to offering demonstrations of the relationship between acts of truth and power in *Du Gouvernement des vivants*, to finally occupying a key place in the history of confession as a discourse of the self in *Mal faire, dire vrai: Fonction de l'aveu en justice*. It is certainly not that nothing changes over the long arc of Foucault's career. As we shall see, Socrates, who is marginalized in the *Will to Know*, comes to occupy a central place in the last years of Foucault's teaching when antiquity again becomes his focus. Nonetheless, we fail to understand the full impact of Foucault's enterprise if we neglect the radical nature of his continuing engagement with the central questions of the philosophical tradition.

In 1980, Foucault's work makes two decisive turns, which form the primary subject matter of this book. First, as announced at the start of his course at the Collège de France for that year, *Du Gouvernement des vivants*, his topic will be the modalities through which power constitutes itself in relation to "acts of truth," for which he coins the neologism, *alèthurgies*, pronouncements or manifestations of truth that constitute, reinforce, or legitimate specific forms of power and subjectivity. While truth had been a central preoccupation from the beginning, his later work focuses increasingly on the individual as a speaker of truth both to himself and others. This shift of focus, which I have just argued should be viewed with some nuance, is what is often referred to as Foucault's "ethical turn" or his return to "subjectivity."[10] Second, the texts and archives on which he will concentrate will no longer be those of the early modern period, which had dominated his published work from the *History of Madness* (1961) to volume one of the *History of Sexuality* (1976), although in the lecture courses of the late seventies he had shown an increased interest in the Medieval and early church, and, as we have seen, his first course focused exclusively on antiquity. Nonetheless, he begins his course in January 1980 with a vignette from Dio Cassius on the emperor Septimius Severus and then proceeds to spend the next two sessions offering a reading of *Oedipus*, before closing with an extensive exploration of the problem of confession, penance, and the baptismal remission of sins in the primitive church. From that point forward, he concentrates on antiquity.

The early eighties are, of course, the period during which Foucault began work on volumes two and three of the *History of Sexuality* (1984) and was completing a draft of volume four, *Confessions of the Flesh* (2018). Yet while there are clear overlaps between the work he was presenting in his courses and the last books he published before his death, nonetheless the seminars are anything but rough drafts for the published work. They are with one exception largely unconcerned with sexuality in either the broader or the more restricted sense defined by Foucault in volume one (1976). Instead, they offer a sustained encounter with the texts of the classical and early Christian era while seeking to trace a genealogy of the Western subject as a speaker of truth, focusing in large part on the very texts he chose to ignore in his first course: Socrates, Plato, and their Stoic heirs. The central questions in these courses become: What is the Western subject's relation to power when speaking the truth? How is this veridical subject formed? What constitutes these truths and who is qualified to speak them? This book will offer the first detailed account of these lectures, and will examine both the development of their philosophical argument and the ancient texts on which that argument is based.

In many ways, these lectures have proven to be a revelation, particularly to scholars of antiquity. When volumes two and three of the *History of Sexuality* were published in English in 1986, they exploded like an atom bomb in the world of American Classics. To understand their impact, we must recall the context. This was the period of the Culture Wars in the Reagan era. In official Washington, the tone was one of reaction and retrenchment. It was time to roll back the excesses of the sixties, to restore pride in American power, to return to traditional virtues. This was the time of the Moral Majority, of the rise of the power of the Evangelical right in the United States. Lynn Cheney, the wife of the future Vice President and architect of the Iraq War, had just succeeded to the Chair of the National Endowment of the Humanities, where she took over from William J. Bennett, the conservative author and media personality. This was also the period in which a series of books were issued proclaiming the need to restore the canon, to defend traditional civilization against the barbarisms of feminism, the emerging fields of gender and queer studies, subaltern studies, and postmodernism and poststructuralism in general. E.D. Hirsch published *Cultural Literacy* (1987), a combination polemic and list of what every "educated" person should know, which was quickly embraced by the conservative establishment and became a bestseller. In the same year, Allan Bloom, the neoconservative disciple of Leo Strauss, published *The Closing of the American Mind: How Higher Education Has Failed Democracy and Impoverished the Souls of Today's Students* (1987), a polemic against "perspectivism" and "relativism" and in favor of traditional education. It, too, was a surprise bestseller, rapidly embraced by cultural conservatives, many of whom were more comfortable condemning feminism and Marxism than reading the Gadamer, Nietzsche, Locke, Plato, and Aristotle their heroes sought to defend.

In retrospect, neither Hirsch nor Bloom were quite as reactionary as they seemed at the time and compared to today's increasing emphasis on the cash value of a university education, they can seem almost radical in their insistence on the centrality of general education and critical thinking. Nonetheless, the 1980s in the United States was also the heyday of critical/literary theory in humanities departments across the country. This theory took many forms. In the United States, the remnants of formalism and New Criticism held on in many guises. Frankfurt School Marxism was widely taught, and the work of Fredric Jameson was a staple in most graduate programs in English and Comparative Literature. The Russian thinker Mikhail Bakhtin and the circle around him, who remain difficult to categorize in Western terms but who emphasized both the formal structures and social determinants of discourse, were also important players. Nonetheless, when one said "theory" in the eighties, one inevitably spoke of French theory: structuralism, poststructuralism, psychoanalysis, deconstruction, and feminism. In the 1980s in the United States, a peculiarly American version of deconstruction was the dominant force in theoretical reflection on the humanities, and all other contributors were either assimilated to this form or seen as critical responses to it. These were the forces of anarchy and relativism that Bloom, Hirsch, Bennett, and Cheney were arrayed against, and it was into this environment that Foucault's *History of Sexuality*, with its focus on the conception and theorization of ancient pederastic and marital practices, made its appearance and to which it was often assimilated by both friends and foes alike.

Yet this constellation of discourses was highly unstable and buffeted by a number of transverse forces that would further complicate and color the reception of what struck many anglophones as Foucault's sudden and (to some) inexplicable turn to antiquity (Said 1984; Macey 1993: 475). First, the dominance of French theory in general and deconstruction in particular was about to be dealt a self-inflicted blow. In 1988, Paul de Man, the deceased Sterling Professor of Comparative Literature at Yale and arguably the chief architect of American deconstruction, was revealed to have published extensively in the Belgian collaborationist newspaper, *Le soir*. At the same time, details about his personal history were made public that showed ethical lapses and possible violations of law. The particulars of these scandals have been covered elsewhere and do not need to be rehearsed here, and in fact Foucault himself had nothing to do with de Man, and he would have rejected any assimilation to deconstruction or the work of Derrida.[11] Nonetheless, in the highly charged atmosphere of the 1980s, the revelations concerning de Man seemed to tar all French theory with the same brush and gave credence to the worst accusations by conservative critics that the theoretical enterprise was an exercise in nihilism and moral bankruptcy.

Foucault was also a gay man who died before his time in the era of AIDS. In 1980, the first cases of AIDS were reported. In 1982, the disease was named. By the spring of 1983, Michel Foucault may have been symptomatic and possibly had a definitive diagnosis by the end of the year. In June 1984, he died at the age of 57, shortly after correcting the proofs of Volumes two and three of the *History of Sexuality*. For those of us who remember, it was a time of horror. Friends, colleagues, brothers, and sisters began dying by the thousands. People we all knew. People we loved. Mainstream heteronormative society by and large did not seem to care until it became obvious that this was not simply a gay plague visited on Sodom by a wrathful god, but a blood-borne illness that could be more easily and effectively transmitted by a medical transfusion than anal penetration. It was not till 1987 that the President of the United States, Ronald Reagan, so much as uttered the word "AIDS" in public. "Enlightened" socialist regimes in countries such as Cuba rounded up homosexuals and placed them in quarantine. To many this seemed like genocide by other means. The actual cause of Foucault's death was not revealed till two years later by his longtime partner Daniel Defert, who founded the French AIDS activist and support group AIDES, although rumors had circulated for some time before.[12]

It was in this environment that the *History of Sexuality* entered classical scholarship, one of the last conservative redoubts in American humanities in the late eighties. In the autumn of 1987, Georg Luck, the editor of America's oldest journal in Classics, the *American Journal of Philology* (*AJP*), published a manifesto, "*AJP* Today." *AJP* is a journal that until very recently sported on its cover "Founded by Basil Lanneau Gildersleeve," the pioneering American philologist, slave owner, and Confederate apologist.[13] To many in Classics and in the popular media,[14] Luck's manifesto seemed like another salvo in the

Culture Wars. It situated the journal firmly within traditional philology as practiced by Gildersleeve. It announced that it would reject articles that were "speculative" and all that was "fashionable and *outré*." The statement was taken as an attack not only on poststructuralist methodologies, associated with deconstruction, but also on feminism. For a variety of complex historical reasons, feminism within American Classics had become the main vehicle for theoretical work in the field. A special panel on "*AJP* Today" was quickly organized by the Women's Classical Caucus at that year's meeting of the American Philological Association, and Luck's dry polemic became a *cause célèbre*. A subsequent book, *Classics: A Discipline and Profession in Crisis?* was published based on the panel and as a response to Luck (Culham and Edmunds 1989). The Culture Wars were now fully under way within the staid environs of classical philology.

Within Classics, Foucault's text was appropriated for a variety of polemics. Having been received in North American Classics largely in abstraction from his ongoing teaching and absent a sophisticated understanding of his previous work and its place within French philosophy, the *History of Sexuality* was taken by many for what it seemed to say it was, a history of sex. And if that's what it was, then, it was clearly a failed experiment, typical of the hubris displayed by French theory and its disregard for traditional scholarship. There were any number of critiques.[15] Why focus only on fourth-century BCE Greece and second-century CE Rome? Why focus only on philosophical and medical texts? Where are the poems, the plays, the novels? Where are the women, the slaves, Jews, the Egyptians? Particularly shocking in a context where Feminist scholarship was the banner under which most political and theoretical opposition marched was Foucault's neglect of writers like Sappho or the plight of women in antiquity. Whose sexuality was this anyway? There seemed a strong phallic bias. Amy Richlin asked, "Foucault's *History of Sexuality*: A Theory Useful for Women?" (1998). Lynn Foxhall published, "Pandora Unbound: A Feminist Critique of Foucault's *History of Sexuality*" (1998). Where Foxhall offers a corrective, Richlin articulates an indictment:

> My major difficulty with the *History* is that it is not historical. It does not give a consistently accurate impression of the sources it does use and it would have needed to use a much wider range of sources to give an accurate impression at all. It leaves out women, and I no longer take narratives that

leave out women to be historical. That bothers me particularly in a work that makes such a big deal out of being historical.

Richlin 1998: 167–8

At the same time, Foucault had his advocates. He was embraced by many LGBTQ classicists but also by others who were looking for more sophisticated ways of understanding sexual practices and expression than could be gleaned from traditional readings of canonical texts, which often took refuge in politically loaded notions of nature, tradition, or normality. Important in this regard were three books that came out in 1990, David Halperin's *One Hundred Years of Homosexuality and Other Essays on Greek Love*, Jack Winkler's *The Constraints of Desire*, and Halperin, Winkler, and Zeitlin's *Before Sexuality: The Construction of Erotic Experience in the Ancient Greek World*. These texts sought to denaturalize and historicize erotic experience in the name of constructing new possibilities of expression, for which the binary terminology of homo- and hetero-sexuality was increasingly problematic. Together these books, which drew their inspiration from Foucault, fundamentally changed the way ancient sexuality was studied.[16]

Subsequent texts found it necessary either to answer or extend on these fundamental works. Polemics were drawn and the divisions within the field became very sharp. On the one side, there was a group associated with the Women's Classical Caucus that felt not only that Foucault had neglected the role of women in antiquity, but also that the gay and queer activists associated with Halperin and Winkler had failed to credit feminist scholars for the fundamental work they had done in opening-up ancient sexuality as a field of study. This sense of resentment culminated in an incendiary article by Amy Richlin entitled "Zeus and Metis: Foucault, Feminism, Classics" (1991) that accused Halperin and Winkler of plagiarism. Very quickly one had to choose sides.[17] If the most extreme characterizations were to be believed, then the feminists stood opposed to the gay activists[18] and both of them were seen as the death knell of traditional philology as practiced by Luck and Gildersleeve. Foucault's text stood in the middle of these swirling controversies able to be perceived as an example of the amoral excess of French theory, another in a long dreary line of masculinist erasures of women from history, or a model of a new queer sexuality and political activism, tailor-made for the age of AIDS and Act Up.

All of these characterizations have some truth to them. Foucault's sources in the *History of Sexuality* are almost all men and only really concerned with men's experience, although Foucault would have found it presumptuous to think that he should or could speak for women or any other group. For him, the role of the intellectual was not to represent the interests of others or to speak for the universal, but to call into question the truth of the present: to open it to interrogation, problematization, and new possibilities of thought and action.[19] While the problem of representation is a complex one and cannot be treated within the compass of a short introduction, similar problems confront all those who are not members of a marginalized or oppressed group who can neither speak in their place nor responsibly remain silent. Foucault was certainly aware of this problematic, even if one can legitimately question the way he chose to address it. Similarly, Foucault's *History of Sexuality* no doubt did as much as any text to help denaturalize heteronormativity and make possible a much richer, less binary discourse about sex, sexuality, about, in the words, of the finale of volume one, "bodies and pleasures" (1976: 211). Lastly, Foucault's work was not in any sense a philological commentary on ancient texts or even an attempt to write a history of sexual conduct or expression (1984a: 15, 36; Rajchman 1991: 87–8). Sexuality for Foucault was not a thing, and it certainly was not natural. It was a discourse, a set of enunciations that provided definition and unity to a disparate group of behaviors, sensations, and biological functions, creating a singular entity (i.e., sex) that was not there before (1976: 198–207). There is no word in Greek, Latin, or Old French for sex. There is a vast vocabulary for emotions, desires, acts, organs, and positions, but no word that covers the full semantic range of our word sex or its articulation as a particular sexuality (homo, hetero, bi, poly). Thus, from a Foucauldian perspective the *History of Sexuality* is not the history of sex, sexes, gender, or erotic expression, it is the genealogy of the series of enunciations that became over time—through myriad shifts, adaptations, and displacements—our discourse of sexuality, and it chooses its textual examples accordingly. In this respect, its aims and methods were very different from one of its chief predecessors, Dover's *Greek Homosexuality* (1978). It seeks to study "the games of truth in the self's relation to itself and in the constitution of the self as a subject, by taking as its domain of reference and field of investigation what one could label 'the history of the man of desire'" (Foucault 1984a: 12).

And so, in the end, sexuality in Foucault is not a matter of organs and acts but a question of truth. It is a question of the way a discourse comes to be that is not only more or less adequate to the entity it seeks to describe, but also one that creates that entity *qua* entity through the act of description. It is not that there was no there there before, but naming something and producing a discourse about it delimits the phenomenon in fundamental ways and changes the kinds of statements we can make about it and hence the way we can experience and understand it. It is in fact not an accident that volume one of the *History* was entitled, *The Will to Know*. Sexuality becomes the fact about us that the discourse of sexuality produces—we are hetero, homo, trans, queer, perverse, normal. This fact explains who we are. It assigns to us our truth, whether we want it or not.

The *History of Sexuality* is the history of how that discourse came about. It poses a classic philosophical question: What is our truth and how did it come to us? And while sexuality is not simply a random example, it would be a category mistake to assume that Foucault was writing a history of sexual acts or practices rather than dominant discourses. Nonetheless, this fact was not understood by many of his initial classical interlocutors, most of whom had not read deeply in his other works, or understood their philosophical context; nor were they aware of the broader context of his teaching at the Collège. Thus, my own early essay on the topic, while focused on broadly philosophical topics and attempting to understand the categories and concepts under which Foucault was operating, was under-informed about the broader context in which his work should be understood (Miller 1998).

The present work is an attempt to offer redress. Focused on the lecture courses offered between 1980 and 1984, it will examine Foucault's understanding of four select topics: (1) *alèthurgies* or "acts of truth," in which truth is shown not to be simply a property of things or of propositions, but an activity, something done; (2) the truth of the self, in which the technologies through which the subject forms itself and is formed by others are described; (3) spiritual practices, in which the ability to know the truth is predicated on acts and exercises undertaken by the subject; and (4) *parrhēsia*, the courage to speak the truth whether to the assembled citizens, the prince, or oneself. Each chapter will take up one year of lectures and we will read them both with and against the source materials they cite. In the process, we will see how Foucault's thought develops from one course to the next, giving a fuller philosophical contour to his later work than can be had from volumes two and three of the *History of Sexuality* in isolation. In the end, we will see that his central preoccupation in these last years remained, as it was in the beginning: what is the truth, what is its relation to power, how do we come to speak it, and how do we know our own?

# 1

# The Government of the Living: Acts of Truth from *Oedipus* to the Primitive Church

> The question that I would want to pose ... is this: how does it happen, in a society such as ours, that power is not able to be exercised without truth being manifest and manifest in the form of subjectivity and without, in addition, one expecting from this manifestation of truth in the form of subjectivity certain effects that are beyond the order of factual knowledge, that are of the order of salvation and deliverance for each and all? In a general fashion, the themes I want to approach this year are these: how, in our civilization, are put in place relations between the government of men, the manifestation of truth in the form of subjectivity, and salvation for each and all?
>
> Foucault 2012b: 74

On January 7, 1980, Foucault began his lectures for the year by describing an audience hall in the palace of Septimius Severus. On the ceiling, the emperor had painted an image of the night sky as it appeared on the day of his birth: a representation of cosmic truth that served to legitimate and actualize his power. Foucault asks us to imagine what is the purpose of this manifestation of truth in the constitution of an absolute imperial power that might seem to require no intellectual legitimation. While the title of the course, *On the Government of the Living*, seems to indicate a continuation of Foucault's concerns with biopower, governmentality, and their implication within systems of knowledge, which had been his primary subject matter since 1976, the shift of scene to the display of power in late imperial Rome signals an inflection point in his thought. It is not so much that Foucault has left his previous concerns behind as that he had determined that their adequate investigation required more historical depth. *On the Government of the Living* asks the question: why is a manifestation of the truth necessary for the government of human beings? Such a question is clearly related to Foucault's earlier concern with knowledge and power, but it is not precisely identical to the previous problematic, as he makes clear at the beginning of the course. This new topic is explored through a close reading of, first, *Oedipus Tyrannus* and, then, of a variety of texts from the primitive church on baptism, penance, and confession. In each case, the question Foucault poses is: what relation obtains between the subject, its acts of manifesting or producing truth (*actes de verité*), and that subject's adherence to a larger institutional structure, which both makes the truth possible and is made possible by the truth—i.e., the *polis*, the church, a government (Foucault 2012b: 51). "This ... is what I want to study a bit this year, that is to say the element of the first person, the element of the 'I,' the element of the '*autos*,' ... in what might be called *alèthurgie*[1] or veridiction or the rights and procedures of veridiction" (Foucault 2012b: 48).

When Foucault published volume one of *the History of Sexuality*, he advertised on the back cover an ambitious plan of publications, most of which never saw the light of day. The subsequent three volumes of the *History* are in fact very different from those initially projected. The original series was to number six volumes and would include, *La chair et le corps*, which would focus on confession in the post-Lateran Council church (1215), when it became institutionalized for the laity, and *Populations et races*, which would take up the idea of biopolitics, as introduced in volume one of the *History*. Biopolitics would remain a central idea for Foucault's thought on governmentality and politics (Foucault 2012b: 371). It would also go on to have an independent career in the work of political theorists such as Giorgio Agamben (Miller 2020a).

Thus, out of the initial conception of the *History of Sexuality* came two ideas that would guide Foucault's thought for the next decade: the importance of institutionalized processes through which the subject comes to speak the truth about itself; and the organization of power to produce a subject that governs itself in accord with structures that do not merely serve a sovereign but promote the life of a population or community, i.e., a nation, state, or race. Within this conceptual structure, confession serves as the point at which truth is inscribed within the self-governing subject. Through confession, subjects come to know and speak the truth of their most intimate secrets to themselves, their confessors, their therapists, their party comrades, or to whomever else it may be necessary in order to produce "normal," disciplined, human beings

(Fejes and Dahlstedt 2013: 1). This demand to speak the truth became especially strong in matters of sex and sexuality, and that truth had a definite history. As Foucault writes at a key moment of volume one:

> Confession has been and remains still today the general matrix that regulates the production of the true discourse on sex. Nonetheless, it has been considerably transformed. For a long time, it was framed by the practice of penitence. But little by little, since the beginning of Protestantism, the Counterreformation, the pedagogy of the 18th century and the medicine of the 19th, it has lost its exclusive ritual localization; it has been diffused; it has been used in a series of relationships: infants and parents, students and teachers, patients and psychiatrists, delinquents and experts.
>
> Foucault 1976: 84–5

Confession has become the way we render ourselves governable and self-governing. As modern governments have increasingly assumed the affirmative task of promoting life through hygiene, pedagogy, and surveillance, as opposed to merely asserting sovereignty in the person of a monarch or through forms of aristocratic violence and display, the importance of the subject's will to know and speak the truth about itself has become ever more central. It is the genealogy of that truth and its relation to the phenomenon of governmentality that Foucault proposes to investigate in *On the Government of the Living* (Senellart 2012: 329, 336–7).

The scope of what Foucault undertakes here has changed from volume one (1976) and presages what became the very different project developed in the lectures of the coming five years and the revamped *History of Sexuality*. We can chart this evolution by paying special attention to his work on the phenomenon of confession. An early draft of *La chair et le corps* provided the substance for Foucault's discussion of confession in his 1975 course, *Les anormaux*. He later found this analysis inadequate and drafted a whole new text on the same material in 1977 and 1978, working increasingly thematically and historically, eventually pushing his genealogy of our modern practices of confession back to the church fathers. By 1980, he had destroyed these previous drafts as well and had come to focus exclusively on the early church. A first draft of what would become *Les aveux de la chair* was complete by 1980 when he began his new course (Elden 2016: 77–8, 97, 102; Senellart 2012: 334, 344–7). As Stuart Elden observes of this draft:

> Confession is the crucial element in both the abandoned and unfinished plans. But Foucault remained unhappy with the introductory material to this volume, which he says discussed antiquity ... All of Foucault's future lecture courses treat this period. Antiquity becomes the focus of his ongoing "history of the relations between truth and subjectivity."
>
> Elden 2016: 133

The question of how the subject produced the truth about itself, and how that truth rendered the subject governable by both itself and others was central to the problematic of the *History of Sexuality*. But the problem of the constitution of the subject was also central to Foucault's larger concerns about how truth was produced and how the truth of individuals could become a means of both their subjection and their resistance. Power, he would argue, is both produced and resisted as subjects reflect on, criticize, and respond to the truths they produce and are produced about them. The relations between truth, power, and subjectivity are never simple or unidirectional. In perceiving, formulating, reflecting, and revising their truths, subjects devise new modes of veridiction and verification that make possible new forms of truth and power, new forms of existence (Fimiani 2012: 123; Fejes and Dahlstedt 2013: 15, 26; Elden 2016: 204–5).

The truth, as Septimius Severus recognized, is a locus of power. There can be no claim to govern nor basis for governance that does not assert a vision of what is real and that does not claim a privileged access to it through the truth (Foucault 1997: 22; Brion and Harcourt 2012: 289). Governmentality requires not only knowledge, a certain kind of know-how or *technē*, but also an apparatus for discovering, producing, and making known its truth (Foucault 2012b: 8, 80–1). The government of the living is grounded in the formal production and recognition of the truth, or at least the claim to such. "You would have great difficulty finding an example of a power that was exercised without being accompanied, in one manner or another, by a manifestation of truth" (Foucault 2012b: 6).

More precisely, behind every claim to power, there is an implicit statement, "X is the case," which always, at least in theory, is vulnerable to the following types of response: "No, Y is the case"; "No, X is really Y"; "Yes, but in addition to X, there is also Y"; "X only exists in a set that includes Y, Z, and a series of other terms"; "X only exists because of Y, Z, and a series of other terms", etc. There is a kind of dialogic structure to power that aspires to monologism and may enforce that aspiration through violence, but in its very structure offers the possibility of a response, and for Foucault it is precisely the task of the intellectual to intervene in that dialogue, to offer a critique of the ways in which truth is produced. It is this process that allows alternative claims to be made and alternative forms of power, governance, and hence subjectivity to come into being, alternative ways of forming the self in relation to the world it receives and makes. In this context, the increasing centrality of forms of confession, of forms of the subject speaking the truth about itself to itself and others, becomes ever more important in the establishment of the forms of knowledge and subjectivity that make governing and social organization possible. The kinds of truths we produce and are produced for us have a direct relation to the ways in which we govern ourselves and others. Thus, what had become increasingly clear to Foucault over the course of his research in the seventies and into the early eighties, is that any critical genealogy of the practice of confession, and hence of the way our modern subjectivity is constituted in relation to the truth we produce about ourselves, could only be adequate to the present situation, could only be cogent and consistent, by pushing back the historical horizon to the very period he had first covered in *Leçons sur la volonté de savoir*. He came to this conclusion not through some axiomatic declaration, but through the concrete practice of repeatedly trying to write a genealogy of our confessing practices (Martin 1988: 10; Bannet 1989; Rouse 1994: 108–9; Halperin 1995: 59–60; Brion and Harcourt 2012: 270; Kelly 2014: 71).

In what follows, I will begin with a short section on the theoretical postulates of the course. The bulk of this chapter will be devoted to Foucault's reading of *Oedipus Tyrannus*, which not only represents a point of continuity with his first course at the Collège but also sets the stage for the remaining courses, all of which focus on classical antiquity. I will finish with an overview of his work on early Christian practices of confession.

# I

> Let us make the masks fall away, discover things just as they happen. Let each one of us become conscious of the society in which we live, the economic

processes of which we are unconsciously the agents and the victims. Let us become conscious of the mechanisms, the exploitation, and the domination, and immediately the government will fall. The incompatibility, consequently, between the evidence finally acquired of what is really happening, evidence acquired by everyone, and the exercise of government by some! A principle, therefore, of universal consciousness as the overthrow of governments, of regimes and of systems. This is what Rosa Luxembourg[2] formulated in a famous phrase, "If everyone knew, the capitalist regime wouldn't hang on for 24 hours."

Foucault 2012b: 16

A regime of truth is therefore what constrains individuals to these acts of truth, what defines, determines the form of these acts and establishes for these acts certain conditions of effectuation and certain specific effects. In sum, if you wish, a regime of truth is what determines the obligations of individuals with regard to the procedure for manifesting the truth.

Foucault 2012b: 91

While in certain ways we have thus far emphasized the broad continuities between Foucault's theoretical and philosophical concerns throughout his career and his increased focus on antiquity in the last years of his life, nonetheless, it would be a mistake not to acknowledge a certain theoretical shift to which Foucault himself draws our attention at the beginning of *On the Government of the Living*. As Foucault observes, throughout the seventies one of his key concepts was power-knowledge (*pouvoir-savoir*). The term refers to a double conditioning that becomes visible through the Nietzschean critique of the will to know. There is no knowledge that is not also an exercise of power. Humans must wrest their existence from an often-hostile nature and from antagonistic social and political relations. And there is no power that is not predicated on the use and deployment of knowledge. We want to know something for a specific purpose or in response to a specific need, and our ability to know things depends on our abilities to marshal resources, time, energy, and social consent (Senellart 2012: 338–39; Kelly 2014: 88). In many ways, power-knowledge refers to the same matrix of concerns that a classical Marxist vocabulary would label as ideology, with two major differences: for Foucault there is no possibility of a knowledge or science that is completely removed from power; and where in orthodox Marxism, as expressed in the work of the French Communist Party or the USSR, ideology was a reflection of class relations that were "expressed" throughout the social superstructure, for Foucault, power-knowledge names a phenomenon and struggle that also takes place on the microlevel of individual institutions and personal power relations (Foucault 1975: 35–6; 1997: 7–13, 159; 2012a: 239; 2012b: 13; Bertani and Fontana 1997: 240; Senellart 2012: 337–8; Elden 2016: 28).[3]

In *On the Government of the Living*, Foucault proposes to replace power-knowledge with "government by the truth." "Truth," he observes, is not simply "know-how" or an archive but a set of mechanisms for the production, verification, and propagation of the knowledges necessary to constitute and govern our world. "The Truth" constitutes that world's definitional sets of truths. Likewise, government is not simply the existence of power relations, but a set of techniques and institutions used to govern ourselves and others, both in accordance with the "truth" and through producing the truths necessary for governance (Foucault 2012b: 13). Every social formation, therefore, entails a regime (or regimes) of truth: a set of obligations that "would impose acts of belief, professions of faith or confessions" (Foucault 2012b: 92).[4] As early as 1976, Foucault had written:

> Each society has its regime of truth, its "general politics" of truth: that is to say the types of discourses that it accepts and makes function as true; the mechanisms and instances that allow one to distinguish true and false statements, the way one sanctions the ones and the others; the techniques and procedures that are valorized in obtaining the truth; the status of those who are charged with saying what functions as true.
>
> Foucault 1994a: 112

All affirmations of truth include an implicit but not logically entailed demand to accept that truth,[5] and, at the same time, truth always makes the claim that it is, on a certain level, self-evident, that the truth is what it is because it names reality.[6] This is as much the case for Septimius Severus, as it is for Oedipus, the church, and modern science (Foucault 2012b: 93–5). Foucault does not propose to study the relative worth of these various claims to truth. His object of study is instead the ways in which forms of governing the self and others are always predicated on historically contingent regimes of truth and the forms of self-relation established within and produced by those regimes (Kelly 2014: 109).

None of this is to deny the existence of science or even that science produces a truth that can be authenticated by its own procedures, i.e., that it is self-regulatory, but it is to recognize that other regimes exist alongside science and are co-implicated with it: one of the most powerful and deeply rooted is that of confession, the form in which the subject is asked to produce the truth about itself, whether in the form of self-reflection, therapeutic discourse, or a call to authenticity (Foucault 2012b: 97). The genealogy of this self-knowledge stretches from the injunction of the Delphic oracle, "*gnōthi seauton*" ["know thyself"], through Augustine's *Confessions* to Freud's couch and our contemporary reflections on "experiential" learning. Yet each link in that chain has its own rules, its own set of relations to the self and others, and its own point of insertion within the larger field of power relations. The truth of the subject, as the subject knows it, is central to both the way we constitute our lives—who are we?, what do we want?, what is our task?—and how we position ourselves with regard to other forms of truth, governance, and power. It is this twin question of the subject's truth and the truth of the subject that will be the central concern of *On the Government of the Living* and of all Foucault's courses until his death. He demands that we ask, "why, under what form, in a society such as ours, does there exist such a profound linkage between the exercise of power and the obligation for individuals to make themselves, through the procedures of manifesting the truth ... essential actors?" (Foucault 2012b: 79, cf. 73–4). The subject "in a society such as ours," Foucault argues, becomes the locus of truth, both its own, and that to which it is witness. The task he sets himself in this course is to identify how this came to be (Foucault 2012b: 49). *Oedipus Tyrannus* serves as exhibit A. It displays, at the height of the Golden Age of Greece, both a conflict and ultimate harmonization of three competing modes of veridiction through which Oedipus discovers his own truth and that of his community.

There is, in fact, nothing natural or necessary about truth being founded on the presence of an authenticating witness, as Foucault had already argued in *Leçons sur la volonté de savoir*, though we take it as self-evident. Neither the bard of Homeric poetry, nor the prophets of Delphi, Jerusalem, or Egyptian Thebes claimed the authority of the truth they pronounced to be authenticated by their personal witness. The authority of the Confucian gentleman in ancient Chinese society was not predicated on his ability to produce veridical propositions on objects separate from himself that could be authenticated by other similar subjects. The truth Septimius Severus displayed in his throne room was not one that he had witnessed, nor was its power predicated on the existence of such witnesses. Indeed, the generic first-person witness, regardless of status or other forms of authentication, regardless of other forms of trial or proof, is not even accepted as an index of truth in all forms of modern jurisprudence, let alone throughout history. Nonetheless, within our dominant Western regime of truth, it is only once the authority of the speaking subject, qua subject, has been established that it can then constitute itself as a witness to itself and to the truth, that it can make a claim to self-knowledge, to having a privileged access to the truth. There is a strange sense in which the very autonomy of the speaking subject as the subject of factual knowledge is both the logical predicate for all our post-Platonist epistemology, as Heidegger had argued, and for the subject to serve as witness to itself. Self-knowledge, and by extension, the possibility of confession as a privileged mode of knowledge, then, rests on the same logical postulates as the autonomous subject as observer, as separate from the object, and hence as the subject of knowledge in the modern scientific sense, of knowledge that is separable from the subject, as a relation between a proposition made by a subject and an independent object/reality (Foucault 2012b: 49; Miller 2020b).

The question for Foucault then becomes, "how does the subject make itself into the vessel of truth?" As Socrates' quest for self-knowledge shows, such knowledge is hard won. We do not simply awake one day and see the truth, we must prepare ourselves, alter ourselves, undertake practices that make us into a speaking and knowing subject that can recognize the truth (Foucault 2012b: 77–80). Throughout much of history, these forms of practice, these forms of *askēsis*, are conceived of as spiritual practices, actions undertaken by the self whereby the self gains access to the truth: whether through rigorous training in mathematics and the practice of the dialectic, as the *Republic* advocates; through processes of introspection, as practiced by the Stoics; or through various other forms of mental and physical training, as seen among the Cynics and Christian monastic movements. Foucault outlines his project for these last five years of courses at the beginning of his February 13, 1980 lecture as follows:

> It would be a matter of sketching a history of the truth that would take as its point of view the acts of subjectivity, or even the relation of the subject to

itself, understood not only as the relation of self-knowledge but also as the exercise of the self on the self, elaboration of the self by the self, transformation of the self by the self, that is to say relations between truth and what one calls spirituality, or even: acts of truth and ascetics, acts of truth and experience in the full and strong sense of the term, that is to say experience as what qualifies the subject, enlightens it about itself and the world and, at the same time, transforms it.

Foucault 2012b: 111–12

Foucault, thus, seeks not to erect a theoretical edifice that would tell us what truth, power, or sexuality is, but to make visible the ways in which the subject learns to speak the truth, and hence to govern both itself and others. In this way, he hopes to expose the mechanisms of power and render them open, if not to our consent, then at least to our will and resistance (Foucault 2012b: 74–7). Truth is something that is made and thus can be a weapon or a tool.

## II

The circle of *alèthurgie* will only be completely closed when it will have passed through individuals who are able to say "I," by my eyes, my hands, my memory, my testimony: the affirmation of men who say, "I was there," "I saw it," "I did it," "I gave it with my own hands," "I received it with my own hands." Without reaching this point, therefore, of what one might call subjectivation, in the general procedure and in the global cycle of *alèthurgie*, the manifestation of truth would remain incomplete.

Foucault 2012b: 72

All seeing time found you, even if you were unwilling;
It brought to judgement the marriage that was not a marriage,
Which was conceiving the already conceived.
Oh child of Laius!
Would that I had either known
Or never known you;
How I lament
Pouring out an extravagant voice
From my mouth! But to tell the truth,

> I drew breath again from you
> And I have put my eye to sleep.
>
> OT 1213–22

In what follows, I will offer an account of Foucault's reading of the *Oedipus Tyrannus* as presented within *On the Government of the Living*. I will supplement this account with materials drawn from three other published versions of Foucault's reading of the tragedy, the first from his 1970 course at the Collège de France, the second from a lecture that he gave at the University of Buffalo in 1972 and the next year in Rio, which was published with that first course (2011), and the third from a series of lectures he gave at Louvain (2012a), the year after *On the Government of the Living* in 1980.[7] At the same time, I will make reference back to the original text of *Oedipus* both to understand Foucault's work and to shed light on its perspicacity and limits.

In opposition to Freud, the *Oedipus* for Foucault is less a tale of unconscious desires than a treatise on knowledge and how it functions within different regimes of truth (2012b: 24; cf. 2011: 185). Freud had posed the question of why does the *OT* continue to resonate with us more than 2,000 years after its first performance and had proposed in response that the desires it articulates—parricide and incest—are both universal (or at least widely shared) and unavowable (Freud 1965: 294–8; Dawe 2006: 1–3; Armstrong 2012). Foucault, however, sees *Oedipus Tyrannus* not as an allegory for the ways in which social and family structures constrain our desires but as the dramatization of a particular relation "between political power and factual knowledge" (2012a: 74n3). "The entire tragedy of Oedipus is run through with the effort to transform into observed facts the enigmatic dispersion of human events (murders, plagues) and divine threats" (Foucault 2011: 179). More specifically, Foucault argues, the *OT* presents one of the first moments where the modern conception of truth as established by an independent observer, who has neither special access to a supernatural realm nor is endowed with a unique social status, is articulated.

To be sure, the complex and conflicted relationship between Foucault and psychoanalysis has been examined at length by others, and I have discussed it elsewhere.[8] In the present context, though, it should be recalled that Freud's fundamental argument is that the Oedipus myth speaks to the social necessity of shaping and hence limiting our desires (the incest taboo) and the simultaneous drive to transgress those limitations (in fantasy, dreams, and works of art). Foucault's reading does not address this level of analysis (Black 1998). His reading focuses on the *OT* as dramatizing a specific moment in the history of the constitution of truth and its relation to power in the West. These readings are not mutually exclusive.[9] They address fundamentally different registers of existence. Where Freud speaks to the continuing salience of the myth itself—why Oedipus continues to fascinate us—Foucault's interpretation is firmly linked to the performance of the Sophoclean text in its original historical context.[10]

For Foucault, the *OT* is fundamentally about conflicts between competing conceptions or "regimes" of truth. From its first articulation in 1971, Foucault's interpretation argued that *Oedipus Tyrannus* was characterized by "the logic of the *sumbolon*" (2011: 191). A *sumbolon*, from which we derive our word "symbol," is an object that allowed two strangers to identify each other as participants in an agreement or group by putting together (*sumballein*) two pieces of an object, such as two halves of a broken pot, which together constitute a whole. In the *OT*, according to Foucault, the truth becomes manifest through a series of pairs, in which the representative of each of three possible regimes of truth must find their corresponding halves to produce a recognizable form of knowledge, and only when those three pairs are taken together is the truth as a whole revealed to Oedipus and the audience. A *sumbolon* is, in fact, a common metaphor from the period for any form of acknowledgment or recognition, in which one piece of information is matched with another, either to give the truth of a situation or to attest to the validity of an agreement (*LSJ*).

For Oedipus within the play, a *sumbolon* is portrayed as a "clue" required for him to begin the process of solving the crime of Laius's murder. At the beginning of the first episode, he declares, with no small dramatic irony, that since he is a stranger (*xenos*) to this place and to this deed, he must begin his inquiry into who murdered Laius without a solid piece of evidence or a clue (*sumbolon*) that would lead him on the trail (*ikhneuon*) to the discovery of the truth (*OT* 219–21; see Dawe 2006: loc. cit.). One thing needs to be fitted with the next for Oedipus to arrive at the truth that will save the city. He is an inductive thinker. Of course, Oedipus is neither a stranger to the city nor to the deed, a fact that he will come to recognize in a moment of shattering self-knowledge once he has assembled all the relevant *sumbola*, once he has put together all the relevant halves.[11] This is in fact his monstrosity: he is himself structured as a *sumbolon*. His truth can only be fully viewed once he has put his relevant halves together: he is both the son and spouse of his mother; he is both the father and brother of his children. He is irretrievably double.

Likewise, Oedipus's words often say one thing but signify another (Foucault 2012b: 33). It is not so much that his meanings are repressed as in excess. His discourse signifies more than he understands, producing ambiguities that remain unresolved until the play's end. The language he uses to announce his pursuit of Laius's killer reveals his guilt and monstrosity:

> Now, since I happen to have both the offices he had before and his marriage bed, his wife sown with the same seed (*homosporon*), and we would have common children, if his race had not been ill-favored, if they should have been born, but, as it is, chance springs upon his head: on account of these things, I shall engage in this fight, just as for my own father, and to all things I shall arrive, seeking after the self-same hand of murder.
>
> OT 258–63

Every word he speaks to justify his pursuit of Laius's killer is an unwitting confession. *Homosporon* is here a cruelly pregnant metaphor (Telo 2020: 258–60). The "self-same hand of murder" is his own. His knowledge and his ignorance, each signifies the other, as over the course of the play he finds both that he does not know what he thought he knew, and that what he seeks to find out, he already knew (Foucault 2012b: 50, 66). He is subject and object of this pursuit (Foucault 2012a: 75n3).

In his 1971 lecture, "Le Savoir d'Oedipe," Foucault defines the three regimes of truth governing the "symbolic" halves operative in the play as the "divine," the human with regard to the death of Laius, and the human related to Oedipus's birth. These halves correspond within the play to the oracle of Apollo and the prophecy of Tiresias, the declarations of Oedipus and those of Jocasta, and the testimony of the Theban shepherd and the messenger from Corinth. The two human pairs are treated as having much the same status, and together they are said to fill in the lacunae left in the oracular discourse necessary to solve the riddle of the plague (Foucault 2011: 228–32). By 1980, however, this analysis has been refined to recognize that these three pairs are arranged in descending order of social importance, from the divine through the royal to the common (Foucault 2012b: 31–3).

This refinement, while perhaps obvious, is of no minor import to Foucault's larger genealogical scheme: for, a principal point in Foucault's argument of 1980 is that the *Oedipus* marks a particular inflection point in the way truth is understood within the West, one that anticipates Heidegger's arguments about Plato and the beginning of metaphysics referenced in the "Introduction" and earlier in this chapter. To wit, the Myth of the Cave offers the first full articulation of a correspondence model of truth in which an autonomous subject apprehends the truth of the object by correctly referring to it by the category or type to which it belongs (Miller 2020a). For Heidegger, the story of Western philosophy as metaphysics begins with Plato, and by "metaphysics" he means representational thinking, in which truth is defined as the adequacy of the representation possessed by the subject in relation to the object (Heidegger 1998: 181; Mortensen 1994: 80–2; Jones 2011: 43). This understanding of truth is anything but natural (Heidegger 1982: 145). It refers to a particular mode of being a subject, limited in time and space. What we see in Plato, Heidegger argues, is a fundamentally new concept of truth, in which the world is grasped as a "picture." What is only *is* to the extent it enters representation, and that representation can be more or less correct (Heidegger 1998: 129–31). This new vision of truth as "what has been seen" (*idea*) is not the exclusive way in which truth is constituted for the Greeks, who at the time of the *Republic* still possess the earlier notion of truth as what Heidegger translates "unhiddenness," but which might be more accurately termed "that which escapes oblivion" or *alētheia*. The truth of the *Iliad* is not fundamentally what Plato imagines in the Myth of the Cave.[12] The "honor" or *timē* of Achilles is not a universally agreed upon abstract standard or code, which can be perceived and referenced by an observing subject, but the receipt of his war prize, Briseis, whom Agamemnon takes as his own (Detienne 1996: 16, 26, 45–52). The *OT*, although performed some fifty years before the writing of the *Republic*, reveals the first steps in the process of creating this modern subject of knowledge. It does so in part through its deployment of these ordered pairs of *sumbola* and the divisions they indicate between their respective regimes of truth.

In point of fact, Sophocles' audience was living through a time of radical epistemic change and uncertainty. In the midst of the Peloponnesian War, which would bring the democracy to its knees, Athenian citizens were simultaneously experiencing what is popularly known as the Greek

Enlightenment (Beer 2004: 97–9). Circa 429, when the *OT* was first performed, Socrates roamed the city's streets, challenging the leading citizens to show how they knew what they claimed to know. Herodotus invented what we today call history. Philosophy and medicine were constituting themselves as disciplines with their own vocabularies. The sophists were offering instruction in rhetoric, argumentation, political theory, and the art of arguing both sides of a question (Long 1968: 24–5, 166–7; Wilson 2012: 538–43). A radical interrogation of traditional modes of speaking and authenticating the truth was underway, and new forms of veridiction and verification were being forged (Detienne 1996: 104–6, 116–18; Beer 2012: 108–10). Oedipus, the man who saved the city of Thebes by the power of his own "unsurpassable skills of ratiocination" (Liapis 2012: 88), who solved the riddle of the Sphinx, was in many ways the very image of the emergence of these new forms of truth and of their disruptive power within traditional culture.[13] At one point, he challenges Tiresias:

> Come then and tell me, where are you clear sighted, prophet? How did you not pronounce what would free these citizens, when the rhapsodic hound[14] was here? And yet the riddle was not just for any man who came along to solve, but it required skill in prophecy, which you were shown not to possess from the birds, nor something known from the gods. But I came along, Oedipus who knew nothing, and I stopped her, having acquired this by thought, but having learned nothing from birds.
>
> *OT* 390–8

Where the chorus speaks in terms of luck, prophecy, and bird signs (e.g., 52), referencing the preexisting regime of truth, of which Apollo and Tiresias are emblematic, Oedipus seeks the "clue" (*ikhneuon* ... *sumbolon*, 221) that leads to the "trail (*ikhnos*) of ancient guilt" (109). He follows an inductive process based on his powers of reason and perception. He does not fear what Creon says when the latter returns from the oracle. He will attend to Creon's *logos*—signifying not only his speech itself but also its logic, its argument, the relation between its words and the truth they present (88–9). After the messenger from Corinth comes and presents Oedipus with the information that he was not in fact the son of Polybus but a foundling, even as Jocasta warns him against pursuing the matter further, Oedipus says he will take up the "signs" (*sēmeia*) and follow them where they lead (1058–9; Foucault 2012b: 56).

Oedipus is the man of reason who seeks "evidence" or "signs": (*tekmēria*,[15] *sēmeia*) to confirm his intuitions. His truth, at least at the beginning of the play, is apart from that of Tiresias and hence of a different order from that of the prophets and poets of Homeric and Hesodic *alētheia*. It is a truth centered in the subject of knowing and his experience. Foucault cites the Pythagorean Alcmeon of Croton as an avatar of Sophocles' Oedipus. Alcmeon, in a fragment preserved by Diogenes Laertius, claims "the gods have certainty, but we men, we have the *tekmērion*, we have the indication, the mark" (Foucault 2012b: 56, citing 8.83; cf. 2012a: 65). Human beings are subjects of knowledge who reason from one indication or sign to the next. For the gods, knowledge is immediate. Foucault observes that *sēmeion* or "sign" in the Greek of the period has a strong medical coloring, often referring to the symptom by which a disease and its cause might be identified (Foucault 2012b: 57). In the context of the plague ravaging Thebes, Oedipus's desire "to take up the signs/symptoms" (1058–9) of his own past so that he may "learn clearly" (1065) what they signify *vis-à-vis* the murder of Laius can only add a further ironic resonance. As Jocasta exclaims in reply to this expression of Oedipus's implacable will to know, "oh ill-fated man, may you never know who you are!" (1068). Yet he cannot stop. When the Theban shepherd is about to reveal his true identity and fears to say the terrible truth, Oedipus replies: "But all the same listen I must" (1170).

Oedipus, then, as Foucault observes, has a certain *tekhnē* for discovering the truth, meaning "a skill that can be taught and learned," and it is this method or procedure of inductive reasoning from signs or symptoms that over the course of the play will allow him to begin to reconstruct the past (what happened to Laius, who was there, who is his father) and will require him to go beyond this reconstruction and seek confirmation from direct witnesses in the persons of the shepherd and messenger (Foucault 2012b: 65; 2012a: 67, 71). It is this *tekhnē* that initially gives him confidence that he has avoided the decrees of the gods—that he will slay his father and marry his mother—by fleeing from Corinth and solving the riddle of the Sphinx (Liapis 2012: 93). It is also a skill that he denies Tiresias to possess (357, 389), and it is that by which he defines his position as "tyrant" or "sole ruler" of the city (*tekhnē tekhnēs*). It is the skill that warrants his rule, the claim to truth that founds his power (380). But it is this same rational art that leads him to follow the signs of his own monstrosity to their logical end and to demand the testimony that will show the prophecy he thought to have escaped to be fulfilled (Liapis 2012: 93). It will, once all the *sumbola* of truth are assembled together at the play's end, convict him as the cause of the plague, blinding him by the power of his own insight.

Oedipus's frame of reference in the course of his inquest is resolutely materialist. When he questions the story told concerning the attack on Laius, the reality of Apollo's prophecy, or Tiresias's reasons for accusing him, the motives he cites for what he considers their fabrications are either financial or self-interestedly political (124, 345–9, 385–9). The same can be said of Jocasta, who in response to Oedipus's charge that Creon had suborned Tiresias, proposes to offer sure proofs that the prophecies and omens of mortal men are not to be heeded, "Now letting go of the things you are saying, listen to me and learn why nothing mortal possessing the art of prophecy should concern you: I will make the signs (*sēmeia*) of these things appear to you in short order" (707–10). It would be difficult to imagine words like these in the mouth of Agamemnon, Achilles, or Hesiod. Oedipus is cast as the model of a new subject of knowledge. He relies on his own experience and reason to track down a truth that is both external to him—he must find the clue, recognize the evidence, conduct an inquest—and a product of his rational capabilities.

Yet Oedipus is also the representative of institutional political power. He had acceded to that power through the force of his intellect, but his warrant to rule rests, as he himself makes clear, on his marriage to Jocasta (258–9) and thus on the claim to dynastic rule that Creon as her brother shares with her.[16] As Creon observes, when Oedipus accuses the former of plotting against him, why would Creon prefer to be "tyrant" (592), when he can already exercise "the painless rule and collective aristocratic power to which he was born" (*arkhēs alupou kai dunasteias ephu*, 593; Foucault 2012b: 52). Thus, while Oedipus may be *tyrannos*, a secular title referring to the ruler of a city who acquired power by his own devices, as Pisistratus had in sixth-century Athens, he nonetheless addresses Creon as *anax* (85), a traditional term widely used in Homer for the chieftains or kings who led the various armies, like Agamemnon, Menelaus, Odysseus, or Achilles (Kamerbeek 1967: loc. cit.; Macintosh 2009: 15). It is here the equivalent of "lord" and will be used by Creon of Oedipus, in turn, in what seems a purely honorific fashion but is laden, as is so much in this play, with dramatic irony (96, 103).

The subject position from which Oedipus seeks and speaks the truth is thus a conflicted one. He is the representative of rightful rule, vouched for by the fact that he shares the bed of the previous ruler's wife and thus shares the claims to power that accrued to her family. He is the self-made man who arrived in Thebes and reached the pinnacle of power by the force of his intellect. The contradictions of his position are felt most vividly in his initial inability to produce a truth that reconciles, through the force of his intellect, his recollections and perceptions with the prophetic truth announced by the god. For this, he will require the authentication of the third pair of *sumbola* or epistemic halves, the testimony of the Theban shepherd and the Corinthian messenger concerning his birth: eyewitness testimony from those who neither represent the traditions of divine authority nor their political analogues. The ultimate response to Apollo's oracle is not given by the wise or the powerful but by a slave who had been a witness, who had *seen* (Foucault 2011: 179). His sight will rob Oedipus of his own, revealing him not to be the self-made tyrant of the play's traditional title, but the true son of Laius. Only once this is revealed does the chorus address him as *basileus*, the hereditary and hence sacred king (1202; Knox 1979; Dawe 2006: loc. cit.). Oedipus, through his pursuit of new forms of empirical truth that purport to debunk traditional powers of prophecy ironically restores them, losing his tyranny in the moment he is revealed as Laius's rightful heir.[17] And though the line is much debated (see Rusten 1990: loc. cit.; Hogan 1991: loc. cit.; Dawe 2006: loc. cit.), one sense of the chorus's observation in the second stasimon, "Hubris begets the tyrant" (872), must be that while the *tyrannos* claims to arrive at the pinnacle of power under his own steam (a form of arrogance if there ever was one), Oedipus is dethroned the moment he is recognized by the lowest inhabitant of Thebes for what he is, the son of the king, the legitimate heir to the throne, and the one who has fulfilled all that was foretold and so now must be expelled as the final result of his own implacable will to know (Foucault 2011: 249–50).

Each of the regimes of truth operative within the play has its own set of rules, its own phenomenology. The truth as articulated by Apollo and answered by Tiresias, Foucault argues, would have been fully recognized in the world of Homer and the archaic age that followed in the sixth and seventh centuries BCE. In the Homeric world, he contends, veridiction is the manifestation of a truth exterior to the speaking subject. The Homeric bards, the rhapsodes, the prophets speak the truth in the same manner as a dream or vision, not through a process of personal observation and verification, but through the emergence of another speaker within the self: the god, the muse, the voice of "eternal fame" (*kleos aphthiton*).[18] Neither Apollo nor Tiresias are knowing subjects in the manner of either Plato's dwellers in the cave or of those philosophers who through their own efforts and strict training are able to see beyond immediate appearance to the nature of things themselves. They do not formulate propositions that are then tested against observed reality or through dialectical interchange. If Tiresias speaks the truth, it is precisely because it is *not* he who speaks. He becomes the voice of the Other. He like Homer is blind. His truth is authenticated by the fact that he is not the person who possesses it (Foucault 2012b: 48–9). By the same token, the god is never simply a witness. Apollo's will and his perception are one. "There is not … any difference between what Apollo sees and what he wants: he wants what he sees, he sees what he wants, it suffices that he has seen it for it to become effectively, over a longer or shorter term, the truth and reality" (Foucault 2012a: 57). In Homer, his will may only be thwarted by another god or by fate itself, but not by the reality that is the object of our experience. Certainly, within the context of the play and within the context of oracular pronouncements and actual cultic practice, what is said by the god is true by definition and requires no external validation or process of verification (Foucault 2012a: 56–7). This is why Plato says in the *Symposium* that the gods do not desire, because that would mean they were imperfect and functionally indistinguishable from men: in the realm of the divine there can be no distinction between what is wanted and what is. They are coterminous. The god and his prophet therefore can see the future because the god's will and the future are one, whereas the knowledge that Oedipus has as the man of *tekhnē* is a backward facing knowledge that rejects prophecy and believes it can escape the future by its own resources, it can escape fate (Foucault 2011: 242–3).

That said, while Oedipus and Jocasta operate within a very different regime of truth than that of the god and his prophet, they are not simply the average person. They are not interchangeable subjects with the slaves who will prove to Oedipus who he is and what he has done. Oedipus and Jocasta occupy positions of power and status that give their words special relevance, but which they are unable to validate themselves (Foucault 2011: 225–6). As Foucault makes clear in a set of lectures given at Louvain, *Wrong Doing, Truth Telling: The Function of Avowal in Justice*, within the context of the play, acts of truth-telling by the divine are not able to be sufficient to themselves, even if, as the play unfolds, they are shown to have been accurate as originally stated (2012a: 53). They require a supplemental confirmation. It is the same with Oedipus and Jocasta:

> And then, there is a second production of truth. This second production is the work once again of two characters who complete one another: Jocasta and Oedipus who, recalling their memories ... say together, the one and the other, the totality of things that would allow one to recognize Oedipus as the husband of his mother and the assassin of his father. This second veridiction, this second *alèthurgie*, again, remains in suspense and is not accepted: it is not validated, it still has an element of uncertainty.
>
> Foucault 2012a: 54

Of course, one of the greatest ironies, as Foucault observes, is that when Oedipus and Jocasta offer their most persuasive proofs that the predictions of prophets are not to be trusted, they in effect confirm their accuracy. Jocasta advances that Laius had self-evidently not been killed by his son, since he had been exposed. Oedipus responds that he had self-evidently not killed his father, since he had left Polybus in good health in Corinth (Foucault 2012a: 60). There are times during their interchanges when the dialogue reads like one extended parapraxis in which the voice of the Other speaks.[19] The audience shivers as it recognizes the implications of what is being said:

**Oedipus**   What time has elapsed since (the death of Laius)?

**Jocasta**   Just a little before you appeared as ruler of this land, it was announced to the city.

**Oedipus**   Oh Zeus, what have you determined about my actions?

**Jocasta**   What is troubling your mind, Oedipus?

**Oedipus**   Never ask me. But say what he was like when he set off, was he at the height of youth?

**Jocasta**   He was large, his head having a recent dusting of white, but his shape was not so different from yours.

OT 735–43

It is hard to imagine that they do not realize, on some level, what has happened, when Jocasta observes that Oedipus and Laius bore more than a passing resemblance to one another. The coincidences pile up in an unsustainable manner. Yet what is really new on the epistemic level, as Foucault observes, is not that the gods are in the end proven to be correct, or that the rulers of Thebes are shown to be subject to the laws of fate, the will of Apollo, and the vision of Tiresias, but that these truths can only be accepted, only be verified, when confirmed by the eyewitness testimony of slaves, of those who have no claim to the authority of truth other than their status as knowing subjects (Foucault 2011: 225–26; 2012a: 58–9). As the chorus says after Oedipus's confrontation with Tiresias, "Zeus and Apollo understand and know the affairs of mortals, but of men, the prophet carries off more than I, there is no judging (*krisis*) of truth. And a man excels wisdom with wisdom" (498–503). Oedipus and Tiresias confront each other with truths of different orders and for the chorus at this point there can be no choosing between them.

At the same time, it is precisely Oedipus's self-confidence in his own rational powers that will engender the investigation that confirms prophecy. No *deus ex machina* intervenes to bring the plot to a close or to reveal the superiority of divine to human wisdom. It is Oedipus's relentless inquiry that exposes his and Jocasta's crimes. Indeed, at the play's beginning, he imagines himself as an earthly Apollo: the sun who makes the darkness dissipate and the hidden appear:

**Oedipus**   What great evil at your feet, when his rule (*turannidos*) had fallen, barred you from knowing the killer of Laius?

**Creon**   The Sphinx of riddling song led us to look only at things that lay at our feet, giving up on those not apparent.

**Oedipus**   I will make these things appear again, from the beginning: for rightly has Phoebus, and rightly you, turned attention to the dying man.

*OT* 128–34

But "these things" do not appear by royal decree, or by the powers of Oedipus as *tyrannos*, ruler of Thebes. The truth only fully emerges once it has been confirmed by the direct observation of third parties, whose position as knowing subjects is open to all.

There is a dialectic of truth and power that Foucault seeks to expose in *On the Government of the Living*.[20] On the one side of this dialectic, there is the necessity of the manifestation of truth for the exercise of power (2012b: 71). Truth is an adjunct to and underwrites the existence and exercise of power. Oedipus must find the cause of the plague if he is to remain as *tyrannos*, a power granted in the first instance by his ability to solve the riddle of the Sphinx. In this respect, he is no different from Septimius Severus or any other ruler whose claim to power must rest on a claim to truth. Within the play, his will to know is the structural principle that drives its plot. In seeking the cause of the plague, Oedipus discovers he must also solve the murder of Laius. The *OT* is our first murder mystery. At every turn within the play, Oedipus's continued exercise of power depends on acts of discovering and manifesting the truth (*alèthurgies*). On the other side of the dialectic, the truth determines the nature of power and is not wholly determined by it or a simple adjunct to it. Within the play, the truth does not reside fully either in the hands of the gods and their oracles or in the hands of those who exercise constituted power, but their veridictions must be verified and their power ratified by a larger set of individuals who can authenticate them (Foucault 2012b: 71–2). These individuals take the form of witnesses and of the chorus itself as the citizen body (Foucault 2012a: 57; 2012b: 29). This truth is open to certain forms of revision, to certain forms of resistance, that in themselves can contest, shape, and reshape power:

> The circle of *alèthurgie* will only be fully closed when it will have passed through individuals who are able to say "I," by my eyes, my hands, memory, testimony, the affirmation of men who say: I was there, I saw, I did, I gave with my own hands, I received with my own hands. Without this point, then, of what we could call subjectivation, in the general procedure and the global cycle of *alèthurgie*, the manifestation of the truth would remain incomplete.
>
> Foucault 2012b: 72

Power, then, is constituted by the intersection between the truth it manifests, as its claim to legitimacy, and the mechanisms established for its ratification, which within the context of the *Oedipus* are made decisively dependent on the presence of subjects of knowledge who can say that they saw the things in question, not as kings or prophets, not as functions of their position, but as subjects of knowledge who can say "I." Foucault's reading of the *OT* in 1980 places at its center, then, not only the necessity of the manifestation of truth for the exercise of power but also the role of the self as the guarantor of that truth, and this is what allows him to join this reading of the *Oedipus* to the second half of the course, which is concerned with early Christian practices of confession (Senellart 2012: 326–7).

The *OT*, it should be remembered, ends powerfully with the publication and recognition of fault. When the truth has finally been established through the testimony of the messenger and former shepherd from Corinth and his analogue, the servant of Laius first charged to dispose of the infant Oedipus, it is Oedipus himself who recognizes and publicizes his fault on stage for all to see, inflicting the most graphic of symbolic punishments upon himself, gouging out his eyes with Jocasta's brooches. As Foucault observes near the end of the course, when making explicit the linkage he sees between the *Oedipus* and the practices of Christian confession he studies in the second half:

> You regularly find in pagan religions, in Greek and Roman religions, the necessity or in any case the efficacy, when you have sinned, of a solemn publication to the god, to manifest that you are wretched, according to the rite of supplication to which someone submits when misfortune has beaten down upon them, but also when you have committed a fault and, *a fortiori*, when the fault and misfortune are joined together. We see it very well in the *Oedipus* of Sophocles; when he arrives blind and a suppliant, he manifests his misfortune and his fault. A sort of exomologesis[21]: I am a criminal, I have committed a fault and I am wretched.
>
> Foucault 2012b: 223

Thus, at the end of the *OT*, we see the confluence of four kinds of veridiction. There are the three sets of *sumbola*, in which each pair of symbolic halves requires the next set in order to confirm and actualize the truth the previous pair has announced: Apollo and Tiresias, Oedipus and Jocasta, the Corinthian messenger and the Theban shepherd. But these pairs are only finally ratified and accepted by the chorus as incontrovertible truth with the confession of Oedipus, now stripped of his power and reduced to the figure of the suffering subject. "Yes, I have done this. Yes, it myself—*autos*—I have seen it, I have heard it, I have given it, I have done it" (Foucault 2012a: 69)

## III

On January 30, 1980, at the beginning of the fourth week of lectures, Foucault, after summarizing his reading of the *Oedipus*, pivots to the topic that will occupy him for the rest of the course, early Christian practices of penance and confession. He marks the shift as follows:

> Here then are three themes that I wanted to underline: first, the relation between the manifestation of truth and the exercise of power; second, the importance and necessity, for this same exercise of power, of a truth that is manifested, at least in certain points, but in an absolutely indispensable fashion, in the form of subjectivity; finally third, the effect of this manifestation of truth in the form of subjectivity, the effect of this manifestation beyond, let us say, certain immediately utilitarian relations of factual knowledge. The *alèthurgie*, the manifestation of truth, is much more than providing something to know.
>
> Foucault 2012b: 73

There follows a brief discussion of what Foucault understands to be the stakes of this undertaking before he turns to the texts of early Christian fathers such as Tertullian, Clement of Alexandria, and Cassian, who are also the focus of the posthumously published volume four of the *History of Sexuality*, *Les Aveux de la chair*. In these texts, the practice of confession is initially the answer to a specific theological problem, how can one repent from sin after baptism has offered absolution, since baptism is not a repeatable process? How, then, does one stay in a state of grace? Foucault traces, over the course of the next two months, the movement from an initial attempt to answer this problem to the later development of doctrines and procedures that sought to establish the nature of the confessing subject, the procedures whereby the truth of that subject could be established, and the relations of power produced within and through these procedures.

The stakes of this seemingly esoteric inquiry, Foucault argues, are critical: tracing how truth-telling came to be authenticated by the speaking subject as the possessor of truth (2012b: 49). How is it that our experience became central to the game of truth? In answer, Foucault proposes to undertake a history of veridiction, conceived not as the steady progress of a disembodied scientific reason, or as the slow evolution toward ever greater forms of objectivity, but as the recounting of a series of countless acts performed by a subject. Truth on this view is not a constant of the world, nor is it a set of external objects whose reality is slowly revealed by the progression of Spirit, but it is a series of actions performed by people in the world. Truth has a history (Foucault 2012b: 111–12; Allen 2016: 132). And the question Foucault wishes to pose to that history is: how is it that, in a society such as ours, power cannot be exercised without truth being made manifest in the form of subjectivity, without our confession, without our articulation of who and what we are in relation to various structures of power—the family, the state, institutions of education, agencies of public health—and thus without our "consent" (2012b: 73–4, 79). Part of the power of confession is that we must want to confess, and we must be able to articulate our desire for it.

Through this history, Foucault does not aim to create and defend an "ensemble of propositions." He does not propose a general theory that would seek to frame (and thus control) the world. He posits instead a series of critical displacements that, by tracing the genealogy of how we came to be who we are, allows us to become increasingly free, or at least distanced, from the structures of power that constitute our world (2012b: 74–6).

> Let us say that if the great forward progression of philosophy consists in putting in place a methodical doubt that holds in suspension all certitudes, the small lateral alternative movement that I am proposing to you consists in trying systematically to put into play, not the suspension of all certitudes, but the non-necessity of every kind of power, whatever it may be.
>
> Foucault 2012b: 76

Foucault does not seek to do away with power. That is a logical absurdity. There could be no greater power play. But by revealing the "contingency and fragility of history" (2012b: 76), he wishes to show us that there is no power that simply must be accepted, that no power is definitively inevitable, and that every power, every form of governmentality, is open to resistance, and indeed constitutes the force of its own resistance in the moment of its assertion (Foucault 2012b: 76–7; cf. 1976: 125–7).

Truth is a weapon in this struggle. It is not an inert property, nor a metaphysical reality dictating the world in which live, the world that makes us who we are in relation to ourselves and others. "There is always the possibility, in a given game of truth, of discovering something else and of changing more or less such and such a rule, and sometimes even the whole ensemble of the game of truth" (Foucault 1994g: 725–6). Indeed, the problem Foucault had set for himself, as he noted in an interview, was to learn "how truth comes to things" (2012a: 247), and through this knowledge to discover how things can be different, how there can be a "revolution" (2012b: 16). As Leonard Lawlor observes, "the central concern of [Foucault's] thinking is the relation of truth and freedom" (2016: 145).

We should pause for a moment to register how far we are from the common understanding, particularly in Classics, of what Foucault's concerns were during this period. While he is certainly interested in sexuality and its history, it is hardly the case that his animating concern was to produce a history of sexual practices, sexual roles, or even discourses. The sexual is but one grid through which a much larger inquiry into the nature and history of the truth, as related to the subject, is to be undertaken. The sexual does have a certain privilege. He did after all produce three books in the eighties that he entitled the *History of Sexuality* (volumes two to four), but that privilege is related to his larger problematic of the subject's relation to truth rather than the other way around. The privilege of the sexual is related precisely to the ways in which our confessional discourses have seen the sexual as something at once deeply related to our inner truth and as a primary locus of social control through rules, codes, and norms concerning the family, gender, and, within Christianity, the problem of the flesh, the consequences of embodiment.

What Foucault aims to produce, then, is "a political history of truth-tellings" (2012a: 9), beginning with an astonishment that "truth" exists and not simply the world. Critical philosophy since the time of Kant has had two primary forms: an analytic of the conditions of possibility for speaking the truth (epistemology); and an interrogation of the various possible forms of veridiction (genealogy). It is the latter that constitutes Foucault's primary interest. He is less concerned with how one may speak the truth about ourselves and the world, important as that is, than with the "very ancient multiplication and proliferation of truth-telling, the dispersion of regimes of veridiction" (Foucault 2012a: 10). For him, the most general political problem is how do we establish, link, and collate different ways of dividing up the world, of determining the true and the false, and hence different ways of governing ourselves and others (Rajchman 1991: 124–5).

From this perspective, there are few tasks more pressing than tracing the genealogy of the confessing subject and its relation to the church. Foucault begins by reminding us that what we understand as the sacrament of confession is not found in the primitive church. It is an artefact of the thirteenth-century Lateran Council. In the beginning, the word *confessor* simply meant one who made a full and complete profession of faith, even in the face of death. To this day, we speak of differences between sects as *confessional* differences. Each confession involves an act of truth in relation to which the subject assumes both an identity and a specific form of self-relation. Each involves the subject undertaking an act of truth and, in relation to that act, the individual within Christianity has been enjoined, in one form or another, depending on the time, place, and sect, to recognize their own sinful nature and their own need for salvation, their need in some manner to avow their sin (Foucault 2012b: 79–84). In proposing to do a genealogy of the confessing subject from Oedipus to the present, by way of the early church, Foucault proposes to do a history of what he terms one of the most fundamental injunctions in Western civilization for the last two thousand years, "Tell me who you are" (2012b: 143).

The earliest form for a believer to recognize his or her own sinful nature after baptism was a practice termed *exomologesis*, Foucault recounts, in which the sinner would acknowledge their sinfulness to a member of the clergy and request to be accepted as a penitent. This status was public and cast one outside the communion of the faithful. The penitent was required to remain outside the church, wear torn clothing with ashes on their head and other visible signs of mourning until such time as the congregation decided to welcome the penitent back into their midst (often on Good Friday), with a public display of contrition. *Exomologesis* did not involve a detailed inventory of the sins committed, let alone of sinful thoughts, with a prescribed schedule of acts of contrition that could be repeated again and again. This would come later (2012a: 176). It was rather a public and dramatic recognition of one's sinfulness and an equally public return to the community after a period of exclusion and contrition (Foucault 2012b: 220–1; cf. 2012a: 101–14; 2018: 78–105; Elden 2016: 118).

Such processes were essentially improvised by the early church. There is no biblical guidance on how sin after baptism should be addressed. As Foucault observes, for Saint Paul baptism was a re-enactment of the death and resurrection of Christ. It was a singular and unrepeatable act in the life of the believer, which erased all that had come before (2012b: 152). The decision to seek baptism is, Tertullian observed, a moment of fear and danger as one discovers the helpless and fallen nature of the self and prepares for its death and transfiguration through Christ. The prospective initiate into the mystery of the faith must first discover their own inner truth in order then to have access to salvational truth. The time before baptism, therefore, is a time of self-scrutiny and contemplation. Tertullian's articulation of this double movement represents a decisive moment in the history of Western thought, Foucault argues, because it is the first moment when the possibility of becoming the knowing subject and having access to the truth is dependent on the prior recognition of an inner truth, which is not so much part of salvational truth as the recognition of an absolute separation from it (Foucault 2012b: 124, 140; cf. 2018: 52–77). This is a very different form of self-relation than that through which Oedipus becomes the knowing subject. The fullness of knowledge may only come to Oedipus once he as a subject recognizes his past deeds, but this recognition is neither the confession of an essential nature nor is it the predicate for the reception of a larger transcendental truth that redeems the knowing subject from the sinful nature it acknowledges.

The question for Christianity, however, becomes, once one has access to salvational truth, first through introspection and recognition, and then baptism, how is it possible to forget it? How can sin recur in the face of access to divine verity? This problem for early Christian thought was one largely unknown to either Greco-Roman or Hebrew antiquity: if one has attained a state of purity and perfection, how could one return to a state of imperfection? It was a logical conundrum that required a novel solution (Foucault 2012b: 175, 183), which was the development, over time, of a variety of forms of self-examination, confession, and penance/submission to authority. These techniques, as Foucault shows both in this and the following years of his course, would draw upon a panoply of techniques of self-examination already developed by ancient philosophers and spiritual directors in the Platonic and Stoic traditions, even as they transformed those traditions. By the same token, these technologies of the self would take on an afterlife in various forms of religious, judicial, disciplinary, and medical practices that depend upon subjects examining themselves, verbalizing their shortcomings and desires, and seeking redemption, remediation, and transformation through this process of verbalization and submission to the power of the priest, the therapist, or the judge. Oedipus's confession is the final affirmation of a public truth that leads to the expulsion of ritual pollution. It in no way exposes Oedipus's hidden secret nature or procures his salvation (Foucault 2012b: 180).

Where Foucault argues ancient philosophy from Socrates to Epictetus sought self-knowledge as a way of mastering and forming the self, a largely ethical pursuit, the goal of Christian self-examination was the recognition of the need for submission, *patientia*, the confession of powerlessness before one's own fallen nature, before the perversity of our desires. We are not transparent to ourselves but constantly subject to delusion (Foucault 2012b: 224, 261, 298; 2008: 320; Geuss 2017: 103). Tertullian, for example, translates *exomologēsis*, a Greek word, by the Latin *publicatio sui*, a term borrowed from Seneca. In Seneca, it refers to a form of self-examination where, at the end of each day, philosophical subjects ask themselves what have they done and what they could they do better tomorrow. It is a process of rational self-improvement, ordered toward the future. Seneca's vocabulary, Foucault notes, is administrative rather than prosecutorial. This Stoic examination of conscience takes place within the self and thus is very different from the public displays of exclusion and contrition that characterized *exomologēsis*. Our *logos* or reason gives us the power to judge and moderate our behavior. We have judgement, *discretio*. Ancient ethics sought to free the self. Christianity sought to dominate the self, examining the root causes of sin and seeking to eradicate them through their articulation to another. The penitent sought not to exercise their own *discretio*, but to submit to the *discretio* of another (Foucault 2012b: 235–40, 288–9; 1988b: 42; Elden 2016: 159–60).

In this regard, Foucault argues that, to understand how Christianity emerged, we need to understand how it built upon and transformed pre-Christian relations to the self (Elden 2016: 159). In place of self-examination aimed at the recognition of ignorance and the attempt to replace it with knowledge, Christianity reorganizes the relation of the self to itself as an "obligation of the soul to say what it is" (Foucault 2012b: 142). This inquiry into the emergence of the centrality of the subject as a speaker of truth became Foucault's main concern and led directly to his interest in *parrhēsia*, or "frank speech," which he would explore in his final three years of lectures, examining the modes by which the subject in the ancient world formed itself as a truth-teller in the political, the philosophical, and the spiritual sense (Brion and Harcourt 2012: 295).

Thus while in ancient philosophy one might have a relationship to a philosophical teacher or master, such as that described in Plato's *Seventh Letter*, which we will examine in Chapter 4, or to a Stoic director of conscience, such as Seneca's relationship with Lucilius, which we will examine in Chapter 3, that relationship was fundamentally different from what would grow, under the influence of monasticism, into the relationship of a penitent to a director of conscience. Under the Platonic and Socratic model, the goal was through questioning and mutual examination to produce the spark of insight that led to knowledge. In the case of the Stoics, it was to train the student to use reason to avoid suffering. The philosophical director seeks a kind of perfection: the tranquility of the soul, self-mastery, "beatitude." He seeks to produce a certain relation of the self to itself (Foucault 2012b: 227). The Christian director, in contrast, seeks to avoid the illusions and deceits of the devil:

> The problem, the question, the danger in Christian direction will be illusion, that illusion, that non-discrimination between the representation of good and the representation of evil, between the representation, the suggestion that comes from God, that comes from Satan, [and] that comes from myself.
> Foucault 2012b: 291

In the end, Foucault argues, the joining of the verbalization of fault to the exploration of the self cannot be understood outside the practice of the direction of conscience (2012b: 224). What the Christian director seeks is not the subject's autonomy, but its obedience (2012b: 302).

Christianity fundamentally changes the relationship between the government of men and the manifestation of the truth, Foucault argues. It is not, at least at its origins, the opiate of the masses. It does not aim to produce the sleep of reason beneath the veil of ideology, but rather it requires the positive recognition within the self of that which is other, of that which is alien to the Truth writ large, and in the production of this recognition, in the creation of this inner truth, there is a necessary submission to external authority, a submission that both guarantees the existence of that truth and offers the possibility of redemption. The history of penance, and hence the history of the confessing subject, is the history of the techniques by which the self makes itself public, from the public enactment of the return to imperfection dramatized in the rituals of *exomologesis*, to the detailed verbalizations of the medieval confessional, to repeated forms of self-exposure on the therapist's couch, to Maoist self-criticism sessions, and, finally, our zeal for self-improvement (Foucault 2012b: 105–6, 157, 206). Our obsession with hidden desires, secret perversities, and hence with true identities that we must verbalize and assume, is, Foucault argues, an invention of Christianity (Rajchman 1991: 89). "The subjectivation of western man is Christian, it is not Greco-Roman" (Foucault 2012b: 231).

## IV

[Descartes's] evil genius, the idea that there is something inside me that can always deceive me and that has a power such that I am never able to be completely sure that it will not deceive me, this is the absolutely constant theme of Christianity. From Evagrius Ponticus or Cassian till the sixteenth century, there is something in me that can deceive me and nothing assures me that I will not be deceived, even if I am sure not to deceive myself.

Foucault 2012b: 298

In sum, you no longer need to be king, to have killed your father, to have married your mother, to have reigned during the plague, to be constrained to discover the truth of yourself. You can be anyone. You need not be Oedipus to be obliged to search for the truth. No people prey to the plague demands it, but the entire institutional system, the entire cultural system, the entire religious system, and soon the entire social system to which we belong.

Foucault 2012b: 306

In January of 1980, nine years after his first course at the Collège de France, Foucault returned to Oedipus. While he recapitulates many of the themes from his previous lectures on the *OT*, the context has changed (Senellart 2012: 377). Where in *Lessons on the Will to Knowledge* the emphasis is on the elaboration of a Nietzschean genealogy of factual knowledge, in *On the Government of the Living* the emphasis is on the knowing subject, its status as a subject, and how it comes to know itself. In fifth-century Athens and throughout the history of ancient philosophy, Foucault contends, self-knowledge becomes a predicate for knowledge *per se*. The subject's self-awareness is what warrants its status as one who knows, as one who can observe and speak a truth separate from itself.

This is the subtle dialectic between self-formation and veridiction that Foucault will pursue over the coming years: the relationship between the ability to speak the truth about myself and the ability to speak the truth about the world. In the cases of Apollo and Tiresias, or of Homer and Hesiod, there is no assumption that the truth of a statement originates from the speaking subject's ability to separate itself from the object of observation and hence to report on it accurately. Just the opposite! Indeed, it is difficult in these cases to speak of a knowing subject in any normal sense of the term. Likewise, if we consider the heroes of the *Iliad*, their ability to speak the truth is dependent on their status as *anaktes*, "lords, kings." When Thersites in Book 2 gives voice to complaints from the common soldiers at Troy, Odysseus clubs him with the scepter that signals the right to speak in the assembly. Oedipus and Jocasta are also empowered to speak by their social position. But, as Foucault observes, what is remarkable in the *OT* is that neither of these traditional regimes of truth, the divine and the aristocratic, remains adequate in themselves. Their truths can only be confirmed when they have first been ratified by the testimony of two slaves and then assumed by Oedipus, no longer as king or tyrant, but as the humblest of men, the blind beggar.

Like the Corinthian messenger and the Theban shepherd, the knowing subjects of Plato's cave are without status. They are neither kings nor prophets. Nor are they slaves in the conventional sense, though they are certainly bound. Their ability to break free of their chains, to make their way to the upper air and see in the full light of the sun, is not dependent on their social class or the possession of divine insight, but on recognizing the fact that they are bound. Their knowing is dependent on self-knowledge, on their privileging the inscription of the Delphic Oracle on which Socratic practice rests, *gnōthi seauton*, "know thyself."

Ancient philosophical self-knowledge takes many forms, but in no case, Foucault argues—and I would submit that he is right—do they require confrontation with the radically alien within the self, the monstrous, whether in the shape of the devil, Descartes' evil genius, or unconscious desires

(Foucault 2012b: 156). What is new with Christianity, Foucault argues, is not the drive toward self-knowledge, and the forms of self-care that form its predicates, but the relation to the radically other and perverse within. And this is why the culture of confession—the demand to articulate the presence of the other within to *others* without—becomes the lynchpin for Foucault of Western modernity, its forms of governmentality, its drive toward disciplinary self-surveillance, and its subjectivation within discourses of sexuality, the panopticism of the workhouse and the prison, and the biopolitical, neoliberal state. It is also why he will spend the next four years of his life exploring alternative forms of self-care, alternative spiritual practices, alternative ways of learning to speak the truth in Greco-Roman antiquity. "What I am searching for is a permanent openness to possibilities" (Foucault 2012b: 260).

2

# Subjectivity and Truth: From the Interpretation of Dreams to the Philosophic Life

> I think I can stop there and simply remind you how... it would be somewhat inadequate and entirely insufficient, with regard to the extent and complexity of the problems, to want to do a history of sexuality in terms of repression of desire. Rather, on the basis of a history of technologies of self, which seem to me a relatively fruitful point of intelligibility, on the basis of a history of governmentalities—governmentalities of self and others—we should show how the moment of desire was isolated and exalted, and how, on the basis of this, a certain type of relationship of self to self was formed that has itself undergone certain transformations, since we have seen it developed, organized, and distributed in an apparatus (*dispositif*) that was first that of the flesh before becoming much later that of sexuality.
>
> Foucault 2017: 288–9

> We have to ask ourselves about the fact that there exists, beyond simply things, discourses. We have to pose this problem: why is there, beyond the real, the true.
>
> Foucault 2017: 240

Foucault's lectures at the Collège de France in the 1980s are dedicated to antiquity. During this same period, he is drafting volumes two and three of the *History of Sexuality*, the sole work published in his lifetime devoted to the ancient world. It is natural to assume that these lectures function as drafts of the later published work. Yet as the initial course from this period demonstrates, that would be an oversimplification. While much of the work on Christian confession finds echoes in the posthumously published volume four, *Les aveux de la chair* (2018), the lectures on *Oedipus*, on Septimius Severus, and on truth and governmentality find no place in the *History of Sexuality*, nor does much of the work from the later years, 1982 to 1984. Yet this is not the case with

*Subjectivity and Truth*, delivered in the spring of 1981. If any set of lectures forecasts the eventual scope and content of volumes two and three of the *History*, this is it. First drafts of the readings of Artemidorus's *Oneirokritikon*, Plutarch's *Erōtikos*, Xenophon's *Oikonomikos*, and Musonius Rufus on marriage can all be found here. In the *History of Sexuality*, they are presented with more detail but in a narrower philosophical frame. The questions there are centered on the "use of pleasures" in terms of dietetics, economics, and erotics (volume two), and the "care of the self" in terms of the body, women, and boys (volume three). The topic in 1981, however, is "subjectivity and truth" (Gros 2014: 319; Kelly 2014: 173). In this chapter, we shall focus less on what is well covered in the *History* and the literature surrounding it, and more on the larger philosophical question of the genealogy of the subject as a locus of truth.

The lectures start where the previous year's left off. Foucault asks: how does self-knowledge in antiquity, as a qualification for speaking the truth, whether in the tragedy of Oedipus or among the inhabitants of Plato's cave, differ from the confessional knowledge produced by the monastic direction of conscience and later generalized through the sacrament of confession to become the basis of our modern therapeutics of self-disclosure? (Elden 2016: 151, 127). The study of this history allows us to move beyond any notion of a universal model of the subject, one that maintains a substantially identical relation to itself and others across time and space. In the modern world, this subject has been seen as containing a quantum of desire that is either expressed or repressed in accord with dominant social structures. Such a vision is most recognizable in a certain crude psychoanalytic model that likens the psyche to a hydraulic machine, in which the pressure of desire continually accumulates unless and until it is ex-pressed.[1] Such a model is clearly phallic, if not simply ejaculatory. It is also static. But, if in fact the relation of the self to itself and others, to the world without and within, has substantially changed over time—as can be seen in the changing concept of truth as it relates to the speaking subject—then the self cannot be represented as an unchanging constant whose quantum of desire must be managed and directed, re-pressed and ex-pressed, rather the desiring subject, as the modern West has understood it, must be constituted or made. What we must study is not repression *per se*, which assumes a constant countervailing force or pressure, but rather the entire range of forces and technologies that have shaped and could shape the subject, and which under certain conditions can make the repression of sexual expression one aspect of the broader array of forces that constitute a specific mode of governing the self and others, but one that is also for that very reason open to change, open to a recasting of the problematic in which it conceptualizes itself. And this is the point at which the genealogy of the veridical subject and the genealogy of the desiring subject meet, the point at which the history of sexuality and the history of the subject and truth intersect (Foucault 2014: 301; Gros 2014: 309).

As Foucault notes in the *Resumé du Cours*, which he was required to pen each year for the yearbook of the Collège and which he used to reflect on the contents of the course and how they were tied to the larger concerns of his work, *Subjectivity and Truth* seeks to join two recurring themes, "the history of subjectivity and an analysis of the forms of governmentality" (Foucault 2014: 300). What is involved is not so much a "return to subjectivity," as has sometimes been alleged—as though Foucault were returning to a Sartrean or humanist model—as a genealogy of the occidental subject. He is less interested in what we are (e.g., the ontology of freedom) than in how we came to be (Gros 2014: 307–8). He is undertaking "an inquest into the constituted modes of self-knowledge and their history: how the subject has been established at different moments and in different institutional contexts as a desirable or even indispensable object of possible knowledge" (Foucault 2014: 299).

Foucault opens the course by observing that from Kant to Plato the question of the subject's relation to truth has been dominated by the question of "how and under what conditions can I know the truth, or even: how is factual knowledge possible insofar as it is an experience proper to a knowing subject" (Foucault 2014: 12)? In short, insofar as there is no knowledge that is not independent of the viewing subject (i.e., objective) and there is no knowledge that is not known by a subject (i.e., there are no true statements in a world without subjects), how is truth possible? To answer this question, traditional philosophy has sought to resolve on a formal level the tension between two ideas: on the one hand, there cannot be any truth "without a subject for whom this truth is true," and on the other, "if the subject is a subject, can it really have access to the truth?" (Foucault 2014: 12).

In this regard, Kant for Foucault represents a turning point in the history of the Western conceptualization of knowledge, and we will return to his importance for Foucault on more than one occasion in this book. It is not beside the point to recall that Foucault's minor thesis for his doctorate—his major thesis became *Histoire de la folie*—was a translation of Kant's *Philosophical Anthropology*. After what Kant termed his "Copernican revolution,"[2] he poses another question, one which Foucault terms "positivist": "what is the truth of the subject"? Can we treat the subject simply as another object of knowledge, even in the study of its activity of knowing *qua* knowing? This positivist question can be reformulated, Foucault says, as: "how can there be a truth of the subject, when there is no truth except for a subject"? (Foucault 2014: 13). This is the basic question at the root of all the human sciences and the problematic that Foucault outlines at the end of *Les mots et les choses*.

In *Subjectivity and Truth*, however, Foucault asks still a further question: "what experience can the subject have of himself, when he finds himself faced with the possibility or the obligation of recognizing, in himself, something that passes for truth"? This question represents a fundamental displacement from traditional epistemology—how can I know, and what are the conditions of that knowledge—to what are the experiences the subject has of itself insofar as it knows itself, insofar as it recognizes a truth in itself. "The question thus formulated," Foucault reminds us, "is ... fundamentally a historical question" (2014: 13). It inverts the classical epistemological question to ask: what experiences can we have of ourselves that show both the existence of a certain discourse or regime of truth and the obligation to link oneself to this discourse? (Foucault 2014: 27–8). The question is less what constitutes knowledge *per se*—although that remains a question—than what are our experiences as knowing subjects and how do those experiences, insofar as they require us to accede to regimes of discourse and verification beyond ourselves, render us able to govern ourselves and others and to be governed *by* others (Foucault 1988b: 17–18; Brion and Harcourt 2012: 287).

These classical philosophical questions, as well as Foucault's refinements on them, are in no way tangential to these lectures. Foucault's longest single exposition in the thirteen years of lectures he delivered at the Collège de France was his extended meditation on the relation between true discourse and reality that occupies two full weeks of lectures in the last half of the course and returns to the questions about knowing subjects posed at its beginning (Gros 2014: 317). He poses these questions, moreover, specifically in terms of the changing understanding of marriage we see in works such as Xenophon's

*Oikonomikos*, Plutarch's *Erōtikos*, and later Stoic and Cynic texts. Thus, classical philosophical questions—what is the nature of truth, what is knowledge, how are we to understand subjective experience—are reframed in terms of reflections on the erotic behavior of the elite, educated males of the period and their spouses.

What we see in these lectures, more than is ever made explicit in the *History of Sexuality*, is what Foucault saw as the actual philosophical stakes in these texts, which in their intense practical focus seem far removed from the sublimity of Plato's *Phaedrus* or *Oedipus Rex*, or Kant, Hegel, and Marx. There is, in fact, a kind of double movement or dialectic to Foucault's reading. On the one hand, texts such as Artemidorus's *Interpretation of Dreams*, Plutarch's *Conjugal Precepts*, and Musonius' reflections on whether the philosopher should marry are marshalled to perform an implicit genealogical critique. On the other, contemporary philosophical questions are reframed by the demands of ancient practical life, even as those same practical concerns are shown to pose rigorous and important philosophical questions on the relationship between truth, discourse, and subjective experience (Gros 2008: 354). Foucault's central questions in the 1981 lectures are not what was the nature of ancient pederastic desire or how does one understand the Roman figure of the *cinaedus*, but how does the conception of sexual acts we deploy take part in a certain "game of truth"?; how does that conception objectify them (literally turn them into objects)?; how does it impose a certain analytic grid? Indeed, how does it modify our very existence as subjects? (Foucault 2014: 224–5).

When Foucault returns to his larger analytical frame at the end of the course, after his readings of the ancient texts, he begins by disposing of the idea that these texts by Plutarch and others on marriage exist because they are true, because they reflect a shift in actual practice from the time of Xenophon (early fourth century BCE) to that of the early- to mid-empire. Such a correlation may well have existed. And while it may be true that the marriage practices of Roman elites during this period shifted toward a valorization of monogamy and mutual fidelity, Foucault argues that nonetheless the existence of something in the real in no way produces a true discourse about it, that a shift in marital practices does not in itself produce a shift in the discourses on them (Foucault 2014: 247–8). If that were the case, and one accepted this as a general rule, then one could not explain the emergence of true discourses at all, since everything that was real should spontaneously produce its own true discourse, and every shift in discourse would likewise signal a change in the real. Such a position is clearly absurd. It is not the existence of a referent in reality that gives rise to a discourse, however true it may be (Foucault 2014: 224). True discourses are processes of veridiction and verification that respond to specific human needs and desires: "the cacophony of games of truth" that constitute the historic reality of the subject's experience of himself (Gros 2014: 318). To do a history of the practices, the economics, and the politics of speaking the truth means that you can never content yourself with saying that speaking the truth makes it real. We must rather examine the real of the practice itself, its position and power within the particular configuration of government and governmentality, and the kinds of moves it allows the individual and forms of power to make within that configuration (Foucault 2014: 223).

Nor can these philosophical texts on marriage merely be understood as *post hoc* rationalizations of existing behaviors, since that would neither explain the existence of the behaviors nor of the discourse *per se*. By the same token, the existence of such a discourse does not make the behavior rational in itself.

> In the end, to say that these general principles [of monogamy and conjugal fidelity] are rational principles implies a very curious conception of marriage and of reason, and perhaps of both at the same time. In any case, it is necessary also to wonder why it would be rational to rationalize the real and the practical. Here is the general question that we must ask when speaking of the rationalizing functions of discourse (of the discourse of truth, of knowledge, etc.) in relation to real practices. Do we really believe that a practice, the moment it is rationalized, is in some way more rational than when it is not? Is it not the most absurd of practices to want to rationalize the real?
>
> Foucault 2014: 246–7

As Foucault continues on to remind us, if in fact the real were rational (as Hegel claims),[3] then it would effectively cease to be real. There would be no distinction between discourse and the world, and hence the notion of a true discourse would become meaningless, since the elaboration of any coherent discourse would necessarily be true and that discourse could not differ from the real. We would not discover the world so much as confabulate it. *Geist* would be all. As Foucault observes in an ironic aside that we find in the manuscript version of the lecture but not in the audio recording on which the published version is based, "it's lucky that the rational has such a slight grip on the real: that is perhaps what permits it to exist" (Foucault 2014: 247).

Our processes of veridiction and verification do not, then, reflect the world so much as transform it (Foucault 2014: 241–2; Gros 2014: 318). They allow our effective intervention in the real, and their truth is measured by the efficacy of those interventions relative to the limited ends for which they might be deployed. There is no one unified game of truth that unites all those possible interventions under a single overarching concept or set of rules, not even in science (Foucault 2014: 239–41). What Plutarch, Musonius Rufus, Epictetus, and others are doing in their texts on marriage is less passively reflecting what is happening around them or offering after the fact rationalizations of behaviors than responding to a changing set of circumstances, both intellectual and political, by offering new ways of thinking about the self, new ways of thinking about our relation to others in our most intimate affairs, and thus creating new possibilities for life. These practices regulating marriage and erotic life, which originated from different social classes, "and perhaps even from geographically distinct regions, [the philosophers] set out to transform into a sort of universal rule of conduct" (Foucault 2014: 245). In the end, Foucault asks us less to think about the relationship between discourse and the real, than for us to examine the real of discourse, for us to see discourse, even philosophy itself, and especially true discourse, as a force within the real, as a way to do things with words (Foucault 2014: 223, 225; Kelly 2014: 97–8). As Nietzsche reminds us:

> Henceforth, my philosophic colleagues, let us be on our guard against this dangerous ancient mythology which has set up a "pure, will-less, painless, timeless subject of knowledge"; let us be wary of the tentacles of such contradictory notions as "pure reason," "absolute intelligence," "knowledge-in-itself"—in these theories an eye that cannot be conceived has to be conceived, an eye which is turned in no direction at all, an eye in which the active and interpreting functions are supposed to be suppressed, absent.
>
> Nietzsche, *Genealogy* 3.12, 2013: 105

In the remainder of this chapter, we shall examine three broad areas, framed by this understanding. We shall first turn to Foucault's reading of Artemidorus. Rather than summarize it in detail or cover ground already well covered in the opening of volume three of the *History of Sexuality*, we shall focus on three specific areas that are central to Foucault's larger philosophical preoccupations and have gone either uncovered or attracted little attention: first, his polemic with Freud; second, his account of the dream's relation to subjective experience and hence its truth; and third the relation of the dream to Descartes' *malin génie* and hence to Foucault's ongoing argument with Derrida and the latter's critique of *Histoire de la folie*. Next, we shall look more closely at his account of the changing status of marriage in the early imperial period, its relation to governmentality and the subject's self-relation. Finally, we shall turn our attention to what Foucault labels variously technologies of the self and *tekhnai peri bion*. To this end, we will examine his distinction between *bios* and *zōē*, its appropriation by Agamben, and then return to the problem of confession.

But first we should tarry a bit with the story of the elephant. Foucault opens his course by recounting the mating habits of the elephant as told by Saint Francis of Sales in the early seventeenth century in his *Introduction to the Devout Life*, chapter 39. There, the good Saint informs us that the elephant mates only every third year and then only for five days in utter secrecy. The elephant is completely monogamous. After the mating period, it bathes extensively before rejoining the herd. Saint Francis, however, was no naturalist doing personal observation and, as Foucault shows us, versions of this story had been in circulation for almost two thousand years, both in scientific and spiritual writings. One of the earliest Christian versions was in a text called the *Physiologus* (second to fourth century) that synthesizes a wide variety of pagan naturalist writings, offering biblical and allegorical glosses on their work. But both Aelian and Pliny also picture elephants in their sexual habits as paragons of virtue and praise their moderation and monogamy. Now clearly Aelian and Pliny do so in a different context from the later Christian writers, and naturally they do not include such details as are found in *Physiologus*, like the elephant always facing toward the Garden of Eden during the act of congress and thus both re-enacting the fall and demonstrating appropriate human behavior in its wake (i.e., monogamy and abstinence). Nonetheless, aside from certain iconographical and dogmatic details, the story and the moral drawn from it are much the same, showing there is no clean break between later pagan conceptions of marriage and erotic behavior and early Christian conceptions. Indeed, as Foucault observes, both paganism and Christianity are retrospective constructions that mask the great internal diversity within these discursive formations as well as major axes of continuity between them (Foucault 2014: 171–2).

At the same time, while this story of the elephant persisted in its broad outlines for a very long time, it is neither universal nor has it always been accepted in the West. The earliest version in Aristotle's *Historia Animalis* contains certain details that are found in the later tradition, such as elephants preferring to copulate near water, but the general structure is quite different and there is no attempt to draw a moral lesson. Plato, Herodotus, and other earlier texts show none of this narrative/moral complex (Foucault 2014: 11). What we see, then, in this brief history offered by Foucault is how a discourse based on purported facts—elephants are monogamous and mate near water— becomes invested with and appropriated by a variety of discursive structures and forms of institutional power. Moreover, many of those same elements are deployed again and again over a wide period of time creating a recognizable discursive unity. The role that unity plays and the accent borne by its individual parts can vary over time as it is adapted to different circumstances, and those adaptations can eventually cause the unity itself to collapse—we no longer retell the story of the mating of the elephants. The telling and retelling of this myth has, therefore, both a beginning and an end, and the deployment of the basic narrative has served different ideological, institutional, and personal ends at different times.

The story of the elephant is an allegory of Foucault's genealogical approach. As with the elephants, so it is with many verities in our culture. To take one of Foucault's most prominent examples, sexuality. It is not that the basic acts, organs, and sensations have changed much over time. What has undergone significant change is the way they are labelled, combined, and endowed with meaning to create a discursive unity. Those unities in turn are able to be deployed for and against structures of institutional, political, and personal power. Foucault identifies three major headings under which erotic activity and its social determinants have been grouped in the West over this period, fully recognizing that these are schematic generalizations that mask a great deal of local variation and do not account for every individual case or necessarily correspond to what is happening in the extradiscursive real. These three headings are: *aphrodisia*, the flesh, and sexuality. Without going into detail at this point on the differences between them or the evidence supporting these generalizations, *aphrodisia* refers to the use of pleasures and the ways in which the ancient world saw erotic pleasure less as an inner essence or as a sign of the fall, and more as something to be managed or shaped. Sexual identity or object choice was less important than the role one's pleasures played within the management of the community and the household. For this reason, Xenophon's *Oikonomikos* becomes for Foucault an exemplary text. The flesh is a Christian concept. It conceives desire as a secret that lurks within. It is a sign of our fall from grace and the need for redemption. Our erotic desires function as a deceptive inner truth that must be brought to the surface and confessed if we are to rejoin the external truth that is manifest through Christ, as the word made flesh. Sexuality, according to Foucault's schema, functions as an inner identity: it tells us who we really are (Foucault 2014: 78, 102, 287, 292; Gros 2014: 316; Lorenzini 2016: 140). We are homosexual or heterosexual. We are normal or perverts. We are cis- or transgender. Nineteenth-century sexology created a whole menagerie of types and identities that continue to be operative today within the discourse of sexuality. These identities assume an inner stability that dictate not only sexual objects and pleasure but family roles, modes of dress, pronoun usage, and political positions.

As in the story of the elephant, the basic objects and actions in the real to which these narrative and discursive matrices refer do not change. Under all three regimes, there are penises, vaginas, hands, mouths, anuses, and orgasms. There are children, marriages, and rituals of courtship. There are erotic pleasures between men, between women, and between the two genders, and between those of indeterminate or fluid gender. What changes under these different regimes is how the relations between these subjects, objects, and actions are articulated, the ways in which the phenomenal world is segmented and made meaningful, the power relations as well as the points of leverage and resistance created by and within those regimes. These complex, historically bound regimes of discourse and power make possible different relations of the self to the self, and different articulations of that self's relation to institutional power and knowledge, that is to say different forms of subjectivity. Broadly speaking, the position of the subject as the head of the household in Xenophon, the penitent in the medieval church, and the normalized sexual subject of 1950s America and 1980s France are not superimposable. They have, in short, different relations, different articulations, and different forms of *subjectivity and truth*.

# I

> The problem posed has been the following: how have the philosophical and medical techniques of life, on the eve of the development of Christianity, defined and regulated the practice of sexual acts—the *khrēsis aphrodisiōn*? You see how far we are from a history of sexuality organized around the good old repressive hypothesis and its habitual questions (how and why is desire repressed?). It is a question of acts and pleasures, and not of desire.
>
> Foucault 2014: 301

> The Greeks and Romans did not have a concept like sexuality, nor did the Christians. You will say to me that the fact that they did not have the idea does not mean that reality wasn't cut up in the same way for them. But I think, all the same, the conceptual field is very important.
>
> Foucault 2012a: 253

Artemidorus's *Oneirokritikon* is hardly a mainstay of classical literature. Foucault's decision to devote the majority of two lectures to an explication of this text and to open the third volume of the *History of Sexuality* with an extended reading of it cannot be justified by its immediate historical importance or the influence exerted on later authors (Foucault 1984b: 13–50; 2014: 49–92). If you were interested in the history of sexuality as a reflection on the types, forms, or categorizations of conduct, there are many texts and evidentiary sources you might choose first. Yet, as the reader will have gathered, such a history is not Foucault's project, despite the title of his final published work. If, however, you were aiming to do a genealogy of the sexual subject as the locus of truth (Foucault 1984a: 12; Kremer Marietti 1985: 247–8; Martin, Gutman, and Hutton 1988: 4; Goldhill 1995: 44–5, 74, 161; Calame 2016: 99), then you could do worse. First, the dream is central to Freud's concept of the desiring subject, and one of the few places where Artemidorus makes a significant appearance before Foucault is in the *Interpretation of Dreams* (1965: 130–2). Second, the dream, since Plato's *Republic* has presented a central problem for the subject of truth (Miller 2015b). How do we know what we perceive is real and not a dream? How do we know we are not mad? This latter question is central to the debate Foucault carried on with Derrida for twenty years, which focused on the problem of the evil genius (*Malin Génie*) in Descartes. Artemidorus becomes Foucault's focus not because he is representative but because he offers a particular point of leverage for the way Foucault understands subjectivity and truth in contradistinction to both Freud and Derrida.

Freud tells us that dreams are forms of wish fulfillment (1965: 155–66). In their simplest form, they are a psychosomatic mechanism to allow sleep to continue. I am thirsty; I dream of water. I need to urinate; I dream I do. We are familiar with sexual dreams that function in the same manner. But, Freud observes, many of our dreams are less easily parsed. Their narratives are fragmented. Parts are missing, one thing is substituted for another. He terms this process "condensation" and "displacement." In other contexts, these tropes are referred to as metaphor and metonymy (Freud 1965: 311–44; Ragland-Sullivan 1986: 83–4; Fineberg 1991: 10, 158; Janan 1994: 43). While Freud resists the notion that there is a universal key to all dreams, and this is one of the things for which he criticizes Artemidorus, arguing that each dream must assume its place in the associative chain produced by the analysand (Freud 1965: 130n2, 274–5, 314–15, 561–2), nonetheless, one of the traits common to many of these dreams is that they express desires to which it would be forbidden to give voice in our waking hours. Plato in the *Republic* (9.574e; Freud 1965: 658) and Sophocles in the *OT* (981–2) both acknowledge that dreamers commit acts of violence and sexual depravity unthinkable in the light of day. Freud argues, however, that many of these desires would be too disturbing in their unvarnished form and would wake us from our slumbers, hence the rhetorical devices of what he terms the dreamwork (Freud 1965: 175–8, 508–9). Thus, what often appears innocent in dreams can have a sexual content: trains entering tunnels, gentlemen doffing their hats, and the famous cigar. And while sometimes a cigar is just a cigar, and as Daniel Orrells has shown (2015), Freud almost never uses the term "phallic symbol," nonetheless it is clear that for Freud the metonymic relation of part to whole in a dream is often pregnant with meaning.

Artemidorus, however, says just the opposite. Rather than normal everyday actions referring to forbidden sexual acts, in dreams sexual actions refer to the world of property and politics, the chief concerns of the Hellenistic and Roman elite for whom Artemidorus wrote. Thus, where for Freud money often has a sexual value, for Artemidorus the body, *sōma*, signifies one's wealth. In every case where there is a possibility of a sexual double meaning, Artemidorus interprets the ambiguity in a political and economic sense. A word such as *blabē*, meaning "damage" or "harm," can thus function as a semantic key for Artemidorus, allowing rape to signify financial damage or a political loss in passages such as, "to be raped by one's son means to be harmed (*blabēnai*) by the son" (Artemidorus 1.78.75). Likewise in the world of *aphrodisia* many key terms such as *homilia*, *sunousia*, and *sumplokē* can have both a social and a sexual meaning. Where for Freud dreaming of a financial loss might signify castration, for Artemidorus there is no sexual secret that lies at the core of our identity (Foucault 2014: 58–60, 80). Sexual desires exist on the same plane as our political and social lives. Rather than a sharp break between the manifest and latent content of our dreams, there is a continuity between our waking and dreaming life.

For Foucault, Artemidorus posits a fundamentally different form of self-relation from what he sees at the heart of psychoanalysis. The psychoanalytic truth of our desire is both our inner essence and what lies hidden from us within the regime of sexuality. It must come into speech to be realized and normalized. In the modern world, we are constantly solicited to say who we are, to assume our true identity, to express our "real" selves. Psychoanalysis did not create this regime. It is actually one of the most sophisticated and self-aware of many similar technologies of the self that saturate our popular culture, our self-help books, and our educational theory.[4]

Artemidorus, however, assumes no secret self that must come to expression. Our dreams reproduce the fundamental social and power relations of waking life. They do not reveal our hidden desire. Sexual pleasure is not something that is censored or repressed, and consequently must be ferreted out, but rather it is an extension and reflection of the basic power dynamics that structure society. These phenomena exist on the same plane. This is generally true across a wide variety of ancient literature, from Aristophanes to Catullus to Juvenal: none of which is to say antiquity was an age of sexual freedom, but its problems and anxieties were different from ours (Macey 1993: 458, 468; Nehamas 1998: 178; Gros 2001: 503; Elden 2016: 142). The discourse of *aphrodisia* was characterized by what Foucault calls "isomorphism," where one's position in erotic activity was viewed to have the same form as one's position in society (Foucault 1984a: 82–3, 88, 96, 237; 2014: 82). The free masculine head of household was envisioned as the dominant partner in all relations, and erotic phenomena that threatened that position, from feminine pleasure to the reversibility of dominant and submissive pederastic positions, were stigmatized and marginalized (Foucault 2014: 83, 94; Parker 1997; Boehringer 2016: 42; Ormand 2016: 65; Lorenzini 2016: 141).[5] Hence in satirical and invective literature throughout antiquity, the sexually independent boy or woman is a figure of particular anxiety. "It is something that carries woman into a kind of unnatural nature. Feminine pleasure [in the regime of *aphrodisia*] is an abyss" (Foucault 2014: 90). The gendered and erotic anxiety that characterizes these relations of dominance is not to be underestimated.

One reason why Foucault spends so much time with *Oneirokritikon* is that it offers a window into this world that is all but designed to contrast with that of psychoanalysis. For Foucault, the sexualized subject, while not the same as the confessing subject of Christianity, is inconceivable without it. The first is the condition of possibility of the second, because each assumes a fundamental truth that lurks within the subject, a truth must be verbalized if it is both to be realized (the subject becomes who they really are) and transcended (the subject is saved, liberated, cured, redeemed). No direct line can be drawn from the ancient subject of Artemidorus to the modern sexual subject who sees their desire as an identity that characterizes their being and must be brought to the surface against the forces of repression, denial, and interdiction (Foucault 1984a: 74; 2014: 70; Ormand 2016: 70; Lorenzini 2016: 144–5; Sforzini 2016: 161). Artemidorus not only inverts the Freudian paradigm, more profoundly he demonstrates the possibility of a hermeneutics of the subject, a self-understanding of the subject's relation to the oneiric world, that is fundamentally different from that of the confessing subject.

More profoundly, as Foucault avers, the example of Artemidorus shows that the problem of the dream subtends much of Western philosophy (2014: 50–1). The dream poses special difficulties for the subject of truth because it directly challenges whether the subject knows, sees, or experiences what it is knowing, seeing, or experiencing. The problem that the dream poses is similar to madness but more extreme because the dream is more universal (we all dream) and more total (it is not a distortion of our world, but a replacement, a simulation). The paranoid schizophrenic may hear voices, may believe there are electrodes in her brain, but she does not inhabit a completely different physical reality from that of a posited normal self. From this perspective, Freud's *Interpretation of Dreams* is less the pinnacle of a certain discourse of sexuality, which sees the manifest content of our dreams as a cypher for the truth of our identity, than the heir to a philosophical tradition that finds its first full expression in Plato's myth of the cave: a tradition that asks, "what is the truth of my experience?" (Foucault 2014: 50). If I am the witness to truth, whether as the shepherd or Oedipus in the *OT*, how do I know that what I see is real, that it is not a dream, that I am not deceived? What is the difference between waking vision and a dream? Where and what kind of truth resides in each? Thus Plato argues that the man who believes the truth resides in phenomena is like one who lives in a dream:

> Socrates: The one who believes in beautiful things on the one hand, but who neither believes in beauty itself nor—should someone lead him to the knowledge of this beauty—would he be able to understand it, does he seem to you to live a dream or be awake? Is dreaming not the following: whenever someone, awake or asleep, believes the like is not the like but the thing itself which it resembles?
>
> *Republic* 5.476c1–5

Philosophy, then, begins at the moment the truth of the immediate is questioned, at the moment I no longer accept what seems to be the case but ask what is. The world seems flat. My desires seem natural. It seems just to smite my enemies. But is that the case? At the origin of Western epistemology and metaphysics is the dreamer, the one who poses the question of what does it mean to see/know (*idein*) the truth and what does it mean to be fundamentally deceived.

As Foucault observes, this problematic remains central to philosophy up to the modern era. It is the fundamental problem posed by Descartes in his *First Meditation*: can we find the truth, even though we may be dreaming or bound by a series of illusions so profound as to alter the most basic regulatory laws of our universe: physics, logic, mathematics itself? (Foucault 2014: 50). What is the one thing I cannot doubt? As Foucault goes on to argue, this same problem re-emerges in Kant, Schopenhauer, and Nietzsche in the form of the following questions:

> Is the truth of the truth true? Couldn't one think the truth of the true is not true?, that at the root of the truth there is something else than the truth itself? And if the truth were only true only because it was rooted in something

> like an illusion and a dream? Was not the truth finally only a moment of something that is only a dream?
>
> Foucault 2014: 50

If Artemidorus sees the truth of the dream in the subject's daily life, and Freud sees the truth of the subject in her dreams, both participate in a larger matrix of concerns that see the subject's relation to truth as always connected in a fundamental way to the possibility that she is dreaming, to the possibility that the reality she perceives is not the real and that in some fundamental way the subject is deceived, and that deception must be relieved by being re-grounded in another more fundamental reality to which our dreams, our perceptions, or our experiences refer (the forms, the *cogito*, the will to power, etc.).

This problematic, in turn, is the basis for Foucault's two-decade long debate with Jacques Derrida, and this entire discussion in *Subjectivity and Truth* is acknowledged by its editor Frédéric Gros to be another in a series of Foucault's rejoinders (Foucault 2014: 72n1; McGushin 2016; 120n3). Derrida had argued in his 1963 essay on Foucault's *Histoire de la folie* that Descartes's *Meditations* showed less madness's exclusion from reason at the beginning of what Foucault labels the great confinement, than the necessity, even in the case of the dream and the *Malin Génie*, of all such forms of illusion to function as the other of reason, and hence always to be included within it (Derrida 1967: 75–84). This argument can quickly become quite technical, and Foucault goes deep into the weeds of Descartes's text in his published responses. But the essence of his response is this: for Foucault knowledge is something we do. His concept of the *will to know* casts knowledge as a human activity that is both determined by and determinative of its historical context. There is no such thing as reason or sense outside of a particular context. He therefore places a strong emphasis on Descartes' *Meditation* as a meditation, as a series of acts performed by the philosopher in order to come to know the truth. If we take this seriously, Foucault argues, then the question becomes can a subject who dreams meditate? Is this an action they can perform? The answer for Descartes is clearly "yes," but for the madman, he argues, Descartes would say "no." This will be a topic Foucault returns to the following year at the beginning of the *Hermeneutics of Subject* where he introduces what will become one of the key concepts of his final lectures, "spiritual practice," or a set of actions performed by a subject on herself in order to produce knowledge or truth (Foucault

2001a: 19, 340–1, 351n5; McGushin 2016: 105–9). Philosophy, then, for Foucault, is a set of historically determined acts performed by those deemed competent to perform them (Foucault 1972; Kremer-Marietti 1985: 129–31; Boyne 1990: 48–9).

For Derrida, however, there is always a certain minimal essence of reason. There is always a certain level on which thought and discourse either make sense or they do not. And while what constitutes the outside of reason changes through time, nonetheless, there can be no outside except through its always already included other, through its own externality (Derrida 1967: 79–80, 86; Penfield 2016: 14).

> The sentence is in its essence normal. It carries normality in itself, that is to say *sense*, in every sense of the word, Descartes's in particular. It carries in itself normality and sense, in whatever state that may be, the sanity or insanity of the one who offers it or through whom it passes, and on whom, in whom it articulates itself. In its syntax, even the most meager, the logos is reason, and reason that is already historic.
>
> Derrida 1967: 83–4

For Foucault, this means that Derrida believes there is nothing exterior or anterior to philosophical reason (Foucault 1972: 584). Derrida would not argue with this characterization, so long as it was understood that philosophical reason was constantly transforming itself through the incorporation of its other through time.

Foucault asks us to imagine a world in which what we consider to be thought does not exist, in which truth as we recognize it does not exist, and this is the reason a text like *Oedipus* that seems to inaugurate an understanding of truth and the knowing subject that is recognizably our own is so important to him. If there is an outside to our concept truth, then it is possible to radically rethink the value we attribute to the subject, to the self, to experience and truth (Penfield 2016: 19). Like the tale of the elephant or like the concept of man at the end of *Les mots et les choses*, what constitutes reason, madness, and the dream will one day wash away, and will do so because of the actions we have taken. For Derrida, however, the moment we articulate this dream of our own disappearance or self-transcendence, we step back within the self-overcoming circle of reason and its other that make historicity thinkable (Allen 2016: 132; Evans 2016: 155; Gratton 2016: 254). Where Foucault critically examines historically specific power formations, Derrida is interested in the structure of reason that makes these periodizations possible (Evans 2016: 160; Gratton 2016: 257; Nealon 2016: 240–1, 246; Rekret 2016: 257). The two positions are ultimately irreconcilable—you cannot logically subordinate one to the other—although that does not make them necessarily mutually exclusive—i.e., if one is true the other must be false (Penfield 2016: 21). It is in fact possible to imagine a world in which the *logos* of one era, and hence the structures of subjectivity and truth in it, and that of another differ quite radically and yet retain a certain minimal formal universality in the moment of their constitution, in their transcendental condition of possibility. Artemidorus gives uniquely powerful testimony of this for Foucault through offering a fundamentally different vision of the relation of the waking subject to its dream life and hence of the subject to truth from our own and yet one that remains intelligible and so offers to us the possibility of thinking differently.

## II

Socrates: "Isomachus, I would happily learn from you whether you trained your wife how she should be or you took her from her mother and father knowing how to manage the things appropriate to her." "And, I said, how would I have taken her already knowing, when came to me not yet being fifteen, and having lived before that time under much care, so that she would see, hear, and question as little as possible?"

Xenophon, Oikonomikos 7.4–6

"I taught her that even in well ordered cities it did not suffice to the citizens that they write fine laws, they must also choose guardians of the laws, who keeping watch would praise the one doing lawful things and punish whoever violates the laws. And so I ordered the wife to consider her self the guardian of those in our household, and to inspect the stores whenever it seemed right to her, just as the commander of the garrison inspects the guard, and to test whether each acted properly, just as the counsel of the city tests the cavalry and their horses."

Xenophon, Oikonomikos 9.14–15

Some men force their wives who bring small dowries to do household management (*oikonomia*) and keep slavish accounts. They quarrel daily and beat them.⁶ Others want children more than wives, like cicadas who emit their progeny into a lily or such, they swiftly beget with their bodies, harvest the fruit, and leave the marriage or, if it continues, they do not think it worthy of love. But the fact that "loving" and "covering" differ by just a few letters shows me the shared good will produced by time and companionship. The man whom Eros leans upon and inspires, just like the man in Plato's city, has no "mine" and "yours." For things are not common among all men or even friends, but only among those who, though their bodies are separate, bring together and join their souls with force, neither wishing nor believing themselves to be two.

Plutarch, *Erōtikos* 21

One of the principles that organizes Artemidorus's reading of sexual dreams, as observed above, is "ismorphism." Isomorphism in simplest terms means that sexual relations should have the same form as other social relations, at least on the level of thought and discourse if not in actuality. Thus in Athens of the fourth century, at the time he is producing his manual of household management, the *Oikonomikos*, which Foucault cites both in *Subjectivity and Truth* and *The Use of Pleasures*, Xenophon makes clear that the household should be the reflection of a well-ordered city. At the apex of that city sat the free male citizen, whose task as a husband was to train his wife to reign over matters within the house. She normally came to him young and inexperienced. He could be ten to fifteen years her senior. His task was to occupy himself with external matters such as agriculture, trade, and participation in civic life (Xenophon 7.8). She was expected to organize the slaves within the house to be a reflection of the polis, a city in which he alone enjoyed full rights. At each level within the social hierarchy, forms of dominance and submission were conceptualized as being homologous with those above and below, and each of those levels reinforced the dominant position of the active, adult male citizen. The man took the wife to produce children and to run the household. Their sexual relations were a reflection of this larger structure, which meant her pleasure was always subordinate to his, but his pleasure was not limited to her. He could avail himself of all the household had to offer, regardless of gender, so long as he did not endanger his dominant position within the *oikos* and the community (Foucault 1984a: 56, 82–99, 237). This set of isomorphic relations that Xenophon articulates with clarity in the fourth century BCE is still very much in evidence in the world of Artemidorus in the second century CE. And while neither of these works do justice to the kinds of complex inner experience we see in erotic writers like Catullus or the Latin elegists (Miller 1998, 2004), let alone to the experience of their partners and slaves, nonetheless the assumption of the existence of an ideal continuity in the power relations that structure sociopolitical and erotic life, an assumption that Xenophon and Artemidorus share, is part of what has made the work of Catullus and the elegists seem so subversive. They both acknowledge and transgress that assumption, when they portray themselves as involved in adulterous affairs or as slaves of love (*servi amoris*) beholden to the whims of their mistresses (*dominae*).

At times Foucault's descriptive methods, particularly in his early work, can make it seem that epistemic and discursive changes happen only in major shifts, with little or no explanatory logic internal to the formations themselves.[7] But the situation described in *Subjectivity and Truth* is more complex. Much of the course is given over to describing a fundamental shift in the way marriage is conceptualized among the Roman elite, a change that happens not as a seismic shift but as a gradual evolution with multiple competing formations present at the same time. For, even as Artemidorus in the second century continues to give voice to an ideal set of isomorphic sexual, political, social, and economic relations, his contemporary Plutarch is offering a different concept of marriage, the family, and Eros (Gros 2016: 27; Lorenzini 2016: 141–3). Plutarch's *Erōtikos* casts itself as a revision of Plato's *Symposium*. The latter, whose main body consists of a series of speeches devoted to the praise of Eros, focuses primarily on pederastic love and mentions marriage only briefly. Plutarch argues, however, not only for marriage as the locus of love but also sees that love as existing in a separate and discontinuous relationship with the larger power relations that structure Roman imperial life. For Plutarch, marriage, rather than replicating the power relations of the larger society, creates a new unity of souls in which there is no longer a "mine" and a "yours."

Plutarch inhabits a very different world from the classical polis of Xenophon. As part of a vast cosmopolitan empire, the relation of governmentality in which the masculine citizen, his spouse, and other members of the household exist is fundamentally different from that envisioned by Sophocles, Plato, and Xenophon. The aristocracy of competitive elites that dominated the culture of the classical city-state and the Roman republic found itself increasingly displaced, increasingly forced to develop new ways of conceptualizing the self and its relations to the social and symbolic structures of the community (Foucault 2014: 277–8).[8] This change in the way the self governs itself and others, as exemplified in the conceptualization of marriage, Foucault shows, is found not only in Plutarch but also in a larger, predominantly Stoic philosophical literature of the period that purports to advise others (Foucault 2014: 46, 215–20, 245–6).

> These new arts of living, conveyed—or rather, formulated, elaborated—by certain philosophers ... find their reason for being in the fact that they are addressed to a particular layer of the population, the aristocracy, which only maintained its self-consciousness, its self-recognition, on the condition that its old system of values would be effectively maintained and that it could effectively judge, gage its own behaviors from that, even if henceforth it was no longer able to apply itself to the social field, to the field of socio-political differentiations ... This system of valorisation ought to be effectively put to work inside marriage ... on the condition, of course—this is what was necessary—that there was a reorganization of the self's relation to itself. Philosophical discourse proposed, conveyed certain techniques, presented effectively as such, precisely in order to be able to live, to be able to accept forms of behavior proposed and imposed from the outside, techniques that made them literally liveable.
> 
> Foucault 2014: 279

The shift in the value and conceptualization of marriage, he argues, reflects and enacts a more general shift in the subject's relation to itself, how it understands its desire, and where it locates and understands its truth. Thus where Xenophon has Isomachus teach his young wife to enforce the laws of the household as the city enforces its own, Plutarch in the passage above decouples married love from both household management, *oikonomia*, and the production of children, to instead promote a vision not only of shared goods, as in Plato's ideal city, but shared being, a spiritual joining that is discontinuous from the surrounding world and thus possessed of a certain autonomy.

Where *aphrodisia* constituted a form of natural unity that required the self-mastery of the male-citizen head of household and demanded an ordered distribution of duties and pleasures, for the husband of Plutarch's married couple it is a very different relation. He is not training a household manager and mother of legitimate citizen children but a partner to whom he owes fidelity, a soul mate. He must monitor and control his own sexual desires, not simply so as not to endanger his position within the community and the household but as an affirmative duty to his spouse. His desire becomes the object of scrutiny. "The technology of the self of the married man demands henceforth that he grasp desire at it first 'budding,' a desire no longer understood as a mechanical preliminary to pleasure but crystalized under the form of 'temptation'" (Gros 2014: 315–16; cf. Foucault 2014: 170 ). It is impossible to imagine Xenophon, Plato, or Callimachus, Caesar, Catullus, or Horace engaging in that same act of internal inspection. *Aphrodisia* (or *voluptates* in Latin) were an activity to be engaged in, a potentially powerful and disruptive pleasure to be enjoyed in a limited, responsible manner, not a fundamental dimension of subjectivity *per se* (Foucault 2014: 287, cf. 268–9). Erotic pleasures were not conceptualized as secrets to be ferreted out and eliminated "at the first prick of the needle of desire" (Foucault 2014: 292). The transformation of *aphrodisia* into the "flesh," then, occurs not simply as a passive reflection of changed social circumstances but also through the specific intellectual work produced by philosophers, thinkers, and writers—through the truths they produced (Foucault 2014: 71).

In the work of Stoics like Antipatros, Hierocles, and Musonius Rufus, Foucault traces the development of a new conception of what it means for marriage to be considered *kata phusin* ("according to nature"). First, it is increasingly asserted that the end of sexual relations is procreation. Since the time of Xenophon and before, lawful procreation to produce citizen children had occurred within marriage, and for this reason marriage had been primarily the concern of the elite for whom issues of property and succession were central. But throughout this period, the sexual activity of the adult male in no wise needed to be limited to his spouse or subordinated to the production of children. Second, the pleasure of erotic activity was now increasingly seen as a natural spur to the affection of the conjugal couple, a pleasure not only to be used responsibly but subordinated to the emotional and affective life of the couple, conceptualized as its own unity rather than as a moment in a larger series of isomorphic relations (Foucault 2014: 144, 230). One consequence of this reconceptualization of marriage was a calling into question of pederastic pleasure (Gros 2014: 314).

At this point, it is worth paying closer attention to the work Foucault observes being done by Plutarch's text. The *Erōtikos* is staged as a dialogue occasioned by an unusual situation. Ismenodora, a chaste and wealthy widow, has fallen in love with the Bacchon, the object of Peisas's affections. This is a very different situation from that envisioned by Xenophon. Rather than a young woman taken from her parents' home and molded into a household manager by her citizen husband, who enjoys a monopoly of power and pleasure, Ismenodora is an older woman, possessing her own means, who becomes enamored of a youth still considered the object of legitimate pederastic affections. Not only are the normative positions of the isomorphic relationship inverted, but, when Ismenodora's advances fail to meet success, she decides to force the issue by kidnapping Bacchon. There ensues a debate on the relative merits of pederasty versus marriage as forms of love, ending with Plutarch's extended praise of marriage in his final speech, which is intended to replace Socrates' speech near the end of the *Symposium* where he recounts Diotima's lesson on the ladder of love, whose highest form moves from the love of beauty in the pederastic object to the love of beauty in itself (Foucault 2014: 194).

Traditionally, pederasty is seen as more high-minded than utilitarian marriage. In the *Symposium*, Pausanias speaks of two forms of Love, earthly and heavenly. The earthly is concerned with the satisfaction of the body and the production of children. It is what unites us with the animals. Whereas the love of boys, the heavenly love, whatever the initial physical attraction, is founded on mutual regard, the ability of the older lover to take the younger under his protection and develop a spiritual relationship that will blossom into a lasting friendship (180d–182a). Likewise, Diotima in her speech recognizes that love is ultimately predicated on a desire for what we all lack, immortality, and while a terrestrial immortality can be found in the production of children, spiritual immortality, founded on the love of a boy whose perfection recalls beauty itself, is the highest form (206b–209e). Similarly in the *Phaedrus*, part of what makes Lysias's initial speech so astonishing is the perversity of its argument: a boy should only yield to one who is not in love! The audacity of such an argument is designed to convince the listener that Lysias can indeed make the weaker argument the stronger. As such, it stands as a remarkable calling card for the speechwriter's talents. The sublimity of Socrates' great speech by contrast becomes all the more marked, as it envisions a pederastic love that leads men to the gods, but only if they are not betrayed by those baser desires that pull the chariot of the soul from heaven to earth, only if they focus more on the transmission of truth than the use of pleasure (Foucault 2014: 166–70).

These pederastic virtues are defended in the *Erōtikos* by Peisas and Protogenes. Protogenes' main argument in favor of the spiritual superiority of pederastic love is precisely its unnatural nature (*para phusin*). Rather than being a form of "hunger" (*orexis*) like any other bodily need (750d), pederasty is a conscious choice, the product of reflection and culture. Its very artificiality is the sign of its spiritual superiority. If the aim of sex is pleasure, the aim of pederasty for Protogenes is virtue.

> Boy love is the true love, "not glistening with desire," as Anacreon says of the love for girls, not "shining and covered with balsam," but you will spy this love smooth and unspoiled among the philosophical schools or about the gymnasia and wrestling grounds, a clear and noble love urging those who are worthy of care (*epimeleia*) toward virtue (*aretē*) concerning the pursuit of young men.
>
> Plutarch 751a; cf. Foucault 2014: 186–9

Rather than beginning in hunger, leading to desire, and ending in pleasure, as does the love that follows the tracks of nature, ideal pederastic love begins in friendship, leads to care, and ends in virtue (Foucault 2014: 189–90).

Plutarch in his final speech calls this conception of pederasty into question, even as the dialogue acknowledges the continued currency of the classical position. Within that tradition, marriage, while valued, is seen as a continuation of power relations within the community. Marriage is "according to nature" because it produces not only pleasure but offspring, as seen among the beasts of the field. Xenophon in Isomachus's instructions to his young wife repeatedly makes reference to *phusis* or "nature" (7.21–8). But Plutarch in the passage cited above and throughout his speech makes a very different argument. Marriage is neither just for children nor is it simply an extension of the isomorphic power relations that characterize society as a whole. It becomes the locus of both truth and virtue, as Plutarch transfers the traditional attributes of the pederastic relationship to the married couple, making them the site of a friendship and a union nurtured by pleasure and care (Foucault 2014: 185). "These things with married women are the beginning of friendship, just like the sharing of holy rites. There is a small amount of pleasure, but honor, charm, trust and mutual affection grow from this pleasure" (Plutarch, *Erōtikos* 769a). The relationship thus envisioned is neither the classic marriage of Xenophon, nor the high-minded pederasty of Plato and Protogenes: both of which, while concerned with virtue and pleasure, do not see them as existing exclusively within the conjugal realm.

Marriage on the model of Plutarch and the Stoic philosophers seeks to establish a domestic realm that is ontologically separate from the political world defining the traditional concerns of the Greco-Roman aristocracy. Where the erotic poets of first century BCE Rome had begun to imagine worlds of love and care that were discontinuous and at times at odds with traditional aristocratic self-conceptions, these were never done so within marriage, which was promoted under the rule of Augustus and seen as a means of reinforcing traditional values while producing support in the form of citizens and soldiers. What we see in the thought of Plutarch and the other writers Foucault cites is marriage becoming a realm where desire and pleasure are developed to create a new model of self's relation to itself. This realm is invested in the sexual as never before, but not so much in its indulgence as in its monitoring, its surveillance, and its control. In marriage we see the development of an ethics of fidelity, understood as self-mastery, that in turn creates the warrant for a private, domestic realm at a remove from the traditional demands of the politics of competitive elites.

> The problem is no longer the limitation of the recourse to these [sexual] acts according to a quantitative regime. It requires a permanent taking into account of the self by the self, it requires that one constitutes sexual activity inside oneself, or rather the principle, the root even of sexual activity as an object of surveillance, of a permanent observation ... We have here the principle of what one could call objectification.
>
> Foucault 2014: 289

In short, when the subject in his masculinity becomes separated from the larger field of social relations, he then becomes an object for himself.

## III

All these discourses that promote matrimonial life, that want to indicate both the necessity of marriage and how one should conduct oneself in marriage, etc., they absolutely do not present themselves, or not exactly, as rules or as a code. They also don't present themselves as a purely theoretical discourse on the essence of marriage, the essence or nature of *aphrodisia* or of good conduct. These are neither codes, nor exactly prescriptive systems, nor theoretical ensembles. They present themselves as *tekhnai* (techniques) *peri ton bion* (that have life as an object).

Foucault 2014: 252–3

As for the procedures by which these arts of living are able thus to lead to a change in the ontological status of the individual, and to give it certain qualities of existence, one can summarize them by saying that it is a question in these arts of living of defining the complex work through which one will be able to attain this ontological status of experience: first, a relation with others; second, a certain relation with truth; third, a certain relation to oneself.

Foucault 2014: 34

*Subjectivity and Truth* begins and ends by posing basic philosophical questions: What is the relation between truth and subjectivity? How has that relation changed over time? How do those changes manifest and produce modifications in these terms' respective natures? And what does this say of the relation between truth and the real? Foucault undertakes his investigation not by establishing universal definitions and pursuing a series of deductions, or by allowing "the facts to speak for themselves," or by gathering data to populate pre-existing grids of rational categories. He is neither a rationalist nor an empiricist in the classical sense. Instead, he examines the history of certain discourses that frame and constitute our experience. He asks: how have we understood certain phenomena?—in this case, marriage, the household, erotic experience, and their relation to governing and governmentality. He does so to reveal the given as the wrought.

In Foucault's genealogy of some of our most intimate experience lies the essence not only of his Nietzschean project to rethink and transcend the human but also of a more Marxian project to rethink and transcend the structures of power and exploitation inherent in our struggle for existence, in the daily labor of *homo oeconomicus* to govern himself and others. *Subjectivity and Truth* offers a reading of texts that, while not necessarily representative of actual erotic experience, reveals fundamental shifts in the way that experience was conceptualized during the 800 years that separate the ascendance of Christianity from the performance of *Oedipus Tyrannus*. Those shifts reveal not only the complex genealogy of our own categories of sexual and subjective experience, but also the contingency all such categories have in relation to their material, social, and discursive contexts. The *History of Sexuality*, it turns out, is but one chapter in the history of subjectivity and truth.

The increased importance of marriage as an object of reflection, which Foucault brings to light in his reading of Plutarch, the Stoics, and figures as diverse as Pliny and Statius, creates alongside the official masculine world of law, commerce, military conquest, and imperial politics a parallel world of normative private life (Foucault 2014: 263). What this literature allows, or makes possible, is the elaboration of a certain kind of relation of the subject to itself, a form of life or *bios*, a relation of the self to itself that, at least in theory, through this theoretical elaboration becomes available to the society as a whole (Foucault 2014: 256). The *tekhnai* themselves,[9] these prescriptive documents he gathers from the philosophical and scientific tradition, outline the procedures of self-transformation that allow the subject to practice this new regimen. Marriage is only one component in this broader project of the elaboration of a form of parallel existence through a set of practices that regulate and constitute a self at one remove from the isomorphic structures of traditional life, structures that remain in evidence (Foucault 2014: 262). It is in fact the history of these techniques that will be a central feature of Foucault's investigations of antiquity from this point forward, beginning in earnest with next year's *Hermeneutics of the Subject* and his introduction of the concept of "spiritual practices."

At the beginning of *Subjectivity and Truth*, Foucault argues that each of these various *tekhnai peri bion* contained three elements: *mathēsis*, *meletē*, and *askēsis*; or instruction, reflection, and practice. The self (*bios*) that is the object of these techniques of elaboration and shaping must first receive a certain instruction—Platonic, Stoic, or Epicurean philosophy in addition to a basic level of general culture and literacy. Within these traditions, there are forms of reflection and meditation that are developed over time, whether through philosophical dialogue, the exchange of letters, or practices of reading and writing. The instruction (*mathēsis*) is made real through these forms of active reflection and elaboration (*meletē*). Then, there is the practice itself (*askēsis*), a form of daily testing where the life (*bios*) at which one aims meets the life one actually leads. This testing, in turn, leads to a new round of learning, reflection, and practice in what becomes an ideally virtuous circle of knowledge, care, and action that governs and produces the subject's relation to truth (Foucault 2014: 35). The *bios* is both the object of that subject, the thing on which its labors are expended, and the necessary correlative of the possibility of the subject modifying that life itself (Foucault 2014: 36). These *tekhnai peri bion* are of interest to Foucault because they make clearly visible the link between subjectivity and truth, between a certain form of self-relation and the recognition of a certain truth (Foucault 2014: 37–8).

For the philosophers engaged in this reflection, the topic of the ideal life had long been central. As we shall see in Chapter 4, Foucault spends a great deal of time reflecting on Plato's *Seventh* Letter, which is closely focused on philosophy, not as a body of doctrine but as a form of life. In general, for ancient philosophy the highest form of existence was considered the *bios theōrētikos* ("the philosophical or contemplative life"). The *bios theōrētikos* was opposed to both the political life and the life of pleasures, in so far as each exposed the individual to forces beyond their control (*egkrateia*) and led to various forms of slavery, dependence, and disruption (Foucault 2014: 153–5). *Aphrodisia*, as violent forms of pleasure, were of particular danger in this regard, and while no school of ancient philosophy to my knowledge advocates complete abstinence or virginity, and though each had its own doctrinal variations, all see giving oneself over to the life of pleasure as incompatible with the pursuit of truth, the distinguishing characteristic of the philosophical life (Foucault 2014: 255).

What was new, then, in Roman imperial philosophy was both the increasing emphasis on marriage as the legitimate arena for erotic expression, and the consequent emphasis on the monitoring and moderation of sexual desire. Domestic life may, as many writers of the period noted, interfere with the philosopher's pursuit of a pure life of *theōria*, and to that extent marriage may be a distraction. Moreover, while every reasonable man, or every man who has subjected his life to reason, may wish to be freed from the paroxystic pleasures of *aphrodisia* and the prick of their desire, nonetheless, it was widely recognized that, to the extent a philosopher remains a man, he will continue to feel pleasure's pull. Thus, it was generally proposed that he should serve as an exemplar to other men by marrying and subordinating his pleasure to the pursuit of truth (Foucault 2014: 111–12, 162–3).

What is to be noted here from Foucault's perspective, however, is that the emphasis in this literature is less on the managing of sexual desire *per se* than on the formation of one's *bios*, the taking of one's life as an object of learning, care, and practice, which includes *aphrodisia*. *Egkrateia*, in this regard, is a primary means toward the fashioning of an existence one desires rather than the fashioning of one's desires as the key to existence. Each person possesses a *bios*, a form of subjective life. The question is what does one make of it. The Academic philosopher, Heraclides of Pontus, Foucault observes, thus outlines three basic forms of *bios* or "modes of life," which he attributes originally to Pythagoras: those who seek glory, those who seek possessions, and those who seek the truth.[10] The last is the *bios theōrētikos* of the philosopher. *Bios* in this sense is not biological life (*zōē*) but the taking of our existence as an object (Foucault 2014: 253–56). It designates "a plane of immanence susceptible of taking on a determined form and oriented by practical objectives" (Gros 2014: 308–9). When Socrates tell us in the *Apology*, *ho de anexetastos bios ou biōtos anthrōpōi* ("the unexamined life is not liveable for a human being," 38a5–6), he is referring to "life" as both an object of examination and an object of care, a thing we shape. An individual's *bios* is characterized by the form of relation he or she chooses to have with the things around them, by the way a person positions their freedom in relation to those things. Indeed, as Socrates argues just a bit earlier, his great contribution to the polis, one for which he deserves to be fed and sheltered at city expense, was to approach each citizen and try "to persuade him to care for himself and not merely his things" (36c4–7).

The philosopher and political theorist, Giorgio Agamben, makes much of this separation of *zōē* from *bios*, claiming that in this separation can be found the whole subsequent history of Western political life. The abstraction of bare life from human existence, he argues, is what makes mass murder and genocide possible in the modern world, inasmuch as "bare life" designates a form of life to be managed and manipulated, fostered or culled. Western politics is, according to Agamben, predicated on the opposition between *zōē* and *bios* and has been from Plato and Aristotle to the present. He attributes this insight to Foucault and his concept of "biopolitics," which is first elaborated in volume one of the *History of Sexuality*. But Agamben argues that Foucault does not go far enough. Where Foucault see "biopolitics" and "biopower" being born from the same discursive matrix that gave rise to phenomena as diverse as the penitentiary and the disciplinary state, the discourse of sexuality, Malthus, and various forms of eugenics and population health, for Agamben the biopolitical state was all but fated from this originary split between *zōē* and *bios*. There is, for him, a straight line from Aristotle to the camps. "Western politics is a biopolitics from the very beginning" (Agamben 1998: 66, 88, 181).

I have argued elsewhere that Agamben's reading of the strict separation of *zōē* from *bios* as determinative of Western politics and leading to the modern biopolitical state is unsupported in terms of both the philology and Foucault's philosophy (Miller 2020a). What I want to focus on here is less the separation of *bios* from considerations of biological existence as Agamben sees it, than on what Foucault sees as the ethical and political possibilities of *bios* as the power to shape one's existence, the power to create a form of life that anchors itself in the search for truth. It is this focus on the nexus of existence and truth as an ethical and political phenomenon that will be Foucault's central concern as, in the next three years, he focuses on concepts such as: *parrhēsia* (frankness, truth-telling), the *bios theōrētikos* (the philosophical life), and spiritual practices. *Bios* in this sense is not to be thought to the exclusion of the life we share with all living creatures. Nor does the existence of this term mean that the bare fact of living (*zēn*) is therefore necessarily "unqualified" and can thus be taken as an object to be manipulated in itself, both protected and exterminated, separate from considerations of existence (Agamben 1998: 1). Rather, for Foucault, *bios* and its *tekhnai* are to be thought of as precisely offering the possibility of an intentional existence, a chance to think and live (*zēn*) differently (Gros 2014: 308, 320–1).

At the same time, it is the elaboration of these very *tekhnai peri bion* that will form the material and practical substrate on which is predicated the subsequent production of the Christian concept of the flesh and the consequent creation of the confessing, penitential subject. It is only once the self becomes an object of care, separate from the social world in which it is embedded, and only once the desires of that subject become a particular problematic that reflection can be transformed from a form of meditation and self-shaping into a process of decipherment and uncovering, a process in which a true self is revealed and that true self can be understood as our hidden desires, as the burden of the flesh. There is not then so much a transition from a world of pagan freedom to one of Christian repression, one from which we must be freed through our modern compulsion to find liberation by expressing our sexuality—as the repressive hypothesis would posit—but rather there is a gradual repurposing of certain discursive techniques that elaborate a model of the self and its *bios* in relation to different material and theoretical contexts, elaborations that produce new forms of subjectivity and new relations of that subjectivity to truth, both its own and that of others.

> Perhaps there is no more important principle for any kind of history than the following, which, though difficult to master, *should* nonetheless be mastered in every detail—that the origin of a thing, as opposed to its ultimate utility, that is, its practical application and incorporation into a system of ends, are *toto caelo* opposites; that everything, anything, which exists and which has come into being anywhere, will always be interpreted from new perspectives, will be seized upon again, will be transformed and turned to new uses by a force superior to itself; that everything which occurs in the organic world consists of *overpowering* and dominating, which in turn consists of new interpretation and adaptation, within which the old "meaning" and "purpose" must necessarily be obscured or absolutely obliterated.
> 
> Nietzsche, *Genealogy* 2.12, 2013: 62–3, emphasis in original

3

# Hermeneutics of the Subject: Spirituality, *Parrhēsia*, and Truth

This year I would like to extract myself a little bit from ... this particular material concerning *aphrodisia* and the regime of sexual comportments, and I would like to take from this precise example the more general terms of the problem, "subjectivity and truth." More precisely, I would not in any case want to eliminate or annul the historical dimension in which I have tried to place subjectivity/truth relations, but I would want all the same to make them appear under a much more general form. The question I want to approach this year is: under what historical conditions in the West were the relations between these elements, the "subject" and "truth," tied together, elements that have not normally been the object of historical practice or analysis?

Foucault 2001a: 4

What I want to talk to you about this year is the history that made this whole cultural phenomenon (the general incitation, acceptance of the principle that one should occupy oneself with oneself), a cultural phenomenon for the whole of Hellenistic and Roman society (for its elite in any case), and at the same time ... an event in thought! It seems to me that the wager, the challenge that any history of thought should take up is precisely to seize the moment when a cultural phenomenon, of a certain size, can ... constitute, in the history of thought, a decisive moment in which the modern subject's mode of being is still engaged.

Foucault 2001a: 11

In 1982, Foucault began to present work on what he thought would be a new book. This book too centered on antiquity but no longer focused on sexual comportments or the sexual subject. Rather, it examined a series of practices of the self on the self, which Foucault following Pierre Hadot labelled "spiritual," practices that produced a fundamental shift in the subject's relation to itself and truth. This book was tentatively titled, "The Care of the Self." Of course, this same title was later used for volume three of the *History of Sexuality*, which includes a brief chapter on "The Culture of the Self." The repurposing of the title occurred when volume two had grown to such a size that in the final redrafting it was divided in two, and another title was needed (Foucault 1984b: 51–85; Gros 2001: 489, 496–7; Pradeau 2012: 134; Elden 2016: 153).

Some of the material presented systematically in *The Hermeneutics of the Subject* first appeared in lectures given in North America at Dartmouth and Berkeley in 1980. These lectures are conventionally labeled "The Hermeneutics of the Self." Dating from the same period as *On the Government of the Living*, they focus on the practices of Christian confession discussed in Chapter 1 but also feature a reading of Seneca and an emphasis on the different forms of self-care and self-knowledge that characterized the Hellenistic and Roman period. These lectures show that by 1980 processes of self-constitution, self-fashioning, and self-knowing had become of primary interest to Foucault as he moved beyond a focus on the genealogy of the sexual subject to the constitution of the self across a range of behaviors (Foucault 1997; Elden 2016: 121–2).

The 1980s are known as Foucault's ethical turn or his return to the subject. Like all such periodizations, there is both an element of truth here and a degree of simplification. In the early eighties, Foucault offered several retrospective views of his career in which he advanced the thesis that he had, in fact, always been interested in a history of the subject and in the consequent possibility of a radical thought from the outside that would reconstitute both the subject and its relation to truth (Foucault 1986: 260; Penfield 2016: 7; Gratton 2016: 260). Such a view is not an untenable reading of his career (Foucault 1994h: 581; 1997: 150–1; Jaffro 2003: 72–3), but it is also difficult to argue that the problem of the subject and the self did not loom progressively larger for him in his final years (Rajchman 1991: 4; Gros 2001: 506–7; Taylor 2009: 8–9).

For Foucault, the purpose of thought was never simply to find the solution to problems already posed but radically to revise the way people understood themselves and thereby create possibilities of real change (Foucault 1994d: 612). The subject of ethical conduct, of morality, is a subject who has taken a portion of itself as the object of observation, elaboration, testing, and transformation. To change the nature of this self-relationship is to change the nature of the subject. To think philosophically, at least since the time of Socrates, is, Foucault argues, to have such a concern for oneself and thereby for others (Foucault 1984a: 35; Rajchman 1991: 7). It was, in fact, Foucault's need to rethink the history of the subject in its powers of self-constitution—that is to say, as a confessing and truth-telling subject—that led him to extend his inquiries into antiquity and the rich philosophical and ethical tradition found therein (Nehamas 1998: 177; Gros 2001: 494–5)

From this perspective, what Foucault first proposes in 1980 with regard to truth and power and then elaborates in relation to sexual behaviors in 1981, will in 1982 become his central concept: the subject's self-constitution over time through a series of deliberate practices, what the Greeks called *tekhnai*. We often translate *tekhnai* as "arts," but this can be misleading. The Greek word does not have the same aesthetic charge that "art" has in modern usage, which primarily refers to fine arts. These "techniques" or "practices of freedom," as Foucault terms them, are recommended by and elaborated in Hellenistic and Roman imperial philosophy (Rajchman 1991: 112–13). As Foucault observed in an interview published in 1984, the fundamental problem for these philosophers was how not to be a slave—not only to others but to yourself, to your circumstances or expectations—how to be free (Foucault 1994g: 712). This is the primary task of philosophy in the Hellenistic and Roman period. In the words of Cicero's Fifth Stoic Paradox, "only the wise man is free." Such freedom refers not to a state or ontological reality but to an ethical condition produced in the self through "thought, action, and self-invention" (Rajchman 1991: 111). This work of the self on itself is not a withdrawal from history. It is not an apolitical solipsism. It seeks to produce subjects who are "fearless in the expression of their freedom" (Lawlor 2016: 270). One should always remember that Foucault defined Deleuze and Guattari's *Anti-Oedipus* (1972), which ask the question "how does one keep from being a fascist?," as a "book of ethics" (Leonard 2005: 86; Foucault 1983: xiii). Ethics are complementary, not opposed, to politics.

In what follows, I will first define some of the basic terms Foucault deploys in the *Hermeneutics of the Subject*. These will play a central role in the final two courses as well: "the care of the self," "spirituality," "self-knowledge," and "*parrhēsia*." I will then offer more extended treatments of his reading of Plato's *Alcibiades* and the Stoics, before focusing on his dialogue and debate with

Pierre Hadot, the great French historian of ancient philosophy. I will conclude by returning to Foucault's concept of *bios*, its relation to *parrhēsia* and governmentality as well as aesthetics, and how these concerns are related to the nineteenth century's problematic of revolution.

## I(a) "The Care of the Self"

> ... the famous comparison of Socrates to the gadfly, the insect that pursues animals, stings them, and makes them run and be agitated. The care of the self is a sort of stinger that ought to be planted there, in the flesh of men, that ought to be stuck into their existence as a principle of agitation, of movement, a permanent principle of restlessness in the course of existence.
>
> Foucault 2001a: 9

> The care of the self—or the care that one takes of the care that others ought to have of themselves—appears as an intensification of social relations.
>
> Foucault 1984b: 69

In Chapter 2, we examined briefly the topic of the "care of the self" in the context of Socrates' claim in the *Apology* that the "unexamined life is not liveable for a human being" and the proper role of the philosopher was to urge the citizen body to "care" for themselves and not merely their possessions (36c4–7, 38a5–6), acting as the proverbial gadfly (30e). Where, in the preceding year's lectures, *epimeleia heautou* ("care of the self") was one element in a series that included "learning" and "practice" in the process of taking one's life as an object of interest and elaboration through the *tekhnē peri bion* of philosophy, in 1982 it occupies the foreground. Indeed, Foucault claims it is a central element of ancient philosophical practice that has become obscured from our view in favor of self-knowledge construed as factual observation (Foucault 2001a: 13–15) More precisely, Foucault's claim in these lectures is that the care of the self is not something we do once we have acquired self-knowledge, but the precondition of that knowledge, the precondition of our access to truth.

Exhibit A is Plato's *Alcibiades*. We will provide a more in-depth examination of Foucault's reading in section II of this chapter. But very briefly, the dialogue puts into action the ideas just referenced from the *Apology*. Socrates encounters Alcibiades on the cusp of his majority, ready to take his place as a citizen in the

Athenian Assembly. Alcibiades makes clear to Socrates that he sees his role as becoming a leader in Athens and throughout the Greek world, which, as Plato's audience would know, he subsequently did with disastrous results. In typical fashion, Socrates begins questioning Alcibiades on what he understands governing the city to mean, and it shortly becomes clear that Alcibiades has no real ideas on the subject. He simply assumes that as the ward of Pericles it is his right. As Socrates reveals the scope of Alcibiades' ignorance, the latter collapses and ask Socrates what he should do. Socrates responds that Alcibiades cannot expect to govern others until he can govern himself and that his first task must thus be to care for himself. He must turn his gaze from the world of externals to the self, undertaking a form of meditation (Foucault 2001a: 12). The rest of the dialogue is devoted to defining the nature of the self and what it means to care for it.

There are three important lessons to be drawn from this synopsis. First, to assume one's place in society requires self-knowledge. Second, that self-knowledge is not simply a matter of registering intuitions about oneself but fully recognizing one's own ignorance and inability to govern oneself. Such recognition is a form of awakening from existence as an illusion or a dream (Foucault 2001a: 9; *Republic* 5.476c1–5). Third, one comes to this knowledge only through first understanding the nature of the self as it exists in itself, and this happens through a concerted dialogue with others, as exemplified by Socrates' dialectical examination of Alcibiades, which is itself presented as a form of love and affection. This is not something that one does once and it is done. *Epimeleia* is a form of activity: in wider usage it and its cognates are used for athletic training as much or more than for philosophical reflection (Foucault 2001a: 82)

With this marker laid down, Foucault makes a second claim. In the Hellenistic and Roman world, this philosophical care of the self moves from being a practice addressed to the young and ambitious, like Alcibiades, as a propaedeutic to the assumption of power, and becomes a general obligation of all humankind, at least in principle (Foucault 2001a: 73, 122). While philosophy and advanced literacy remained largely confined to the upper reaches of society, the Stoic paradox that only the wise man is free does in fact imply that many slaves may be freer than their masters and, in the case of Epictetus, who was born a slave, this was literally true. By the same token, the care of the self became an imperative for all the major schools of ancient philosophy in this period, not just the Stoics, but also the Epicureans, the Cynics, and Academics like Plutarch (Foucault 2001a: 10–11). Under these later philosophers, self-care moved from a form of individual examination undertaken with a master like Socrates, who through rigorous questioning led one to the realization that one knows nothing, to a set of exercises that involved reading, writing, oral instruction, and forms of self-examination undertaken with a director of conscience in the context of a philosophical community (Foucault 2001a: 125, 406–7). The care of the self, then, according to Foucault, moves from being a set of practices leading to self-knowledge that prepares one to assume a role in the governance of the self and others to become a generalized culture practiced by trained individuals as an end in itself, as a way of creating and shaping a life livable for a human being in a vast multinational empire (Foucault 2001a: 170–3). It creates and maintains a relation of the self to itself aimed at producing a self-sufficient plenitude incarnated in the ideal figure of the sage (Foucault 2001a: 305).

## I(b) Spirituality

Let us call, "philosophy" that form of thought that questions itself on what permits the subject to have access to the truth, the form of thought that tries to determine the conditions and the limits of the subject's access to the truth. And then, if we call this philosophy, I believe we would be able to call "spirituality" the research, the practice, the experience through which the subject carries out on himself the transformations necessary to have access to the truth. We will then call "spirituality" the ensemble of researches, practices, and experiences, which could be purifications, *askēses*, renunciations, conversions of the gaze, modifications of existence, etc., that constitute, not for factual knowledge but for the subject, for the very being of the subject, the price to pay for having access to the truth.

Foucault 2001a: 16–17

The modern subject does not need to undergo a conversion through *askésis* or *erōs* in order to gain access to the truth. Truth is not a characteristic of the ethos or subjectivity of the subject; it is a quality of propositions. In fact, in modernity truth is true precisely to the extent that it is "disinterested" rather than interested, "objective" rather than "subjective."

McGushin 2016: 110

In 1977, Pierre Hadot, a professor of ancient philosophy, published an essay entitled "spiritual practices," in which he argued that the principal aim of ancient philosophical discourse, regardless of school, was not the elaboration or communication of theoretical truths or of the conditions of those truths but the formation of the spirit of the reader or interlocutor. It is not that the truths elaborated by the ancient schools were immaterial to the work being done, but the work itself was not the discourse. Rather, the aim of the discourse was a transformation of the interlocutor that allowed the self to be shaped and realized through a series of dialogical practices: with oneself, with a master and members of the community, and with texts.[1] These practices involved regular forms of self-examination, taking an inventory of one's knowledge, ignorance, virtues, and vices. These exercises, Hadot contends, become most visible and formalized in the philosophers of the Hellenistic and Roman imperial periods. He uses the term "spiritual" to refer to them because, while words like "psychic," "moral," "ethical," and "intellectual" all cover a portion of what he means, they are each partial in relation to the phenomenon of a specifically philosophical self-formation (Hadot 2002: 20–33, 61, cf. 272–3, 278; 1995: 20–1, 269–71, 412; Davidson 2002: 12). While Hadot became a major exponent of this view, it was certainly not unique to him.[2]

In the late seventies, when beginning his work on the care of the self, Foucault discovered Hadot's writings on ancient philosophy and became a staunch advocate, urging him to present his candidacy for a chair at the Collège de France, which he obtained in 1982. While Foucault was profoundly influenced by Hadot (cf. Foucault 2001a: 218), they were not in total agreement and we will reserve the end of this chapter for a discussion of their differences. Spirituality for Foucault falls under the larger category of the care of the self. Where the latter was primarily an ethical concern, in the sense of the formation of the *ēthos* ("character," "disposition," "self"), the former has a distinctly epistemic flavor, referring to the formation or transformation of the self necessary to have access to the truth (Foucault 2001a: 227–8). Thus as early as his May 6, 1981 lecture at Louvain, Foucault was arguing that one of the characteristic ideas of ancient philosophy was that a certain style of life was required to have access to the truth and that this idea would later, in altered form, be central to Christian monasticism (Foucault 2012a: 125).

Truth, in this spiritual sense, cannot simply mean the correspondence between a given set of propositions and the world to which they refer. The same set of propositions spoken or read by one unable to appreciate or understand the truth will have a different value than they possess for one who does. This is the essence of Plato's critique of writing in the *Seventh Letter*, a topic to which we will return in the next chapter. For the philosopher, truth is a quality of experience, a relation between subjectivity and the world (McGushin 2016: 109, 112). It requires a moment of conversion, a literal turning of one's attention, one's gaze—as we see in the case of those dwelling in Plato's cave—from objects to oneself (Foucault 2001a: 17, 201). In later Hellenistic and Roman philosophy, this conversion will be less a matter of turning one's gaze from the world of temporal change to a world of unchanging truth, than it will be of turning it from the world of external attachments to the interiority of the self, from a world in which one will always be a slave to fortune, fate, and the will of others to a realm of spiritual calm and identification with a larger logic of the cosmos, whether in the form of Stoic *pneuma* or Epicurean atoms dancing in the void (Foucault 2001a: 201–2, 208).

Foucault defines the modern era by the loss of spirituality in the domain of knowledge, by the subject's self-constitution no longer needing to be called into question to have access to truth (2001a: 19–20). This loss of spirituality is, in fact, the precondition of the elaboration of scientific truth, which is by definition impersonal, and, consequently, its loss is also the cause of the alienation of our experience from that truth. The loss of spirituality is what makes possible both the modern world of technology and scientific advancement, and the consequent ability to take humans as a population to be administered (biopolitics); and it is what disqualifies our experience from entering the calculations necessary to that administration. Our subjective truth is cut off from "reality" but also strangely absolutized. In a world in which experience is simply a data point abstracted from the texture of existence, every individual's truth is their own, and this is defined as freedom. We have a right to our likes, our preferences, our beliefs. "You can't tell me what to do." At the same time, this subjective truth no longer possesses any necessary point of contact with the truth of the world. It becomes an impotent solipsism that defines freedom in abstraction from power, a form of slavery in its assertion of individual meaning ("I have a right to . . ."). The corollary to the Stoic paradox that only the wise man is free is the fool is always a slave.

Foucault points to the Cartesian moment as the point at which this transformation occurs, the moment when the self becomes reduced to the *cogito*, a purely punctual moment of apperception that requires no preparation, no transformation to accede to the most fundamental of truths (*sum*, "I am"), and from that foundation to build out a world of truth. Of course, this history is grossly oversimplified, as Foucault quickly admits, though others have taken him to task for his supposed naïveté. It is conceptual rather than empirical. It is not that Descartes single-handedly abolished spirituality or even that it happened at a specific point in time. But it is rather that the absolutization of the knowing subject can be distilled and illustrated in the figure of the *cogito* as the moment of punctual reduction. As Foucault himself observes, this is the result of a long process. Already in the scholasticism of the Middle Ages, we can see an effort to separate spirituality from access to the truth, and as Foucault pointed out with much vigor in his debate with Derrida, it is no accident that Descartes labels his work a meditation, a form of action on the self (Foucault 2001a: 28, 183–4; Hadot 1995: 395–6; 2002: 373; Jaffro 2003: 73, 78; McGushin 2016: 112). Nonetheless, there is a split that occurs on or about the time of Descartes's radical doubt, a split that establishes a knowing subject separated from that subject's actual experience as the foundation of scientific reason and as the foundation of what became modern university-based philosophy. Under this regime, the truth of the self is separated from scientific truth. It becomes the province of art and expression of dissident philosophers like Schopenhauer, Nietzsche, and Heidegger (Foucault 2001a: 29–30; Hadot 2002: 374; Adorno 2012: 54). By performing the archeology of these spiritual practices, Foucault argues, we chart a movement *from* the subject's self-relation as the foundation of truth *to* subjectivity's alienation from truth and the political and spiritual pathologies that result therefrom.

## I(c) Self-knowledge

> Socrates: For me there is never leisure for such [mythological] inquiries. The cause, my friend, is this: I cannot in accord with the Delphic inscription

know myself (*gnōnai emauton*). It seems a ridiculous thing to me when I don't know this thing to investigate other things ... I examine myself whether I happen to be some wild beast more twisted and aflame than Typho or a gentler and simpler form of life (*zōion*).

Plato, Phaedrus 229e3–a5

Within the history of the care of the self, *gnōthi seauton* does not have the same form and the same function. As a consequence, the contents of the knowledge that are revealed or delivered by the *gnōthi seauton* are not going to be the same each time, which means that the very different forms of knowledge put into play are not the same, which also means that the subject itself, as constituted by the form of reflexivity pertaining to a given type of care of the self, will be modified. Consequently, we should not formulate a continuous history of the *gnōthi seauton* that would have as an implicit or explicit postulate a general and universal theory of the subject, but I believe we must begin with an analytic of the forms of reflexivity, insofar as the forms of reflexivity constitute the subject as such.

Foucault 2001a: 443–4

The elements of Foucault's analytic grid now start to become clear. In the ancient world, beginning with Socrates, but building on a history of self-care extending back through various Pythagorean and shamanistic practices into prehistory, there was a fundamental obligation to care for, even to curate, the self (*epimeleia heautou*). This obligation was the foundation of ethics and virtue (*aretē*). One paid attention to oneself so one could form one self into a subject capable of governing oneself and others. Under the Socratic model, this care took two primary forms, dialogue (whether internal or external) and *erōs* ("love," "desire"). Whether we consider Socrates' speech in the *Symposium*, his great speech in the *Phaedrus*, or his approach to Alcibiades in the dialogue of the same name, *erōs* is always seen as a means of instruction, as it had been throughout the history of Greek pederastic practices. The kinds of intense dialogical practices we see exemplified by Socrates' questioning of others are often charged with erotic tension, which then becomes re-cathected to the love of truth (Foucault 1984a: 264–9; Elden 2016: 179). It is no accident that one of the crimes for which Socrates was executed was corrupting the youth.

Under the rubric of the care of the self, Foucault identified what, following Hadot, he labelled "spiritual practices." These were specific exercises and forms of meditation that had the purpose of forming a subject able to accede to the truth. They were aimed at fulfilling the ancient admonition to know yourself (*gnōthi seauton*) inscribed on the oracle of Apollo in Delphi. As Foucault observes, the content of that self-knowledge much depended on the kind of self the subject was engaged in elaborating, the precise nature of the self's relation to itself in a particular context, and the forms of the spiritual practice undertaken to give that subject access to the truth of itself and the world.

Central to all forms of spiritual practice was conversion, the practice of turning the gaze to what is real, the truth and the self. The question of how one performs this conversion, the nature of its techniques, is at the heart of Foucault's inquiry: "how do you establish, fix, and define the relation between truth-telling (veridiction) and the practice of the subject?" (Foucault 2001a: 220). It is important to recognize that the various practices of turning the gaze from the things one possesses to the self that possesses them do not in the Platonic or Hellenistic world make that self a secret to be deciphered, but rather this moment of conversion seeks to shape a self capable of understanding and pursuing its own ends. The self-knowledge this practice produces is more like the concentration of an athlete or a Zen archer than it is the discovery of a secret self, inner child, or forbidden desire (Foucault 2001a: 213; Fimiani 2012: 96). The truth that Alcibiades learns in his eponymous dialogue is the reality of both his ignorance and his desire for Being, for the good. The self-knowledge gained by the Stoics is the recognition of the subject's inability to control the external world and yet its profound solidarity with it. The techniques that produce this knowledge are repurposed in the later Christian direction of conscience and function as a kind of first draft for what will become "the sciences of the spirit, psychology, the analysis of consciousness, of *psukhē*" (Foucault 2001a: 242).

Thus, in Hellenistic philosophical practice (*askēsis*), the self comes to fix upon itself as both the end and object of a technique of life (*tekhnē biou*), not with the goal of becoming the object of a true discourse but the speaking subject of that discourse. Through practices of reading, writing, and discussion, the telos of Hellenistic philosophy is to produce a subject who, Seneca observes, makes the things it learns its own (*facere suum*), aligning itself with the truth and speaking it. Such a practice is not a matter of submitting to an external law but of linking the self to the truth and thereby becoming a subject in the fullest sense (Foucault 2001a: 316–17; Seneca, *Letters to Lucilius* 119).

94   Foucault's Seminars on Antiquity

Foucault's claim is that the traditional history of philosophy has privileged *gnōthi seauton* as though the self and its constitution as a subject were a universal constant, "from Plato to Husserl, passing through Descartes." What he attempts in this course, however, is to recontextualize the meaning of self-knowledge within the history of the care of the self. He flips the script. Rather than self-knowledge leading us to care for ourselves and that knowledge and its object being in some way a constant—while the actual care would be dependent on various political, economic, and environmental factors—the care of the self and its spiritual practices would make possible self-knowledge and the joining of the self to truth. Thus, he argues, the object of our study should not be the truth of the subject, but the way the subject constitutes itself to speak the truth (Foucault 2001a: 442–3). Where we moderns understand self-knowledge to be the "objectification of the subject in a field of factual knowledges," the Greeks and Romans, he argues, understood "the constitution of the world as the spiritual experience of the subject" (Foucault 2001a: 304).

## I(d) *Parrhēsia*

> Throughout the development of the practice of the self ... something very new and important, I believe, developed, which is a new ethic, not so much of language or discourse in general, but of the verbal relation with the Other. And this new ethic of the verbal relation with the other is what is designated by this fundamental notion of *parrhēsia*. *Parrhēsia*, generally translated "frankness" is a rule of the game, a principle of verbal comportment that one should have with the other in the practice of the direction of conscience.
> 
> Foucault 2001a: 158

> The thought of Foucault, seen from the perspective of his encounter with ancient philosophy, is still that of the present of our future in which so many threatening relations constrain us, once and for all, into an identity determined by the mercantile *cogito*; this present in which more than ever we must fashion, at each moment, an ethic of speech in order to have the courage to speak the truth.
> 
> Davila 2003: 207

On March 10, 1982, Foucault offered his first systematic examination of what will become a recurring topic in the last three years of his life, *parrhēsia*, or "philosophical frankness." In this instance, the context is a discussion of a Stoic director of conscience speaking to a student who wishes to care for himself and so arrive at genuine self-knowledge. *Parrhēsia,* here, is a practice whereby subjects are converted to philosophy by being told the truth about themselves. It could take a variety of forms, from Seneca's *Letters to Lucilius* to a Cynic preacher's street corner harangues (Foucault 2001a: 232; Gros 2012: 156–7).

In these last three years, *parrhēsia* will occupy an increasingly central role in Foucault's vision of philosophy as a practice of truth. It will be rigorously distinguished from rhetoric, philosophy's traditional adversary. If rhetoric is the inventory and analysis of the means by which a discourse moves others toward certain ends, philosophy is an ensemble of practices, to care for yourself and others, and hence to govern yourself and others through truth. The capacity to speak the truth is central to any claim to power, whether we are considering the astrological map in the throne room of Septimius Severus, the riddle of the Sphinx as the warrant for Oedipus's rule, or the mandate of Alcibiades to assume the leadership of the Athenian people (Foucault 2001a: 131; Evans 2016: 162). Philosophy as the parrhesiastic practice par excellence is thus always implicated within the structure of power and its claims. By speaking the truth to and for power, it has the capacity both to legitimate and contest that power, if only (but not exclusively) on the level of the subject.

*Parrhēsia*, then, is not simply an ancient technique of life (*tekhnē biou*) or a Greek philosophical concept—although it is all those things and Foucault's analysis of it will be deepened over the course of the next two years—but it is also central to the way Foucault understood the function of the philosopher in modern life: speaking truth to power, whether on prisons, sexuality, or other forms of oppression. There is a sense in which he is performing his own genealogy through his examination of this concept. *Parrhēsia* offers the possibility of a form of critique, a form of truth in which the subject is directly engaged. It is not scientific reasoning, although it may make use of it, because it does not offer a disembodied instrumental reason. Rather, the philosopher who engages herself to speak truth to power, as she understands it, as a form of critique, wagers herself in the act of veridiction. This is not an objective or impersonal truth. It requires the subject to be fully engaged. What Foucault undertakes in his examination of *parrhēsia* is the genealogy and warrant for this form of speech (Kelly 2014: 181–2).

As noted above, the traditional opposite of philosophical *parrhēsia* is rhetoric. Where the goal of rhetoric is to persuade others to do as the speaker desires, which may involve the speaker assuming a variety of personae or even utilizing deceptive or sophistic means, the aim of Stoic *parrhēsia* is to allow others to "constitute for themselves in relation to themselves a relation of sovereignty, which will be the characteristic of the sage, of the virtuous subject, the subject who has attained all the happiness that is possible to attain in this world" (Foucault 2001a: 368–9). *Parrhēsia* is fundamentally concerned with speaking the truth, while rhetoric is concerned with the manner of speaking (Gros 2012: 157). Clearly, these are not mutually exclusive concerns, and as Foucault goes on to clarify, the true enemy of *parrhēsia* is flattery (Foucault 2001a: 357, 369). Seneca, he contends, often used *libertas* to mean *parrhēsia* in Latin, the traditional word for aristocratic freedom of speech under the republic and the sign under which Roman satire as a genre asserted its right to criticize the behavior of others. While satire is often ironic, the ideal speaker of traditional Roman *libertas* presents himself as the speaker of a truth others may not wish to hear, a truth that is useful for reforming the behavior of both speaker and hearer (Foucault 2001a: 356; Miller 2005: 1–14; 2019: see Chapter 1).

What characterizes *parrhēsia* and *libertas* then as a philosophical exercise is the speaking subject's complete engagement in the speech. The flatterer by definition does not coincide with the content of his speech. The rhetorician like the advocate or the professional writer of speeches may or may not warrant the truth of their speech with their being. But the parrhesiast is he who says, "what authenticates the fact that I am speaking the truth, is that effectively I am, as the subject of my conduct, absolutely, wholly and totally identical with the subject of my enunciation." While *parrhēsia* may be spoken in many modes, including the ironic and satiric, it cannot be hypocritical. The servile flattery of the imperial hack has no place. And this, in the end, is what distinguishes the philosopher from the technician of truth: for true philosophy is always in the end a spiritual practice, a practice of the subject in relation to truth, and not the mere elaboration of a theory, the defense of a position (Foucault 2001a: 362–3, 388–9). To be a professor of philosophy is a career choice, to be a philosopher is a vocation.

## II

**Alcibiades**   And so what is the care (*epimeleian*) that I should exercise, Socrates? Can you explain to me? You seem like one who has spoken the truth about everything.

*Alcibiades* 124b7–9

**Socrates**   And so, did you know that when one person is gazing into the eyes of another there will appear in the eyes of the second person, just as in a mirror, in what we call the pupil, the image of the one who gazes?

**Alcibiades**   You speak the truth.

**Socrates**   Therefore, an eye contemplating an eye, and looking into the best part of it, where sight is, would see itself.

**Alcibiades**   It appears.

**Socrates**   But if it should look at any other part of a person or at anything of other beings, except what happens to be similar to it, it will not see itself.

**Alcibiades**   You speak the truth.

**Socrates**   If an eye will see itself, it must look into an eye, and into that part of the eye in which the virtue of the eye is born. Is this right?

**Alcibiades**   Indeed.

**Socrates**   And so, my dear Alcibiades, if a soul will come to know itself, it must look at a soul, and especially into that part of this soul where the virtue of the soul, wisdom, is born.

*Alcibiades* 133a1–b10

**Alcibiades**   We run the risk of exchanging our appearances with one another. For there is no way I will not follow you from this day and you will not be followed by me.

**Socrates**   Good sir, my love will not differ from that of the stork, having hatched a feathered love in you, it will then by served by this.

**Alcibiades**   But so it is, and I will begin at once to care for justice (*dikaiosunē*).

**Socrates**   I would very much like you to accomplish this. Even so, while I do not distrust your nature, I see the power of the city, and I shudder that you might not be ruled by me and you.

*Alcibiades* 135d8–e8

These three passages mark three critical points in Plato's *Alcibiades*. In the first, after extensive questioning by Socrates concerning Alcibiades' plans to assume political leadership, now that he is on the cusp of his majority, the young man admits his aporia, his inability to determine how he should proceed. He does not know what "care" he should exercise, if he is to lead the city, and though he was filled with self-confidence earlier in the dialogue, he now turns to Socrates to seek direction. Such moments of aporia are the primary aim of the Socratic *elenchus* or "examination," the reduction of the interlocutor to perplexity. Many of the shorter dialogues, which are generally assumed to be the earliest, end with that moment. In the more complex dialogues, like the *Republic*, such moments of puzzlement are often only the first step. The recognition of the interlocutor's ignorance serves as a propaedeutic to a more serious and protracted study of the issues at hand. Yet, even in some of the more complex dialogues, which are frequently considered later, such as the *Theaetetus* or the *Philebus*, the dialogue often ends without a firm final conclusion. There is an immense literature on the topic of the *elenchus* and its relation to *aporia*.[3] But, perhaps, no better statement can be found on the philosophical function of this perplexity than Socrates' own in the *Theaetetus*, when, after reaching an initial aporia with the eponymous interlocutor and then attempting to reformulate the definition of knowledge, the object of their discussion, he says, "if we keep going like this, one of two things will happen. Either we shall find what we are after; or we shall think less we know things we don't" (187c). At its best, the aporia that results from closely examining an interlocutor is the first step toward an advance in knowledge. At minimum, it presents a moment of demystification in which what had been assumed to be true is shown to be false or, at least, incomplete. Thus in the *Alcibiades*, the main character, after being questioned extensively by Socrates, recognizes that he in fact does not have the expertise necessary to lead the city, and this must be remedied. But how? His care and attention must first be turned toward a more fundamental object than the city or even politics itself. What is it that he should care for? What should he devote his attention to, if he is to come to the knowledge necessary to govern himself and others?

The answer, of course, is that he must first care for himself, but how? The self is a most elusive thing. As we have already seen in the passages quoted from the *Apology*, it must not be confused with one's possessions. Indeed, it must not be confused with anything separable from the self, including parts of the body. Even should he lose a hand, a foot, or an eye, Alcibiades is no less Alcibiades. Just as the cobbler is separable from the tools he uses and so is not the same as those tools, so the self is separable from its bodily extensions. But what is in us that makes use of our hands, feet, and eyes, indeed of our body writ large, as the cobbler makes use of his knife, his hole punch, or a sheet of leather? That would be what is truly our ourselves, and Socrates argues we should name this "singular and transcendent position of the subject in relation to what surrounds it, to the objects at its disposition" our *psukhē* or "soul" (Foucault 2001a: 56):

**Socrates** What do we say about the cobbler? Does he only cut with his tools or also with his hands?

**Alcibiades** Also with his hands.

**Socrates** And does he use these?

**Alcibiades** yes.

**Socrates** And does he cobble using his eyes?

**Alcibiades** yes.

**Socrates** And are the cobbler and even lyre player different from the hands and eyes with which they work?

**Alcibiades** It seems so.

**Socrates** And in this fashion a man uses his whole body.

**Alcibiades** Completely.

**Socrates** And the user is a different from the used.

**Alcibiades** Yes.

**Socrates** And is a person different from his body?

**Alcibiades** So it seems.

**Socrates** And so what is a person?

**Alcibiades**   I can't say.

**Socrates**   But you can because it's the thing using the body.

**Alcibiades**   Yes.

**Socrates**   And so does anything other than the soul (*psukhē*) use the body?

**Alcibiades**   Nothing other.

129d4–130a2

The soul too, however, is an elusive phenomenon and not immediately visible to ourselves. We, indeed, are not visible to ourselves except with the aid of a mirror, and the mirror of our soul, Socrates argues, is the soul of another: the self of the philosopher who through his love, his care, and his questioning reveals us to ourselves. The *logos* of the other, the honest speech (*parrhēsia*) of the other becomes the mirror through which we are revealed to ourselves, through which we become visible unto ourselves and so can become the object of care, the object of our own spiritual practice (Pradeau 2009: 78, 96).

It is to this game of mutual reflection that Alcibiades vows to devote himself at the end of the dialogue, and through this game, in which he will find himself revealed, he hopes to discover justice (*dikaiosunē*) and thus the power to rule others as well as himself. Even so as Socrates' final lines show, he worries—and history reveals he is right to—that the erotic intoxication of power will be too much and that Alcibiades will once more become the beloved of the people (*dēmerastēs*, 132a3), and not the lover of wisdom and justice that Socrates would have him be. There is a strong sense here in which Alcibiades, it is implied, becomes the erotic object of the entire city and hence absolutely corrupted. He is the object of the care of others but not of himself, and he becomes subject to their flattery and deception.

It is no wonder, then, that Foucault places the *Alcibiades* at the center of his inquiry into the care of the self. He was certainly not alone: the Neo-Platonic tradition began its syllabus with this dialogue as the opening of the Platonic *cursus* leading to the *Philebus* at its end (Foucault 2001a: 164; 1988b: 23; Hadot 1995: 238–9; Denyer 2001: 14). The *Alcibiades* can be considered a natural starting point for any history, Foucault argues, that would foreground the care of the self as an important philosophical concept (Foucault 2014: 299–300).

There are, in fact, questions about the authenticity of the work and its dating, only some of which Foucault was aware. But none of this is material to Foucault's inquiry. The work was accepted as both authentic and important throughout antiquity (and indeed until the nineteenth century), and Foucault's inquiry is not into the value or precise positions taken by Plato, the individual, at a given point in his career, but about the history of a larger discourse on the nature of the self and its relation to truth as an event in thought that continues to shape our own subjectivity today. He reads the dialogue as both a genealogy of our own position and as part of a larger strategy that would allow us to think differently about how we understand truth and our relation to it, about how we govern ourselves and seek to govern others (Foucault 2001a: 68–73; Denyer 2001: 14–26; Elden 2016: 155). In a sense, we all become Alcibiades, as we are asked to justify our aspirations, asked to care for ourselves, and asked to think carefully about what that means for the entire project of self-governance.

One of the distinctive features of the Platonic care of the self, as opposed to its later Stoic counterpart, is its emphasis on the erotic. At the beginning of the *Alcibiades*, Socrates asserts that while many have claimed to love the famously handsome Alcibiades, he alone has been his true lover. He has waited to this day, when Alcibiades has almost reached his majority and is able to address the Athenian Assembly (105b1; Denyer 2001: ad loc), to declare his affection, so there could be no question of impure motives, no suggestion that Socrates loved Alcibiades' youthful body rather than his soul (103a1–105b7). Socrates' goal in the dialogue is to convince Alcibiades that he alone is his true lover and that Alcibiades, as he does at least tentatively at the end of the dialogue, must submit to Socrates: not in the manner of a pederastic beloved, but as a philosophical lover who will only learn how to speak before the assembly, and hence how to rule others, when he has learned how to care for himself through turning his gaze from the adulation of the city to the image of himself mirrored in Socrates' eyes. As Foucault says of the dialogue in an interview later in 1982 at the University of Vermont, "The intersection of political ambition and philosophical love is 'taking care of oneself'" (Foucault 1988b: 23–5).

Alcibiades is naturally intrigued by Socrates' approach and submits to his questioning, hoping to arrive at the answer to the question of how he can rule Athens and ultimately all of Greece. But, as Socrates continues to question him, Alcibiades reaches a point of capitulation, where he admits his powerlessness in the face of the *elenchus*. Foucault draws our attention to the following (2001a: 37):

> **Socrates** What then do you say is this friendship and agreement concerning what we must have to be wise and of good council so that we may be good men? For I am not able to learn what it is or in what class of things it is ...
>
> **Alcibiades** But by the gods, Socrates, I myself do not know what I am saying. I run the risk of having forgotten myself most shamefully.
>
> **Socrates** But have courage. For if you had discovered this thing at age 50, it would be difficult to have cared for yourself (*epimelēthēnai saoutou*): now you are an age in which there is no need for shame.
>
> 127d1–e2

The classic pederastic relationship between an older man and his young beloved is still the frame of reference here, but it has been evacuated of all immediately sexual content, and the fact that Alcibiades is almost twenty makes that all the more clear. Rather, the love that Socrates demonstrates for Alcibiades is a love that will allow the beloved not to submit to the will of the lover, but to find himself reflected there, to assume a relation with himself that were he not mirrored in the eyes of the other would be impossible. He has "most shamefully forgotten himself," but now Alcibiades has the possibility to see himself, perhaps for the first time.

For Foucault, the *Alcibiades* constitutes an event in thought. It is the earliest full-fledged theoretical investigation in the West of what it means to care for oneself (Foucault 2001a: 46). By asking the question of "what is the care for the self," it is also the first text that poses in a systematic way the problem of interior life, of the self's relation to itself. Even if the theme is already touched on to one degree or another throughout the Platonic corpus and arguably posed in poetic texts of an earlier vintage, the dialogue remains unique (*Alcibiades* 127e8; Festugière 1950: 61; Foucault 2001a: 65):

> The question Socrates asks and tries to resolve is not: should you occupy yourself with yourself? It is not, "now you are a man, therefore I ask what is a man?" The question Socrates asked is much more precise, much more difficult, much more interesting. It is you should occupy yourself with yourself, but what is the self itself (*auto to auto*), since it is the self with which you should be occupied?
>
> Foucault 2001a: 39

The *Alcibiades* is a natural starting point for a history of subjectivity defined as the relation of the self to itself. On the one hand, it poses with unusual rigor the question: what is the self and how does the self, defined as soul (*psukhē*), become visible to itself and so the object of care? On the other, it asks this question in the context of what does it mean to assume power within the state and to pursue justice (*dikaiosunē*). The need for Alcibiades to care for himself is deduced from his wish to exercise power over others (Foucault 2001a: 37–8).

In many ways, the dialogue is a mirror image of the *Republic*. In the latter, it is proposed that we look to the composition of the ideal city to learn what it means to pursue justice in the soul, since large things are easier to see than small. In the former, we are told that to understand what it would mean to pursue justice in the city we must first come to know the nature of the soul and how to care for it (Foucault 2001a: 52–3; Pradeau 2009: 96–7).

In the *Alcibiades*, the relation of the self to itself is mediated by and pursued for the *polis*. This is not the case in the Hellenistic and Roman imperial period when the majority of the citizen population was no longer directly involved in governance (Foucault 2001a: 80–1). In the next two years, Foucault will trace how the role of the philosopher as parrhesiast will change during this same period from active citizen and pedagogue to aspiring leaders like Alcibiades to the advisor to princes and the director of conscience for those who seek to rule only themselves and their households. The care of the self becomes a project of self-perfection if not yet salvation. Thus where Alcibiades must care for himself in order to assume power, according to a 1983 interview of Foucault, Seneca expressed the wish to grow old more quickly precisely in order to withdraw from public life and care for himself (Foucault 1994d: 615).

## III

> No one should feel pride in anything that is not his own ... Suppose he has a beautiful home and a handsome collection of servants, a lot of land under cultivation and a lot of money out at interest; not one of these things can be said to be in him—they are just things around him. Praise in him what can neither be given nor snatched away, what is peculiarly a man's.

You ask what that is? It is his soul (*animus*) and the perfection of reason in that soul. For man is a rational animal.

Seneca 1969: 88–9, Letter 41

In the slow development of the art of living under the sign of the care of the self, the two first centuries of the imperial period can be considered as the summit of a curve: a kind of golden age in the culture of the self, being understood, of course, as a phenomenon that only concerns the social groups, very limited in number, that were the bearers of culture and for whom a *technē tou biou* was able to have a meaning and a reality.

Foucault 1984b: 59

The passage from Seneca could almost come from the *Alcibiades*. It identifies the self not with its possessions, even those most intimate, but only with that without which the person would cease to have their core identity, their soul or spirit (*animus, psukhē*). This is certainly not the only passage in the *Letters to Lucilius* or in what remains of the once vast Stoic corpus to voice such sentiments. Letter 9 tells us that, while the wise man will be unequalled in his devotion to his friends, he will consider nothing truly valuable that can be lost. Letter 18 admonishes that while wealth is not bad in itself (Seneca was fabulously rich), the attachment to possessions was. Our internal freedom, in the end, rests on the distinction between the things that are ours and those that are not (Veyne 2003: 47). For the Stoic, beauty, power, and wealth are of no importance except as they can be related to virtue, defined as the soul's conformity to reason and nature (Brouwer 2014: 6). Like Socrates' fear that Alcibiades will be seduced by the enticements of the Athenian crowd, so Seneca too fears for the soul of Lucilius at the end of Letter 89: "how can people hold on to spiritual well-being when no one is trying to hold them back and the crowd is urging them on?" (Seneca 1969: 89, Letter 41). Philosophy for the Stoic in the end is a kind of therapy, a medicine for the soul (Nussbaum 1994: 13–14). It is not a profession, not a trade. It is a spiritual practice or an "art of living" (Letter 108; Veyne 2003: viii).

The Stoics are an important part of what Veyne labels Foucault's "Nietzschean-ethical project," what would have become the *Care of the Self* as a separate project on ancient ethics (Veyne 2003: x). Stoicism was for Foucault fundamentally a way of thinking differently about the self and hence rewriting the scope of its possibilities (Miller 1993: 340). It was never his goal or purpose to write a history of ancient philosophy or to give a complete account of Stoic philosophy, and it should certainly not be received uncritically as such.[4] Foucault is always a genealogist, and his focus remains on the self's ability to transform itself as a weapon in our arsenal, a tool for our survival in difficult times (Veyne 2003: x–xi; Jaffro 2003: 52–3; Pradeau 2012: 146–7).

His interest in the Stoics was hardly unique. Deleuze had already in *La logique du sens* enlisted the Stoics to approach a similar Nietzschean end and to combat what he saw as an idealist, Platonic metaphysics linked to the church (Benatouïl 2003: 20, 30–3; Foucault 1994h). Foucault's later use of the Stoics does not share Deleuze's focus on logic. Ethical practice is his central concern. Stoic *askēsis* is, for Foucault, a means to reveal the fundamentally technological nature of our processes of subjectivation and hence to make visible the possibility of those technologies' reappropriation for other purposes in other contexts (Jaffro 2003: 71–2).

The passage from Seneca continues the basic ontology of self-relations posited in the *Alcibiades*. Yet, the Stoic and more broadly imperial project of caring for the self has two crucial differences. First, as noted above, where Alcibiades must care for himself in order to assume political power, the project of a young man, all of the major imperial philosophical systems promote a model of autonomous existence, which, if it is not separate from the intrigues of the imperial court, strives to be immune from their dangers (Henderson 1993: 128–9; Edwards 1993: 32). It is no accident that one of Hadot's more famous works, on the *Meditations* of Marcus Aurelius, bears the title, *La citadelle intérieure* (1992). The care of the self for the philosopher emperor is less preparatory to governing than a refuge from it (Newman 1989: 1478). Thus, even as Seneca writes in Letter 40, "how can a thing possibly govern others when it cannot be governed itself?," articulating a principle of isomorphism that would have been recognizable to Xenophon and Plato (Seneca 1969: 83), nonetheless there is a subtle difference. Marcus Aurelius does not care for himself in order to govern the empire, but he knows that he will govern the empire well to the extent he also knows how to care for himself (Foucault 2001a: 193, 198).

The second major difference between the Stoic care of the self and the earlier version found in the *Alcibiades* is the lack of a necessary erotic content. It will be recalled that Socrates approaches Alcibiades as a suitor and that *erōs* throughout the Platonic corpus, but most especially in the *Symposium* and *Phaedrus*, serves as a form of spiritual practice that gives the proper lover access to the truth. As noted above and discussed in the previous chapter, this conception builds upon the educational function of pederasty as conceived in archaic and classical Greece and which still formed an active part of the debate in Plutarch's *Erōtikos* in the second century CE. Yet what we saw in that same dialogue was an increasing emphasis on marriage and the relative autonomy of the marital couple from the isomorphic relationship that subordinated sexual relations to power relations in a figure like Xenophon. Thus Foucault charts a kind of double movement in which the care of the self, while certainly not dissociated from political power, gains a relative autonomy and comes to function as a refuge from its harshest unpredictabilities, as the elites of Hellenistic and Roman imperial society are removed from the labor of direct citizen rule as understood in democratic Athens. At the same time, as this private space becomes increasingly elaborated and refined by the philosophers of the period, domestic life functions as a parallel or overlapping sphere of autonomy, making erotic life both more important as an object of care and less directly engaged in the constitution and wielding of political power and the truth claims that legitimate it. According to Foucault's vision—and even he admits this is overly schematized—we move from a situation in which political power, truth, erotic practice, and domestic life exist as a series of mutually reinforcing, homologous relations, to one in which the care of the self, and hence domestic and erotic life, are no longer immediately identified with political and civic power (*krateia*), and in which truth itself is able to be pursued through spiritual practices that are not necessarily subordinated to that power in an immediate fashion. Thus the self and its practices become an object of care and perfectionism in their own right, allowing a new constitution of the subject and a new relation between the subject and the power to govern itself and others (Foucault 2001a: 74, 484–5; Gros 2001: 507; Jaffro 2003: 59; Fimiani 2012: 118–19).

This care consists, in the first place, of a series of practices. One is not simply taught the truth as information and then it is applied, but certain practices (*askēses*) are undertaken in order to make the assimilation of the truth possible, to form a self able to receive the truth. "It is a process of intensifying subjectivity" (Foucault 1994i: 800). As Socrates reminds Agathon in *Symposium*, truth is not something poured from a full vessel into an empty one (175d3–e7). For Seneca, this intensification of subjectivity happens through a process of habituation. The mind must be straightened like the beams of a house that have become warped over time. The process is methodical and repetitive. To learn virtue we must unlearn vices (Foucault 2001a: 92, citing Seneca Letter 50). There must be a constant process of learning, reflection, and self-scrutiny, an "examination of conscience":

> This examination of conscience is a sort of test to the extent that, thanks to this reactivation of [the rules learned] and the memory of deeds ... you can measure where you are: if you still have a lot to do, if you are far from the goal, if effectively you have or have not been capable of translating into your actions the principles of truth that you have in the order of knowledge. Where am I as an ethical subject of truth? ... Am I someone capable of being self-identical as a subject of both action and truth?
>
> Foucault 2001a: 463

The examination of conscience is a daily inventory, a technology for forming the self. It is different in structure and content from anything recommended in the *Alcibiades* or elsewhere in the Platonic corpus (Foucault 1994d: 627).

While only one practice among many, it becomes a central focus for Foucault, as an antecedent of the modern confessing and therapeutic self. It was of importance to Seneca and has roots in the neo-Pythagorean philosophy of Sextius (Seneca, *De Ira*, 3.36; Hadot 1995: 306–7; Veyne 2003: 75–6). For debutant students, such as Seneca's correspondent Lucilius, this examination was performed under the tutelage of a director of conscience, an older, more experienced friend who offered frank advice, not in a paternal or an authoritarian manner but in the manner of Horace's *liber amicus* ("free/frank friend") in Satire 1.4, whose *consilium* will help him remove the few remaining vices that his father's exemplary advice did not. The emphasis on *libertas* and *parrhēsia* in this context is to be observed, even as the tone of interaction is one of civilized conversation between friends rather than hectoring or accusation (Veyne 2003: 125; Hadot 2002: 369; cf. Seneca, Letter 6). Thus in Letter 38, Seneca observes, "Philosophy is good advice (*consilium*), and no one gives advice at the top of his voice" (1969: 81). In the same satire, Horace, who was not a Stoic but had a sound philosophical education, moves from the example of his father and the advice of his friend to turning these examples over in his mind silently (*labris compressis*) to discover how he can himself become a better man. Instruction is internalized as the self becomes doubled: both the subject and the object of examination. Each of us becomes the inspector who "measures" our selves (Seneca, *De Ira* 3.36; Foucault 1984b: 78). Seneca stresses repeatedly the need for critical self-reflection, arguing that what ruins character is a failure of self-examination (Letters 16 and 83).

Self care, then, is not a piece of information. It is not data to be learned and archived. It is a daily incremental practice of reflection, assimilation, and change. It involves study but not just gathering facts. "Each day ... acquire something which will help you to face poverty, or death, and suffer other ills as well. After running over a lot of different thoughts, pick out one to be digested thoroughly that day" (Seneca 1969: 34, Letter 2). The philosopher, as Epictetus notes and as Seneca cites approvingly from the Cynic Demetrius, is a spiritual athlete (Newman 1989: 1498; Foucault 2001a: 479). His training requires daily study and meditation (Veyne 2003: 74–5). This meditation involves both the examination of conscience and the memorization of short passages and *sententiae*, as well as exercises in visualization in which the philosopher imagines poverty, death, and loss to disarm them of their sting (Newman 1989: 1480, 1489).

Stoicism is cognitive therapy. Its object is not sin or depravity, but *stultitia*, commonly translated "stupidity," but closer to what Buddhist texts refer to as "monkey mind," an inconstant and undisciplined spirit that jumps from topic to topic, craving to craving, attachment to attachment, robbing the student of both tranquility and mental clarity (Suzuki 2006: 107). The result is suffering. *Stultitia* is the opposite of caring for the self, of a determined and disciplined spiritual practice (Foucault 2001a: 126–7). The *stultus* ("fool") is one whose will is not free, whose will is controlled by external events or representations, by desires to which one becomes enslaved (Foucault 2001a: 128).

> What is it, Lucilius, that drags us from one place to another and drives us to a place from which we desire to pull back? What struggles with our soul and does not allow us to want anything once and for all? We are tossed between the waves (*fluctuamur*) of differing opinions; we wish nothing freely, nothing absolutely, nothing permanently. You reply "*Stultitia* is that for which nothing is constant, for which nothing long pleases." But how or when do we emerge

from it on our own? No one is strong enough to pull himself out. You need someone to extend a hand, someone to lead you out.

Letter 52

We see this same imagery of drowning beneath the waves of uncontrolled passion, of the self adrift and in need of rescue in Clytemnestra's speech near the beginning of Seneca's *Agamemnon*:

> I am carried by different tides (*fluctibus*). And while the wind drags me here on the deep, and the storm takes me there, uncertain the wave hesitates before the evil to which it should yield. Henceforth I loose the rudder from my hands! Wherever anger, pain, and hope will carry me, there I will drive myself to go. We have given our boat to the waves.
>
> 138–43

Clytemnestra wounded by fate, by the monstruous sacrifice of her daughter, and by her adulterous love for Aegisthus, has let the tiller slip. In the end, the object of a truly free will can only be itself, and *stultitia* ("madness, a lack of control") represents a loss of connection between the self and the will. It is the task of the philosopher to stretch out a hand to the one who so suffers, not to transmit information, not to offer a correct proposition or theory, but to lead the drowning person out from the waves of suffering and indecision (Foucault 2001: 128–9). While for some philosophy may be an entertainment, a pass-time in which one displays their mental prowess before others, for Seneca, philosophy is not real if it does not lead to lasting internal change (Letter 108). The goal of the helping hand is to turn a momentary enthusiasm into a spiritual disposition. There is no happy life without wisdom (Letter 16), or as Socrates argued in court, on trial for his life, "the unexamined life is not livable for a human being."

The goal of the helping hand is not subjection. It does not seek to reveal the individual's need for salvation but emancipation. The *sapiens* ("wise person") who extends their hand to the *stultus* is a vanishing mediator, a means to allow the subject to regain the tiller and develop a relation with themselves, like that Horace imagines for himself (Foucault 2001a: 129–30). Behind this imagery lies a sophisticated cognitive theory that space will not allow us to develop in full. In outline, the role of the *sapiens* is to teach the *stultus* to apply reason to gain mastery over his internal discourse. Stoicism is a thoroughgoing intellectualism (Hadot 1995: 210–11). Every sensory impression for the Stoics is propositional in form. Each impression proposes itself to our soul in the form of a *lekton* or a "sayable," and it is reason's task to assent to those impressions or reject them as fallacious. Once assented to, they can then become sources of impulse or apprehension. It is the role of reason within the soul to criticize those impressions and draw correct conclusions from them (Annas 1992: 64–6; Nussbaum 1994: 327; Frede 1994; Hankinson 2003: 65). Errors in this process harden over time into habits, and it requires repetition and training to dislodge them so the soul may return to health. That health consists in being aligned with its own unitary nature, which Stoic theory defined as reason (Veyne 2003: 50, 61, 63). In this way, the soul regains the tiller and becomes captain of its own destiny regardless of the winds of fate and attachment that may buffet it.

Reason, according to the Stoics, is what separates humans from beasts. Martha Nussbaum has criticized Foucault's understanding of this central tenet of Stoic philosophy. In her monumental 1994 *The Therapy of Desire*, she did not have access to the published seminars and, judging by the single footnote she includes, seems to be working primarily from the short section on the "culture of the self" in volume three of the *History of Sexuality* and from summaries found in Hadot and Arnold Davidson. Thus when she argues that "For Foucault, reason is itself just one among many masks assumed by political power. For the Stoic, reason stands apart, resisting all domination, the authentic and free core of one's life as an individual and as a social being" (1994: 354), I would contend, she offers an impoverished reading of Foucault's understanding of both reason and the Stoics. Certainly, Foucault understood reason in a Nietzschean sense as a form of power that allowed individuals to shape themselves and their environment, but that power was never simply political power, nor did that make reason nothing but power. Reason is indissociable from power, precisely because reason works, because it is effective. Reason is a set of linguistic practices that allow individuals and institutions to take control of themselves, their environments, and ultimately others, and this is not a notion as alien to the Stoic conception as Nussbaum's caricature would make it seem. In the end, what Foucault found fascinating in the Stoa is the power of its technologies to shape a self that was not founded on mere juridical or authoritarian assertions of power, but on a disciplinary structure through which the rational subject takes itself as its own object (Miller 1993: 323).

For the Stoics, Foucault contends, freedom is understood as escaping the "servitude of the self," our bondage to error, habit, and the frailties of the body (2001a: 260). Thus, Seneca in Letter 47 congratulates Lucilius on the good treatment he offers his slaves, since we are all slaves, save the sage, and while our slaves may have had no choice in their fate, our servitude is self-imposed, which makes it all the more disgraceful. Likewise, in Letter 45, he tells Lucilius that he must not be a slave to his body and, should its needs become overwhelming, through sickness, injury, or the threat of torture and death, their partnership may be dissolved (Seneca 1969: 123–4). Similarly, Epictetus tells us that freedom from our fears and desires can be achieved by applying the rule of reason to the entire gamut of representations our mind presents to us and that this weapon is so powerful Caesar himself can do nothing against it (Newman 1989: 1501–2). Stoic philosophy, thus, can be characterized as a form of cognitive therapy that aims at the uprooting of habitual error that inhibits the self's realization of its intrinsic freedom even in the face of actual, physical bondage.

For the Stoic, the study of the natural world, the reading of history, the study of philosophical texts themselves, are only valuable insofar as they lead to a lasting change in the student. Rather than read broadly, Seneca advises picking one or two texts in which you can go deeply, picking out concepts and formulations that you not only memorize but truly internalize. "Precepts have the same features as seeds: they are of compact dimensions and they produce impressive results—given, as I say, the right sort of mind to grasp at and assimilate them" (Seneca 1969: 82, Letter 38, cf. Letter 84). We are to imagine epigrammatically articulated ideas slowly stretching their roots throughout our consciousness as their full potential is slowly realized. I suspect most of us have had the experience of reading something and reflecting on it again and again over the years only to see it reveal new dimensions not only of its meaning but also of ourselves. Similarly, as Foucault reminds us, Seneca admonishes us not to read history with an interest in mere antiquarianism, but the tradition of the Roman exemplum is highly valued: Horatius at the bridge, Mucius Scaevola, Cato the elder, and Cato the Younger can all be models of behavior (Foucault 2001a: 253–4). Stoicism also had a physics, and Seneca himself wrote an entire treatise on *Natural Questions*, but as he observes in Letter 65, you begin with ethics and then move to physics. The Stoic is committed to living according to nature, and that nature is seen ultimately as reason (the organizing principle of inert matter), thus the observation of the self is not in opposition to the observation of nature but each implies and reflects the other, even as nature stands as an admonition to the erring self (Foucault 2001a: 263–5). Stoicism, Veyne argues, is perhaps uniquely powerful in the way it combines an "art of living with a metaphysics or, rather, a philosophy of nature" (2003: 43).[5]

In the end, it is not a question of moving to another world as in neo-Platonism or its later Christian variants. The Stoics like their Epicurean *confrères* remain very much a part of this world. But the Stoic sage, that *rara avis*, and all those who seek to imitate him, do seek a higher, more encompassing perspective. The isolated self by identifying with reason and nature, and thus escaping the slavery of what are now viewed as petty fears and desires, comes to identify itself with the totality of existence. There is a dilation of the self that brushes up against its own dissolution. Seeing oneself and understanding the totality of the world become indissociable from one another (Foucault 2001a: 264–9). The sage enlarges himself to the scale of the cosmos (Veyne 2003: 108).

## IV

> One sees that from a certain perspective dandyism borders on spirituality and stoicism. But a dandy is not able to be a vulgar man. If he were committing a crime, perhaps he would not have fallen; but if this crime were committed for trivial reasons, the dishonor would be irreparable. Let the reader not be scandalized by this seriousness in frivolity, and let him remember that there is a greatness even in follies, a force even in excess. A queer spirituality!
> 
> Baudelaire 1968: 560

> Whether these men be called "refined," "unbelievable," "beautiful," "lions," or "dandies," all are issued from the same origin; all participate in the same character of opposition and revolt; all are representatives of what is best in human pride, of that need, too rare today, to combat and destroy triviality.
> 
> Baudelaire 1968: 560

As we observed at the beginning of this chapter, Foucault's concept of ancient philosophy as a spiritual practice owes much to the work of Pierre Hadot. Yet while Foucault's reading of ancient philosophy in general and his reading of the Stoics in particular is deeply indebted to Hadot's, their perspectives are not identical. In this section, we shall take a closer look at their divergences with three goals in mind: 1) to understand better the nature of Foucault's argument; 2) to judge the pertinence of Hadot's critique; and 3) to come to a fuller understanding of ancient Stoicism.

Hadot grants the interest and the importance of Foucault's reading of ancient philosophy and regrets that their dialogue was cut short by the latter's untimely death. He is, however, concerned that Foucault overvalues the aesthetic dimension of the Stoic care of the self, its emphasis on fashioning a fine (*kalos*) or admirable existence, and undervalues the cosmic dimension, in which the sage becomes identified with the universe as a whole. The result is ultimately less a true spirituality, as Hadot understands it, than an aestheticism or dandyism. We will develop each of these critiques, before then turning to specific responses that can be found in Foucault's text, and finally taking up the question of the dandy.

While there is general agreement between Hadot and Foucault that ancient philosophy presents itself as an "art of living" (*tekhnē tou biou*; Hadot 2002: 300), the difference between them is largely centered on whether we choose to lean more heavily on the concept of *tekhnē* as an "art," whose pleasures are largely aesthetic, or a "technology" or "craft" that presents a means to the end of living, in Socrates' words a "life livable (*bios biōtos*) for a human being" (*Apology* 38a5–6). Like Nussbaum, Hadot draws largely on the abbreviated treatment of the "Culture of the Self" in volume three of the *History of Sexuality*. He pays particular attention to a passage where Foucault highlights Seneca's emphasis on the pleasure (*gaudium*, *laetitia*) to be had in the development of a self whose happiness is not dependent on external possessions, bodily convulsions, or the whims of emperors and crowds (*voluptas*). "Foucault presents the ethics of the Greco-Roman world as an ethics of the pleasure one takes in oneself" (Hadot 2002: 324–5, citing Foucault 1984b: 83). Yet while this statement may be true for the page in question, it hardly does justice to the fuller presentation of the care of the self found in the *Hermeneutics of the Subject*. Certainly, we can find other passages where Foucault emphasizes the aesthetic dimension of caring for the self (1994d: 617). Likewise in the introduction to volume two, he speaks of the ancient "arts of existence" as seeking to fashion a life that is the bearer of "certain aesthetic values" (1984a: 16–17). And Hadot is correct to emphasize that the aesthetic in the ancient world was never autonomous but always linked to other moral and ethical values. The *kalon* ("fine, beautiful") was always associated with the *agathon* ("good"). Indeed, Hadot argues that ancient philosophy was less a culture of the self than of its "overcoming" (Hadot 2002: 308–9; cf. Pradeau 2012: 138–42).

Nonetheless, we may still ask, what exactly does Hadot mean? When Foucault emphasizes fleeing the servitude of the self in his reading of Seneca, does he say otherwise? Likewise, it would be good to recall that in the very same "Introduction" to volume two, where he speaks of the aesthetics and the arts of existence, Foucault defines his entire "essay" as an "attempt to modify oneself in the play of truth" (Foucault 1984a: 15; Kremer-Marietti 1985: 261). Clearly, this essay is not "merely" aesthetic in a narrow or precious sense. Indeed, one must be very careful in the case of Foucault when abstracting the aesthetic from the epistemic, that is from processes of knowledge, truth, or thought. While there is certainly pleasure in thought, and the highest forms of pleasure may be those that are the most lasting and consequential, as Seneca and Plato both would see them, that does not mean that thought itself or the good has been reduced to unmediated pleasure, any more than the fact that reason always involves power means that reason is nothing but power in its most brutal, unmediated form.

It may seem strange that Hadot as Foucault's colleague was not more deeply acquainted with the content of his lectures and not reading the *History of Sexuality* in this expanded context, but nothing could be more natural. Few of us know in detail what is happening in our colleagues' seminars, and we are lucky if we have time to read their published work. It is only natural that the *History of Sexuality* would be the primary focus of Hadot's response, given that the *Hermeneutics of the Subject* was not published till 2001 and the other late lectures largely ten years after.

Hadot, however, voices a second concern with Foucault's understanding of the purpose of the care of the self in ancient philosophy: he accuses Foucault of having neglected the importance of "cosmic consciousness." Now we have seen that this is not completely accurate. Foucault does acknowledge the ultimate understanding of the self in Stoic thought, in the figure of the sage, as coterminous with nature itself, and that this understanding entails a dilation of the self to the dimensions of the very cosmos. But, it is true that this is not the main focus of Foucault's work, and it is worth spending a few moments to understand Hadot's objection.

Hadot claims that Foucault's understanding of the moment of conversion is faulty because while its first movement is a turning of the gaze from the external world of possessions and attachments, there follows a second movement that elevates the self to a higher level: nature, reason, the forms, the universe in its totality (Davidson 2002: 13; Hadot 2002: 328–30). As Hadot observes:

> The Stoic does not find joy in his self but, Seneca says, "in the better part of his self," in the "true good" (Seneca, Letter 23.6), that is to say (23.7) "in a consciousness turned toward the good, in intentions that have no other object than virtue, correct actions," that is to say in what Seneca calls (121.23) perfect reason, that is to say ultimately in divine reason (92.27), since, for him, human reason is only perfectible reason. Seneca does not find his joy in "Seneca," but in transcending Seneca, in discovering that he has within him reason, part of the universal reason, internal to all men and to the cosmos itself.
>
> 2002: 325

Passing onto Marcus Aurelius and Epictetus, Hadot argues that Stoic spiritual exercises aim to overcome the self, to think and act in union with "universal Reason" (2002: 325). Ancient philosophy's liberation happens in the passage from the individual suffering subject to the objectivity of the universal perspective (Hadot 2002: 310, 326, 345; cf. Annas 1992: 43). None of this is explicitly denied in the *Hermeneutics of the Subject*, although it would be legitimate to claim that universal reason is not the aim or primary object of Foucault who is more interested in an ontology of the present than a comprehensive vision of the past. By the same token, it is worth noting that if one turns to the actual text of Seneca Letter 33, cited by Hadot, the crucial distinction is not between reason and pleasure, but between the better part of the self and "the pathetic body" (*corpusculum*) with its "brief ... empty pleasures, to be regretted" (*vanas ... voluptates, breves, paenitendas*) unless "they are tempered with great moderation" (*nisi magna moderatione temperentur*). This understanding is more in line with the distinction made in the *Alcibiades* and the lengthy quotation from Letter 44 cited above than with a schema that would exclude reason from the world of pleasure. As Pradeau observes, in sympathy with Hadot's critique of Foucault, for the Stoics an individual becoming conscious of his freedom is not sustained by the autonomy of his reason, but by his consciousness of universal reason (2012: 142–3).[6]

More importantly, perhaps, we should note that nothing in the texts of Marcus Aurelius cited by Hadot corresponds precisely to his capitalized "universal Reason." Such a reading of the *logos* goes well beyond noting that reason for the Stoics is not limited to the individual who wields it. There is no doubt a transcendental dimension to reason for the Stoics. As Seneca observes, it can be identified with a kind of original difference, an original division and thus a vivifying of inert matter:

> Our Stoic philosophers, as you know, maintain that there are two elements in the universe from which all things are derived, namely cause and matter. Matter lies inert and inactive, a substance with unlimited potential, but destined to remain idle if no one sets it in motion; and it is cause (this meaning the same as reason) which turns matter to whatever end it wishes and fashions it into a variety of different products.
> 
> 1969: 118, Letter 45

This cause in turn can be seen as nature or what Marcus terms *phusis logikē* (nature as determined by the logos/reason/the word; 8.7). But is it a substance in the way Hadot's capitalization of "universal Reason" seems to indicate?

There is a subtle and important difference of opinion between Foucault and Hadot concerning the nature of reason, and it colors the way in which each of them reads the Stoic texts. Hadot, in fact, recognizes that there are larger philosophical differences between him and Foucault that determine this difference. In a passage just following those cited above, he acknowledges the genealogical nature of Foucault's project, casting himself as a more traditional historian of philosophy, but the real nub of the matter comes in the next sentence, "according to a tendency in modern thought, a tendency that is perhaps more instinctive than thought through, notions of 'universal Reason' and of 'universal nature' no longer now have much sense" (2002: 325–6). This is more than a historical observation on the part of Hadot. Twenty pages later, he observes, "For my part, I believe in the possibility for modern man to live out ... an ever fragile, ever renewed exercise of wisdom. And I think that this exercise of wisdom can and should aim at realizing a reinsertion of the self in the world and the universal" (2002: 345–6). He acknowledges that with the rise of the modern sciences, it has been felt that only in the aesthetic mode can we still permit "the existence, the *Dasein* of man, to conserve the cosmic dimension that is essential to human existence" (Hadot 2002: 349). But he considers this a fundamental mistake and argues that it has always been the case that "man must separate himself from the world in order to live his daily life, and he must separate himself from the day-to-day world in order to find once more the world as world" (Hadot 2002: 356). There is clearly a strong Heideggerian and existential element in Hadot's thought, even what could be seen as a religious element. It is perhaps not unimportant to remember that while he had not been an active member of the church for many years when he wrote this, nonetheless he had trained for the priesthood and been ordained before leaving in 1950 and marrying in 1953. Reason for Hadot remains a transcendental reality that defines the universal and into which humans can insert themselves, if only they will withdraw from the distractions of day-to-day life and convert their gaze to the constitution of the world as world and to the place of their existence within it. For Foucault, the genealogist, however, reason is historically produced. It is something we do. It is less *the* Universal that constitutes us and the world, than a shared reality that is always in the process of elaboration by and through us. There is in the end, for Foucault, less *Reason* than a plurality of *reasons*, which does not mean they are not real and have no effect. It does not mean that they are not integral to truth and its history. And it most certainly does not mean that they are not powerful tools in our struggle to produce lives that truly are "livable for a human being."

With this in mind, the difference between Foucault's reading of the Stoics and Hadot's is as much or more about its implications for modern life as it is about accuracy or philological exactitude. Indeed, in the final lecture of the *Hermeneutics of the Subject*, Foucault acknowledges that in Hellenistic philosophy, at its culmination, one lives not for one's possessions, one's power, or any of the other numerous things in the world the Stoics labelled *adiaphora*, "indifferents." One lives "for oneself" in the strong sense that we learn in both the *Alcibiades* and Seneca, the *psukhē*, *animus*, or soul, and living for oneself in this strong sense for the Stoics means to become indistinguishable from reason and God, from the cosmos itself:

> Between the rational God who, in the order of the world places around me all the elements, the entire long chain of dangers and misfortunes, and myself, who is going to decipher these misfortunes as so many tests and exercises for my perfection, between this God and me, there is henceforth only myself.
>
> Foucault 2001a: 430

The self thus becomes identified with the rational principle of the world and henceforth views all its experience, all its suffering from that perspective as a means toward its perfection, toward a final identification with God, the cause that animates matter. The spiritual practices of Hellenistic and Roman imperial philosophy are not aimed at a shallow or immediate pleasure in the self, and Foucault does not argue that. They are aimed at the subject experiencing a plenitude it has never known, an absolute freedom from contingency and error, from the deceptions of attachment, and hence from the illusion of the self's own separation from *phusis* or nature (Foucault 2001a: 125). To reduce this care of the self either to solipsism, to a mere foppish "dandyism," or to an umediated aestheticism, Foucault says from the beginning, would be a mistake (Foucault 2001a: 14–15; Gros 2001: 511).

Nonetheless, it would be equally mistaken to reject the value of the aesthetic for Foucault and to see it as somehow less than cognitive, somehow merely about pleasure and therefore unconcerned with reason or truth. This is a separation that, as Hadot rightly observes, would not be recognized in the ancient world, and we must be wary of reimposing it either through the absolutization of *to kalon* ("the beautiful, the fine") or *to agathon* ("the good") in ancient philosophy or Foucault's reading of it. As Veyne in another context is quick to remind us, all ancient asceticisms are forms of aestheticism: "the ascetic is a dandy of morality ... there is an elegance" (2001: 110–11).

We thus need to think back to those initial passages, at the beginning of this section, from Baudelaire, who makes the connection between the Stoic and the dandy—not because Stoicism is a trivial pursuit of style for its own sake, but because there is always a seriousness and a spirituality in what to the untrained eye seems frivolous—in the strange figure of the philosopher who withdraws from the world to seek wisdom, who leaves the cave of normal life in order to see things in the clear light of the sun, who pursues a vision of spiritual beauty even among the blooming evils of the Paris streets. The dandy for Baudelaire is precisely the "lion" who refuses to accept the triviality of day-to-day existence as constituting the limits of the world. So while it is a mistake to argue that Foucault reduces Stoicism to dandyism, he quite explicitly does not, it is important to recall that as Pradeau observed, his reflections on ancient modes of subjectivation were always a means to find a way beyond the normalized subject of the present (Pradeau 2012: 147–8) and that as such his "queer spirituality" was anything but reductive or trivial.

## V

> If one takes the question of power, of political power, and places it within the more general question of governmentality—governmentality understood as a strategic field of relations of power in the largest sense of the term and not simply the political—therefore, if we understand governmentality as a strategic field of relations of power, in that they are mobile, transformable, and reversible, I believe that reflection on this notion of government is unable not to pass, theoretically and practically, through the element of a subject that would be defined by the relation of the self to the self ... What this means is simply that in the type of analysis I have been trying to propose to you for a certain time you see that relations of power/governmentality/government of the self and others/relation of the self to itself, all this constitutes a chain, a fabric, and that it is, around these notions that one should, I think articulate the question of politics and ethics.
>
> Foucault 2001a: 241–2

The care of the self is neither a withdrawal into dandyism—if by dandyism we mean an apolitical aestheticism devoid of cognitive or ethical content—nor a mere antiquarian interest, the elaboration of an ancient model that we can follow. Under this rubric, rather, Foucault describes the development of a *tekhnē tou biou* ("art of living"), which first assumes clear theoretical definition in Plato's *Alcibiades*. It evolves in the Hellenistic and Roman period from a propaedeutic to the assumption of political power in the classical polis, embedded within the traditions of pederasty, to an end in itself, as the taking of the self as an object of work develops an increasing autonomy from the structures of governmental power. This care involves first the definition of the self as separate from its possessions and the conversion of its gaze from external distractions to a more fundamental truth. It also involves a set of spiritual practices—dialogue, study, and meditation—through which a self was fashioned that was able to access truth, self-knowledge, and ultimately freedom. This freedom insulated it from the vagaries and uncertainties of what had become a vast imperial state where day-to-day governance was abstracted from the immediacy of personal experience but could nonetheless impinge upon it in surprising and arbitrary ways.

The care of the self was not a solitary pursuit. Whether the catalyst was Socrates' approach to Alcibiades, Seneca's letters to Lucilius, the withdrawal into an Epicurean community of friends, or the dialogic interchange imagined in Plutarch's *Erōtikos*, it depended on the frankness of one's friends and interlocutors, a relationship often formalized into that of teacher and student or director of conscience and disciple. *Parrhēsia* was integral to the spiritual practice that provided self-knowledge.

On the larger philosophical level, what Foucault's study demonstrates is that the elaboration of a self is anything but a natural or a given practice. This reality is widely understood but rarely theorized. Whether we are discussing the New Soviet Man, the Japanese company man, the lifestyles of countercultural movements, or the unstated assumptions of university life, we all know on some level that specific institutional and governmental structures create, depend upon, reinforce, and enforce a certain ethos, a certain style that goes well beyond dress and manner of speech to include family and sexual norms, modes of thought, and assumptions about what constitutes the true and the real. This is why deviations from those communal norms are often perceived as subversive and stigmatized. Everything from dietary choice to clothing is assumed to signify. As Foucault notes, the relations between political power, governmentality, the government of the self and others, and the relation of the self to itself are not separate realities but so many links in a chain, so many overdetermined elements in a complex weave.

What genealogy offers is the opportunity to denaturalize these relationships or, in an older vocabulary, to demystify them. The taking of one's life (*bios*) as the object of a *tekhnē* implies the freedom and the choice of the person who uses the *tekhnē* (Foucault 2001a: 405–6). What kind of person do you want to be, what sort of existence do you choose to fashion for yourself? Of course, the options are not infinite, and they are historically determined, but they do not exist until they are made visible, until they are denaturalized, and until the possibility of turning one's gaze is made apparent. If there were not in fact the freedom of subjects to put into play their *tekhnai* as a function of their objectives and their desires, we could not meaningfully speak of the possibility of fashioning a better life, a *bios biōtos*, and the entire ethico-political project would collapse. It is not that ethics determines politics, or simply that politics determines ethics, but the ways in which we organize ourselves to govern ourselves and others cannot be separated from the way we constitute our lives, from the choices we make with our bodies, our pleasures, our genders, our domestic lives, and our economic existences. We become aware of those choices through a searching consideration of their histories, their interdependencies, and the levels at which they are already determined by the situation into which we find ourselves thrown.

It is thus not just a passing remark when Foucault observes in the middle of the *Hermeneutics of the Self* that we need to trace the ways in which technologies of the self in the nineteenth century first become linked to the idea of political revolution in 1848 and beyond, among anarchists, socialists, and various utopian movements. These movements often combined modes of life, dress, and even regimes of diet with attempts at radical political change. How, in turn, did these same technologies later become absorbed within party structures? Who was a true Bolshevik? A bourgeois counterrevolutionary? Whose habits, sexual practices, reading and artistic choices demonstrated the need for re-education? And, equally important, how did we reach the point where one no longer is converted to revolution but its denunciation? "The great converts of today are those who no longer believe in revolution" (Foucault 2001a: 200).

Whether considering the performance of gender, the checking of privilege, or the Culture Wars that rage unabated within the American polity, it would take an act of extraordinary blindness not to see how questions of ethos are inseparable from those of not only political power writ large but also from the thousands of power relations that constitute the fabric of our daily lives. To understand the history and technology of how this ethos has been constructed, its style and content, can never be a trivial matter. It is only through understanding the ontology of the present, the myriad discourses, technologies, and actions that constitute the present, that a future—a politics, a self, a truth, and a beauty yet to come—can be brought into being.

4

# The Government of the Self and Others: Truth-Telling and the Real of Philosophy in Plato's *Seventh Letter* and Beyond

> By posing the question of the government of the self and of others, I would like to try to see how truth-telling, the obligation and the possibility of telling the truth in the procedures of government, are able to show how the individual constitutes itself as a subject in relation to itself and others.
> 
> Foucault 2008: 42

> In the *Apology of Socrates*, you see very neatly the distinction between *didaskalia* and *ōpheleia*. The master is not only going to teach—that is *didaskalia*, to pass the knowledge he possesses to a student who does not possess it—but he ought also to be useful, that is to say make the individual do a certain number of exercises that will permit the disciple to advance on the road to virtue, exercises that are not truly a transmission of knowledge.
> 
> Foucault 2012a: 135

Foucault's 1983 course, *The Government of the Self and Others*, represents a continuation of the project begun in the *Hermeneutics of the Subject*, initially entitled The Care of the Self.[1] His final course, the following year, continued work toward this project, which never reached fruition. The lectures have the feel of work in progress. They are text-centered, and one can see concepts being developed and reformulated as he goes (Gros 2008: 348–9, 358; Elden 2016: 196, 198–9). Throughout, however, the problem of what it means for the self to form itself as a speaker of truth remains central, even as the historical frame is pushed deeper, with a shift in focus from imperial Rome to classical Greece. At the same time, the analytic frame is enlarged from the care of self *per se* to its ability to engage problems of equality before the law (*isonomia*) and freedom of speech (*isēgoria*). The central questions of this course are: who is able to exercise the *parrhēsia* necessary to lead the souls of the citizens or the princes, and what practice leads to this capacity, rhetoric or philosophy? (Foucault 2008: 180).

More specifically, what Foucault proposes to undertake is a "history of thought." It should be recalled that his chair at the Collège de France was in the History of Systems of Thought. By offering this frame at the beginning of the course, he is not only making a claim about the philosophical and intellectual stakes of what is to come, but he is also tying it explicitly to how he wishes to characterize his entire project from *Histoire de la folie* to the present. A history of thought should analyze, he notes, three elements for any given period: possible forms of knowledge, normative matrices of behavior, and virtual modes of existence for possible subjects. Together, these form what he terms "a seat of experience" (*foyer d'expérience*). For any given "seat of experience," we should be able to ask: what kinds of knowledge are possible, what are its matrices for regulating behavior, and how can subjects constitute themselves within those constraints? (Foucault 2008: 4-5). A history of thought focuses less on tracing the progress of different forms of factual knowledge, which assumes that the subjects and objects of that knowledge are functionally equivalent across time, than on "displacing the axis of inquiry" to systems of thought and discursive practices that organize and constitute these systems. A history of thought is the study of these discursive practices as regulated forms of truth-telling across time (Foucault 2008: 6).

Within this frame, Foucault proposes to study the history of technologies of the self as forms of behavior that allow a subject to speak the truth within a given seat of experience. He proposes that we move away from a theory of *the* subject, whether psychoanalytic or phenomenological, which would allow one to trace the subject's different modes of being, toward a more pragmatic history of subjects and their technologies, such as he had begun the previous year with Plato and the Stoics (Foucault 2008: 42). Those technologies did not exist in a vacuum. They were constituted within a field of social relations and entailed the presence of other people, such as the frank friend or the philosophical director of conscience, individuals whose abilities to speak the truth to the philosophical student or disciple were integral to the form of subjective plenitude the student might achieve. In a passage that recalls the *Alcibiades*, Foucault cites the physician Galen to the effect that you can only establish a correct opinion of yourself if you address yourself to another, one who is mature, has a good reputation, and possesses *parrhēsia*, and who, like a mirror, can reflect you to yourself (Foucault 2008: 43–4).

These technologies of the self and their history, as we argued at the end of the last chapter, in no way represent a solipsism or a withdrawal from politics and governance. Rather, as noted there, the discourse of governmentality is "unable not to pass, theoretically and practically, through the element of a subject that would be defined by the relation of the self to the self." Thus, Foucault proposes as his task for this year to launch a history of governmentality that takes as its guiding thread what he terms the "dramatization" of true discourses. By "dramatization" he means something close to speech act theory (2001a: 59), but rather than seeing the act of veridiction as bringing something into being, as is the case in the performative speech acts of Austin and Searle—the paradigmatic example being when the priest says, "I now pronounce you man and wife"—the parrhesiastic act names an external reality. Yet, in the act of affirming this reality, it constitutes the self in a particular relationship to both its enunciation and to the persons to whom it is made in ways that simple observation (the constative speech act) do not:

> Is there a political drama specific to true discourse, and what are its different forms, the different structures of the dramatization of political discourse? In other words, when someone gets up, in the city or before the tyrant, or when a courtier approaches the person who exercises power, or when the politician takes the podium and says, "I am telling you the truth" what type of dramatization of true discourse does he put into effect?
> 
> Foucault 2001a: 65–6

Foucault envisions four modalities of this dramatization, without denying there are more: the ancient orator and counsellor to the prince; the early modern minister of court; the Enlightenment social critic; and the modern revolutionary (Foucault 2001a: 67). Each of these figures embodies a different relation between speaker and enunciation, and between the act of speech and the intended audience.

This history of the dramatization of true discourse he reformulates at the end of the course as a history of the ontology of true discourses. Each true discourse is seen as a practice undertaken by a specific subject, and he posits that this conjunction of forms of subjectivity with specific practices determines the being of these discourses and their effectiveness in the order of the real in ways that cannot be measured simply by a history of factual knowledges (Foucault 2001a: 285–6). Whether as dramatization, though, or as ontology, the key focus is on true discourse: not as a relationship between a proposition and an external reality—which is never denied—but as a practice undertaken by a subject that has been formed within certain matrices or norms, which in turn determine the acts of veridiction possible with the larger play of truth and governmentality.

In what follows, we first look at Foucault's lecture on Kant's "What is Enlightenment," which opens the course. It focuses on the role of truth and criticism in the emancipation of the subject. We then examine Foucault's reading of Euripides' *Ion* as an object lesson in the original political meaning of *parrhēsia* in democratic Athens, before turning to Plato's *Seventh Letter* and the confrontation between the philosopher and the tyrant. From there, we pull back to a larger view of Foucault's understanding of *parrhēsia* and its implication for politics and the role of philosopher.

## I

> *Enlightenment is man's emergence from his self-incurred immaturity. Immaturity* is the inability to use one's own understanding without the guidance of another. This immaturity is *self-incurred* if its cause is not lack of understanding, but lack of resolution and courage to use it without the guidance of another. The motto of enlightenment is therefore: *Sapere aude!* Have courage to use your *own* understanding!
>
> Kant 1991: 54, original emphasis

> We must not consider the critical ontology of ourselves a theory, a doctrine, not even a body of knowledge that accumulates; we must consider it an attitude, an *ēthos*, a philosophical life in which the critique of what we are is at the same time a historical analysis of the limits placed on us and a test of the possibility of their crossing.
>
> Foucault 1994j: 577

Foucault opens *The Government of the Self and Others* with a reading of Kant's "Answer to the Question: 'What is Enlightenment.'" In it, he sets out the philosophical stakes of this year's lectures. As will be recalled, our discussion of the previous year had ended with an examination of his contention that any theorization of governmentality must pass through the relation of the self to itself. To the extent that the "care of the self"—whether in its Platonic or Stoic formulations—offers insight into the ways a subject might constitute itself in relation to truth, how that self-constitution could employ different techniques to become an object of knowledge and care, and how that self-formation could produce forms and relations of power and pleasure, then Foucault's study of these forms, we argued, has direct implications for our ability to reconceptualize what it would mean to have an aesthetics, a politics, an ethics, and even an epistemics of existence. One possible way of understanding this reconceptualization, this ability to think differently, as we saw, was in terms of the *ēthos* of the dandy—if, as in Baudelaire, the dandy is seen as a figure of spiritual significance, as one who refuses the triviality of a conventional life— but it might equally be understood through the figure of the revolutionary, as someone who forms themself in order to receive and actualize a particular truth in the world. Thus, if, as Foucault wrote, the essential problem of ethics is that of freedom, then Kant's reflection on what it means for human beings to assume their majority, to free themselves from the bonds of convention in thought, and hence the unexamined life, is a natural continuation of Foucault's inquiry begun in 1982 and renewed in 1983 (Foucault 1994g: 711–12; 2008: 8–9; Brion and Harcourt 2012: 288).

Foucault had long been interested in Kant, and, while we conventionally think of him as a Nietzschean, if we stop there, we seriously limit the range and complexity of his thought.[2] Before beginning his reading of "What is Enlightenment," he observes there are two main philosophical lineages that come down to us from Kant. On the one hand, there is the epistemological tradition that poses the question: what are the conditions necessary for true factual knowledge? Today, this line of thought is seen most clearly in Anglo-American analytic philosophy, but it was central to German and French neo-Kantianism as well. On the other, there is the tradition of what Foucault terms "the critical ontology of ourselves," which poses the question: what is "modernity," what is our "present field of possible experiences"? This tradition, he contends, is embodied in thinkers such as Hegel, Nietzsche, and the Frankfurt School (Foucault 2008: 22; Lawlor 2016: 168–9; Elden 2016: 195). He locates himself within this second lineage. As he observed in 1981, "I think that philosophy, among the different functions it can and should have, has also this, to ask what we are in our present ... and to this extent I am Nietzschean or Hegelian or Kantian" (Foucault 2012a: 235–6).

As we see in the passage quoted above, Kant's notion of emergence from a state of "tutelage" or "immaturity" into enlightenment, like Plato's progress from the cave, contains within it a necessary temporality, a movement from one position to the next that only becomes possible within a present. This moment of emergence is always poised between a future and a past in the possibility of a present, and it forces us to ask one of Foucault's most basic questions: "what is the ontology of the present, what is the nature of the moment in which we are constituting ourselves." Moreover, inasmuch as that question is addressed to a present, its answer can only be historical or genealogical in nature. There is a past that constitutes the present in its openness to the future (Foucault 2008: 22). That is what the present is.

If the ontology of our present is constituted by our relation to the past, then, the question of that ontology and its genealogy will also be central to our freedom. Our "present field of possible experiences" will both determine and produce the kinds of autonomy we assume in relation to the moral, political, and scientific authorities that constitute our intellectual tutelage, and thus that field of experiences will also produce and determine our ability to assume our majority, our ability to be subjects in the fullest sense of the word (Foucault 2008: 29–30). While this emergence from a state of immaturity is temporal, it is not singular but an ongoing process of self-surveillance and care, a series of decision points. The loss of our autonomy stems from inhabiting a certain kind of self-relation in which the subject cedes its ability to reason independently through "laziness and cowardice" (Kant 1991: 54; Foucault 2008: 32; Brion and Harcourt: 2012: 301–2). Of course, as members of a polity, we must accept that our private thoughts and interests cannot supervene on the authority of the community. We cannot simply wake up one day and refuse to pay our electric bill, obey traffic laws, or replace what is taught in our classrooms with our random opinions and still be members of the community. But, when the obedience necessary to participating within a political or institutional regime "is confused with not reasoning, and when, in this confusion of obedience and not-reasoning, one oppresses what ought to be the public and universal use of our understanding, at this moment there is minority." At this moment, we have ceded our majority (Foucault 2008: 35–6).

Enlightenment is not passive tolerance. It is not a suspension of reason and judgment. Enlightenment gives freedom its most public and universal form, while maintaining obedience in its private role as the guarantor of the subject's position within the social body. The bureaucrat cannot simply impose their private will on others who come for a public function, but they *can* argue for the imposition of that will on the level of the universal and the general, which can, in turn, lead to changes in actuality. "Once the germ on which nature has lavished most care—man's inclination and vocation to think freely—has developed within this hard shell, it gradually reacts upon the mentality of the people, who thus gradually become increasingly able to act freely" (Kant 1991: 58). The project of enlightenment is not a solipsistic pursuit but a public action that participates in the general discourse, the *logos* of reason, and in that capacity has the ability not only to emancipate the individual from the status of minority but to change the lives of the community.

Foucault considered his engagement with Kant of some importance. In May 1984, shortly before his death, he published an extract from this lecture in the *Magazine Littéraire*.[3] He also published in English translation, "What is Enlightenment?," an expanded essay built around the same material (1984c). In this expanded treatment, he makes an explicit comparison between Kant's conception of enlightenment and Baudelaire's project of modernity. Both Kant and Baudelaire stress an acute awareness of the nature of the present as a moment of decision, a moment in which autonomy of judgment can be exercised or refused, a moment in which a consciousness of freedom can arise. Foucault uses this unlikely conjunction of Kant and Baudelaire to ask the question of whether we cannot envision modernity less as a period than as an attitude, "a manner of thinking and feeling, a manner also of acting and conducting oneself, which at once marks our adherence and task. A little, no doubt, like what the Greeks called an *ēthos*" (1994j: 568). Thus if enlightenment for Kant is both the name of the present and a recurring moment in which the self emancipates itself from tutelage to external authority, for Baudelaire, modernity is a recognition of the "will to 'heroize' the present" (Foucault 1994j: 569, citing *Le Peintre de la vie moderne*). It is, as Foucault avers, a moment of "transfiguration," a moment of the difficult interplay "between the truth of the real and the exercise of freedom." This transfiguration of the self requires the practice of a certain "asceticism." "To be modern, is not to accept oneself just as one is, in the flux of moments that pass."

It is not passively to accept, with cowardice or laziness, one's minority, and hence conformity. Rather, "it is to take oneself as the object of a complex and difficult elaboration, what Baudelaire calls in the vocabulary of the time, 'dandyism'" (Foucault 1994j: 570). Foucault is precise with his language here. He does not claim that Kant was a dandy, nor does he claim that what Baudelaire terms a dandy is what it means in the vocabulary of Foucault's time. Rather, he observes that for Kant enlightenment is a process of self-emancipation that can only take place in a present defined as what is actual at this moment, as the active sum of the past that opens into the future, and this process of emancipation necessarily entails a process of self-formation or transfiguration in which the subject frees itself from an unthinking, unreasoning submission to the structures of what has been, to "the flux of moments that pass." By the same token for Baudelaire, modern man "is not he who sets off to discover himself, his secrets and his hidden truth, he is the one that searches to invent himself" (Foucault 1994j: 571).

To experience enlightenment is to have a moment of self-recognition, which requires a separation of the self from its environment. To reason on one's own is to develop a new relation with the *logos* and, hence, with truth. This new relationship to truth and the given is a sign of modernity, the elaboration of an *ēthos* which both recognizes its appertaining to the present and takes that present as a task, as work to be done. This work is inseparable from the elaboration of the truth, not as a private confession or fantasy but as public speech, as reasoning on the level of the universal and the general. Thus the emancipated thinker of modernity is one who must stand before the present and speak frankly. Such a speaker, who fully engages themselves in this moment of truth, is what antiquity would call a practitioner of *parrhēsia*, which is Foucault's central concern for the year and the reason he began by reading Kant (Foucault 2008: 322).

## II

**Ion**  I pray my mother is Athenian,
So that through her I may have rights of speech (*parrhēsia*).
For when a stranger comes into a city
Of pure blood, though in name a citizen,

>   His mouth remains a slave: he has no right
>   Of speech (*parrhēsia*).
>
>   Euripides 1959: 38, Ion 670–5
>
>   **Creusa**  As I cried for my mother's help
>   You led me to bed in a cave,
>   A god and my lover,
>   With no shame,
>   Submitting to the Cyprian's will
>   In misery I bore you
>   A son, whom in fear of my mother
>   I placed in that bed
>   Where you cruelly forced me.
>   Ah! He is lost now,
>   Snatched as food for the birds,
>   My son and yours; Oh lost!
>
>   Euripides 1959: 46, Ion 891–904

On January 12, 1983, Foucault recalls to his audience that his primary focus throughout these lectures has been truth-telling: how has the subject formed itself to tell the truth, what relations of power made those formations possible, and what relations were produced by them? Within this framework, for the last two years, the specific focus has been on the relation between truth-telling and the care of the self in ancient culture, with a special emphasis on *parrhēsia*, "frankness" or "free speech." This year he will trace a series of shifts in the meaning of *parrhēsia*: from a primarily political meaning, such as that seen in the first passage from Euripides' *Ion*, to one in which the individual speaks truth to a powerful figure, such as a prince or tyrant, before later being applied to the philosophical mentor who speaks to students engaged in caring for themselves. The two texts that will occupy Foucault's focus for the year will be Euripides' *Ion* and Plato's *Seventh Letter*.

The *Ion* is hardly one of Euripides' best known tragedies and has exercised a negligible influence on the subsequent development of the genre. It presents itself as an aetiological drama telling us the origin story of the four Ionian tribal names and asserting Athens' hegemony over the Ionian Greeks through claiming their eponymous ancestor for the seat of the Delian League, Athens' fifth-century empire (1575–81). While the exact date of the drama's staging is open to dispute, it is certainly a product of the last portion of the fifth century, when Athens's role in the Delian League was under considerable military and ideological pressure from Sparta and its allies during the Peloponnesian War. The *Ion* presents this just-so story as a series of chance events, misrecognitions, a rape, an attempted murder, and various deceptions all of which, in the end, lead to Ion taking his place as the rightful heir to Erichthonius, the first inhabitant and ruler of Athens. It is hardly clear that Euripides is unreservedly endorsing the Athenian ideology he is dramatizing, rather there is a level of complexity and irony here that at once calls the ideology into question, even as the play asserts its seeming necessity in a time of crisis (Wohl 2015: 27–8).

Ion, we are told, is the son of Apollo from his rape of Creusa, the granddaughter of Erichthonius, the autochthonous founder of Athens. Creusa exposed the baby in a cave and, when the play opens, assumes he is dead. Apollo, however, saved the child and deposited him at his shrine in Delphi, where Ion is a temple servant who believes himself to be a foundling. In the meantime, Creusa has married Xuthus, an Achaean noble who through the marriage has become *de facto* ruler of Athens. The couple, however, remain childless and, at the beginning of the play, they have arrived in Delphi to consult the oracle on how they can conceive an heir. Apollo, wishing his son to assume his rightful place on the throne of Athens, deceives Xuthus, telling him that he already has a son and he will recognize his heir as the first person he meets when he leaves the shrine. That person is, of course, Ion. After an initial astonishment, Ion happily accepts his new identity and immediately begins to wonder who his mother is. He is warned to keep his identity a secret lest Creusa find out and become jealous, since Xuthus will no longer need an heir and the line of Erichthonius will come to an end. Nonetheless, Creusa is told by the chorus of her attendants what has happened, and she plots her vengeance by attempting to poison Ion, thinking him her stepson, when he is actually the child she bore. Luckily, Ion is saved by a bird who after drinking some of the wine served Ion by Creusa dies instantly. Creusa flees in fear to the altar of Apollo as a suppliant, where just in the nick of time the priestess happens to pass bearing the tokens Creusa had left with Ion when he was exposed. A final recognition scene occurs, and mother and son are reunited.

Clearly, it is not owing to the versimilitude of its plot that Foucault has chosen the *Ion*. Yet, as he demonstrates through a series of original commentaries

(Gros 2008: 357), the play, while on one level a representation of Athenian imperial ideology, is on another a dramatization of different forms and genres of truth-telling: oracles, confessions, and *parrhēsia* (Foucault 2008: 77). Within the plot, its human characters are all characterized by ignoroance, and this fact explains how they end up in Delphi. Xuthus seeks to know if he will have an heir. Creusa has come to Delphi in hopes that Apollo will tell her what has become of her son. Ion is ignorant of his origin or heritage. At the same time, Hermes, who in the prologue makes clear to the audience who the characters are and what their relations are to one another, knows and speaks the truth, as evidently does Apollo, the god of prophecy. Lastly, the audience, thanks to the prologue, know the truth. The play dramatizes for Creusa and Ion a move from ignorance to knowledge through a series of misrecognitions and deceptions. This movement, in turn, ensures the future history of Athens as ratified by the knowledge of the audience itself (Foucault 2008: 82–3). Like the *Oedipus*, the *Ion* moves through a series of halting steps, as pieces of truth are unveiled and fit together to reveal the structure of the whole (Gros 2008: 357–8).

Indeed, as Foucault acknowledges, there is much in common between *Oedipus* and *Ion*. He outlines a series of parallels and ironic inversions. First, there is the misrecognition scene between Xuthus and Ion, in which the former throws his arms around the latter, having been misled by Apollo to believe he is embracing his own son. Ion initially interprets this embrace as a potential sexual assault and threatens to kill the man who believes he is his father. The scene ironically recalls Oedipus's murder of Laius after their chance encounter and misrecognition at the place where three roads meet, except there the murder results from Oedipus's failure to recognize his actual father rather than the father spuriously believing to recognize a son. As Foucault observes, in some versions of the story, Oedipus kills Laius because the latter is making sexual advances on the comely young man, as Ion initially believes Xuthus is doing here (and of course there is actual incest in *Oedipus* as well). Other parallels and inversions include the fact that just as Oedipus kills his father and marries his mother, Ion tries to kill his mother while living in the house of his father (Apollo). In the first half of *Oedipus*, we learn about the murder of Laius and that Oedipus had killed someone at the crossroads, and in the second half we learn that the person Oedipus killed was Laius and that he was Oedipus's father. In the first half of the *Ion*, we learn about the rape of Creusa by Apollo and that she and Xuthus, each in their own way, are looking for a son; in the second half, we learn that the child of that rape is Ion and that he will become the heir of Xuthus and Creusa (Foucault 2008: 78–9, 108–9).

> It is thanks to this double paternity of Xuthus and Apollo that Ion is to be able, as opposed to Oedipus, to return to his country, settle there, and recover all his rights. And thanks to this fundamental tie having been found again, thanks to this return to the very land of Athens, he will be able exert his legitimate right of speech, that is say to exercise power in Athens. And therefore, in these two processes of the *alèthurgie* of birth, of the discovery of the truth of birth, you see that you have in fact two different processes that lead to exactly opposite results.
> 
> Foucault 2008: 80

Nonetheless, while both tragedies play a critical role in Foucault's history of truth, they are not the same. The *Oedipus Tyrannus* is crucial for its dramatization of the establishment of a particular form of truth: that which has been validated by a perceiving subject regardless of status. The *Ion* dramatizes two different modes of *parrhēsia*, each of which is crucial to its subsequent history. These different modes are exemplified in the quotations at the beginning of this section.

In the first passage, Ion, having been embraced by Xuthus, prays that his mother prove to be Athenian because only then will he be a full Athenian citizen and possess *parrhēsia*. This is an anachronism. Pericles' restriction of citizenship rights to those who could prove they were descended from a citizen mother and father, was passed by the assembly in 451 BCE, many centuries after the mythic date of the play, although well before the play was staged. *Parrhēsia* here names the essential right of any Athenian male citizen to address the polis and try to persuade it to his purpose. This, too, is an anachronism because Euripides appears to envision the civic machinery of democratic Athens in a period of semi-divine kingship, Creusa being the granddaughter of Erichthonius the offspring of Hephaestus' attempted rape of Athena, whose seed had spilled to the ground and engendered the earth-born Athenians. Yet even the monarch, as *Oedipus* shows, must address the polis to exercise his power, and Ion would not possess this right of speech without being a full citizen. Within Athenian democracy, *parrhēsia*, Foucault observes, is the act of using speech to persuade those over whom you seek to have authority and yet leaving to others who also want to have authority their freedom to speak in the agonistic game of truth and power that was the assembly. *Parrhēsia* in this context is a claim of truth that, through your engagement, you bid others to accept, with the full knowledge that you are not alone in making such a bid. It is a form of speech beyond the simple right to speak possessed by all citizens. It is a form of speech that seeks to exercise power while leaving others their freedom as well. It is not the command of an absolute monarch or god. I stand before you as a citizen making a claim of truth in which I engage my person and bid you to engage yourself as well (Foucault 2008: 96–8, 126). "To speak the truth in order to direct the city, in a position of superiority in which one is in a perpetual contest with others, this, I believe, is what is associated with the game of *parrhēsia*" (Foucault 2008: 145). It is this very mounting to the podium, in the attempt to lead the city, that Alcibiades envisions at the beginning of his dialogue with Socrates.

There were three fundamental principles that governed Athenian democracy, Foucault observes, *isonomia*, *isēgoria*, and *parrhēsia*. The first two are simple rights, but the third is more complex. Drawing on Polybius as well as Plato and Aristotle (Foucault 2008: 69, 137–9, 186), he defines *isonomia* as equality before the law for all citizens.[4] *Isēgoria* is the right of citizens to make their opinions heard in the assembly. *Parrhēsia* is, then, something beyond free speech, and it is important that what Ion hopes for is not simply *isēgoria*, but *parrhēsia* repeated twice. *Parrhēsia*, too, is theoretically open to all, but it is not practiced by all. It is a political practice that allows the constitutional system to function. In democratic Athens, *parrhēsia* is the right to attempt to persuade your fellow citizens to follow you over your rivals, with all the risks attendant on that. If the assembly is displeased, or if they feel you have attempted to assert your power as a hegemon too vigorously, they can vote for your exile through the process of ostracism. *Parrhēsia*, thus, involves a certain risk on the part of the speaker, an engagement that not only seeks to warrant the truth of what is asserted but risks the person of the speaker in that assertion (Foucault 2008: 99, 147, 172; Rajchman 1991: 120–1). Again, the tumultuous career of Alcibiades is a case in point, as one who assumed leadership of the assembly through his oratorical gifts and charismatic personality and later was forced to flee only to return to power before leading the disastrous Sicilian expedition. By the same token, as the case of Socrates shows, after the collapse of Athenian democracy at the end of Peloponnesian War, after the rule of the Thirty, and the return of the democratic regime, the expression of heterodox sentiments even outside the assembly could cost you your life. *Parrhēsia* was fraught.

As Foucault notes of democracy in Athens (but certainly not there alone), you cannot have true discourse, you cannot have the free play of true discourses, unless everyone has access to true discourse. *Isēgoria* is thus a necessary presumption of the existence of true discourse within a democratic regime and so of democracy itself. At the same time, true discourse cannot be equally shared by all speakers, and all speakers cannot have equal access to the podium whether literally or figuratively in the making and offering of true discourse. We see this regularly in scientific and institutional structures within modern democratic societies: the need to establish rules and norms to determine who gets to speak, whose speech is authoritative, and how the truth of speech is validated. Democracy both renders true speech possible and incessantly threatens it. As Socrates observes in the *Gorgias*, the temptation of the speaker to flatter the democratic audience, to say not what is true but what the speaker believes it wants to hear can be overwhelming. Socrates compares such a speaker to a chef who offers his audience sweet cakes, when what is needed is a physician prescribing strong medicine (464c–465d). The *parrhesiast* is the speaker who stands before the assembly and engages his person in making the truth-claim he believes the audience needs to hear. He is the opposite of the flatterer. Political *parrhēsia* of this type, of the type envisioned by Ion, can in fact only exist in a democratic system characterized by *isēgoria* and yet must always be in tension with that same system. It is what is required by that system and constantly threatened by it (Foucault 2008: 167–8).

There is, however, a second form of *parrhēsia* exhibited within the *Ion*. When Creusa discovers that Apollo has told Xuthus that he has a natural son, before she discovers Ion's true identity, she flies into a rage. She is angry at the deception Xuthus has proposed in bringing Ion to Athens to be his heir. But she is even more enraged at Apollo, her rapist who through his oracle has forced upon her a spurious son. The result of her anger is a double public act of truth, the climax of which can be found in the second passage quoted above. It is both an accusation and confession. Although the god is manifestly more powerful than she, she accuses him of rape, "In misery I bore you/ A son." She engages in a public act of proclaiming an injustice, one in which she fully engages herself and assumes the risks associated with the act. At the same time, she also engages in a confession. She admits that it was she who exposed the unwanted child, "snatched as food for birds." Foucault observes both of these acts of truth are necessary to the progress of the plot. They lead to Creusa's attempt to poison Ion, which produces their mutual recognition scene and thus Ion's ability to assume his citizen rights in Athens. In short, Ion's political *parrhēsia* is predicated on this earlier sense of *parrhēsia* as an accusation. Foucault notes that the two senses in which Creusa performs her parrhesiastic act—accusation and confession—will go on to have separate careers after the collapse of Athenian democracy, as speaking truth to power and as speaking truth about the self (Foucault 2008: 102, 125–6, 129). They will each become central philosophical concepts, and it is to this latter evolution that Foucault turns in the second half of the course, with particular focus on the philosopher as truth-teller to the prince in Plato's confrontation with Dionysius the Younger, Tyrant of Syracuse, as recounted in the *Seventh Letter*.

## III

For Foucault ... it is Plato who exhibits this courage. Plato had the courage to tell the truth to the tyrant of Syracuse ... As is well known, Plato's courageous speech act almost resulted in his death.[5]

Lawlor 2016: 171

Dionysius refused ... to choose the long road of philosophy that had been shown him. He had no sooner heard the first lesson of philosophy than he believed he already knew the most important things (*ta megista*) and that henceforth he knew enough and he had no need of any further self-formation.

Foucault 2008: 227

Foucault labels the confrontation between Plato and Dionysius the Younger of Syracuse the birth place of philosophical *parrhēsia*, even if Plato never actually uses the term (Foucault 2008: 50; Lawlor 2016: 252). As in the case of Creusa, Plato's stance before the tyrant is an example of truth-telling in which the speaker while acknowledging an extreme power differential, is fearless and risks their person. As in the case of Ion, the act involves standing before the instance of political power and making a statement in which the speaker is fully engaged and assumes all the consequences. Nonetheless, while the genre of the enunciation remains recognizably similar, there are differences. Plato neither stands before the democratic assembly nor does he make an accusation of a personal injustice. He is likewise not advocating a particular policy, although in other places he seeks clemency for the tyrant's uncle Dion. Rather, Plato is more like Socrates approaching Alcibiades, telling the tyrant that if he is to rule justly, if he is to achieve his goal of uniting Sicily under his rule, he must first care for himself, he must become a philosopher—not because he will then know the truth in some kind of simplistic or formulaic way—but because only then will he have formed himself so as to accede to knowledge, only then will he possess the knowledge of what truth is and its limitations. Plato's act of *parrhēsia* to Dionysius, on Foucault's reading, is an admonition for the tyrant to undertake the kind of intensive spiritual practice that makes truth possible. "It is clear that when Plato responds to Dionysius: I have come to look for a good man in Sicily, implying that he does not find him, there is something on the order of a challenge, of irony, of an insult, of criticism. It is not to persuade him" (Foucault 2008: 53–4).[6]

Plato's *Seventh Letter* presents itself as a missive offering political advice to the friends and family of Dion of Syracuse, shortly after his assassination. Dion was killed in the aftermath of leading a successful effort to overthrow his uncle, Dionysius the Younger. Plato had come to know Dion during his first visit to Syracuse when he visited the court of Dionysius the Elder. He was impressed by the philosophical earnestness of the young man, and he found in Dion an eager student. When Dionysius the Younger acceded to the throne, Plato returned at the invitation of Dion with the intent of initiating the youthful ruler into philosophy and realizing his vision of philosophical rule. The attempt was unsuccessful and Dion himself had to leave Sicily for the Greek mainland to which Plato soon returned as well. Plato would go back to Sicily a third time, again at the insistence of Dion and those around him. He was determined to see once and for all whether Dionysius possessed the philosophical potential Dion attributed to him, and he was hopeful that he could find a resolution to their dispute. When this third voyage ended in failure, Dion led an expedition from Greece to Sicily that overthrew the tyrant, but, in the subsequent political unrest, Dion fell victim to the machinations of one of the "allies" who had accompanied him. It is in this context that Plato seeks to offer his advice in response to a request from Dion's allies and kinsmen.

The letter begins with a brief introduction (323d10–324b8), followed by a section in which Plato recounts how he came to believe that only those who practice philosophy should rule in the wake of the depredations of the Thirty and the execution of Socrates by the restored democracy (324b9–326b4). There follow the stories of his first (326b5–328c3) and second voyages to Sicily (328c4–330b8). He then offers advice to the friends and family of Dion (330b9–331d6). He argues that the courageous counselor is not the one who seeks to advise those in power how to accomplish their own ends, but those of the city, even under the threat of death. Nonetheless, while the potential for violence is inherent in the role of honest counselor, the willingness to use force to get others to accept your political and ethical views is rejected. The friends and family of Dion are urged to pursue their ends through persuasion and the example of an ethical life.

The linkage between caring for oneself and becoming a political subject is made explicit in the next section (331d7–334c3), where Plato recounts how he counseled Dionysius the Younger that he should live each day as master of himself and his desires. If he did, he would acquire faithful friends and allies both within Syracuse and across Sicily, and this would secure his rule and the harmony of the island.

> In the great federation that [Dionysius] organizes around Syracuse, each city ought to have its own voice, but all these voices ought to function together to create a harmony and a symphony. But to guarantee the harmony of the different cities, the leader should be *sumphōnos* with himself, that is to say in harmony with himself.
>
> Foucault 2008: 249

Such harmony would mean abstaining from the rich banquets and sexual indulgences that were typical of the Syracusan court. In this way, Plato contends, Dionysius might achieve the stability and hegemony in Sicily that eluded his father. The young tyrant did not heed his counsel.

Plato draws appropriate conclusions for the friends and family of Dion to whom he is writing (334c4–337e3). He argues that enslaving others benefits neither the enslaver nor the enslaved, and that only souls possessed of small and unfree manners (*smikra kai aneleuthra ēthē*), that is, those knowing nothing of the good and the just, will strive to carry off the goods of others. Political tyranny is thus shown to be a function of the malformation or poor training of the soul. At the same time, Plato argues that the desire to experience what is finest for oneself and the city is necessarily the desire to experience what is wholly correct and fine, and thus incorruptible. Hence enlightened self-interest should lead one to prefer the good and the just. Plato's basic argument is that, as for Foucault and even Baudelaire, there is a convergence between the political, the aesthetic, and the ethical. The tyrant, as in the *Republic* (Book 9, 571a–578c), is the one who has no limits to his desires and therefore, as the Stoics recognized, becomes their slave.

Plato continues with his narrative. Dionysius's court was filled with people who had a smattering of philosophy and loved to recount bits and pieces of what they had heard. There was, in fact, a certain level of culture and learning in Syracuse. Likewise, Plato concedes that the young tyrant was "not altogether unsuited for learning and eager for praise" (338c5–d8). These facts helped Dion convince the philosopher that he should try once more to counsel Dionysius, since "it was not at all remarkable that a young man who had heard philosophical discussions would be seized with a desire for the best life" (339e5). And so it was that Plato decided he should make a test of Dionysius on his return to determine "whether in actuality he had been lit aflame by philosophy as by a fire" (340b1–2).

When Plato arrived in Syracuse, he discovered Dionysius had written a book, a kind of précis or resumé of philosophy. Plato makes clear nothing could be more misguided. Dionysius had taken bits and pieces of things he had heard (341b3), transcribed them, and presented them as his own. He represented himself as a philosopher but had not done the hard work of living a philosophical life. Plato claims he knows nothing of the matters in the book, but he knows others who have written such books and says the authors are completely lacking in self-knowledge: "they do not know themselves who they are" (*hoitines de, oud' autoi hautous*, 341b6). They are not philosophers. They lack the self-knowledge prerequisite to philosophical insight (*Apology* 21b–22; *Phaedrus* 229c–230a).

Self-knowledge changes your life. It is the difference between waking and sleeping or, in Kant's formulation, between majority and minority. This knowledge and the effect it has on the soul is the true matter of philosophy (*pragma* 340b8; Harward 2014: 211). It is philosophy's purchase on the real (Foucault 2008: 210-20). The mere repetition of what you have heard on philosophical topics no more makes you a philosopher than the memorization of the Greek alphabet allows you to read Greek. Philosophy is something you do, not something you memorize. It is not information that you receive and therefore know. As Plato explains to the friends and relatives of Dion:

> [Philosophy] is in no way a discourse (*rhēton*) that is like other forms of knowledge. Rather it is from spending a great deal of time together concerning the matter itself and from living with it (*suzēn*) that all of a sudden a light is kindled, just as when a fire leaps forth, which once this flame has been born in the soul then it nourishes itself.
>
> 341c6–d2

Philosophy is not a body of precepts to be learned or a skill to be honed. It is not a set of truths to be repeated, a faith to be professed, or an object to be exchanged (Nightingale 1995: 48). It is a practice, a form of life (*bios*).

At this point, Plato's narrative pauses, and we begin what is known as the philosophical digression (342a7–345c4). In it, Plato seeks to define the three elements that make up knowledge or *epistēmē*. This knowledge takes up a specific attitude in relation to being. The subject of philosophy is formed through the deliberate and critical manipulation of these three elements to produce ever new relations between knowledge and the being it purports to know, creating an intellectual friction that leads to the spark of enlightenment.

Knowledge as normally understood for Plato is a repeatable structure. It is dependent upon a framework that seeks to align name (*onoma*), argument (*logos*), and image or perception (*eidolon*), the totality of which is called *epistēmē*. For Plato in the *Seventh Letter*, philosophy's concern is not so much with these three elements and their correct alignment to produce factual knowledge, as with the contingency of those structures in relation to what makes them possible, which he calls being (*on*) and the known (*gnōston*) (342a–b). Thus, every identifiable phenomenon has a name (*onoma*). Plato uses the example of a circle. We can then make propositions (*logoi*) about that phenomenon. For example, "circles are round." We can also check those propositions against the images we either receive or make of circles (*eidōla*), either through culture or personal experience, and when we perceive an alignment between these three elements—"yes, the name circle is applied to things that are round"—we then have *epistēmē*.

Now certain forms of empirical research stop there. "The cat is on the mat." "Yes, that is a cat, per our previous definition." "Yes, that is a mat, per our previous definition." "I observe that what we call 'cat' is currently 'on' what we call 'mat.'" Therefore, we can conclude that "the cat is on the mat" is a true statement. This is something we know. Philosophy however, at least on Plato's understanding, is only beginning. To return to Plato's example, the reality of the circle *qua* circle (as opposed to that of any particular circular object), which seemed to inhere in both the name itself and the propositions in which it appeared and to be confirmed by personal perception and the social imaginary, when adequately examined and tested, begins to float free of these empirical constraints and instead comes to constitute the ideal object of geometry, an object that possesses specific and universal mathematical qualities that exist apart from any of its empirical instantiations. For those empirical instantiations are always possessed of a certain contingency, a certain particularity, a certain element of that which is opposed to the thing itself in its intrinsic being. There indeed is no drawing or rendition of the circle that does not contain an element, however small it may be, of the straight (*eutheos*, 343a5–9). No ball is ever perfectly round. A factual part of our existence, the empirical circle, that was a function of our perception and our use of language and reason is now revealed to have its being *as* a circle apart from those elements of factual knowledge in the circle *qua* circle. And hence what is known (*gnōston*) is shown to transcend knowledge as repeatable information (*epistēmē*) and to consist in the experience of both the initial recognition of the correspondence of the first three elements and then, through their progressive manipulation, in the recognition that the reality to which they gesture ultimately exceeds their grasp. If this is true for an object as simple and intuitive as a circle, it is all the more the case with more abstract concepts like the good, the just, and the true, which structure our existence.

The aim of philosophical life, then, is not the production of empirical knowledge but the revelation of its limitations, the demonstration of the ways in which it always falls short of being: of circles *qua* circles, cats *qua* cats, and justice in itself. Philosophy does not seek to confirm the reality of our perceptions or their correspondence to the pre-existing names and categories that make up our daily existence but rather it precipitates the criticism of their preconceived unity, and does so as the predicate to the production of new knowledge, new understandings, new truths possessed of a fuller, more adequate, or at least different, relation to being itself. There is, however, no metalanguage that can be recorded in a book or repeated by others to guarantee this truth. There is no final formulation in which the truth in itself can be captured and transmitted. It is always a process, always a form of life and a practice of the self in the world:

> Indeed, the argument (*logos*) itself concerning argument (*peri logou*), if it consists of nouns (*onomatōn*) and verbs (*rhēmatōn*), is in no way sufficiently grounded in its solidity. There are a thousand arguments concerning each of these four elements [of knowledge] that they lack clarity. But the greatest is what we said before: that concerning these two things, being and quality, the soul seeks to know not what sort of thing something is but *what* it is. Yet each of the four elements offers to the soul, through argument and experience, not what is sought, rather each thing that is said and demonstrated presents itself as being easily refuted by the senses and so fills a man with practically every perplexity and confusion. Consequently, on the one hand, we are not accustomed to seek the truth through onerous training, and on the other, the first image that comes to us suffices, and using them we do not become laughingstocks to one another, even though we are being questioned by those who are able to toss about the four elements and to refute them.
> 
> 343b4–d2

Indeed, Plato argues that in many circumstances, the speaker who is glibly able to manipulate the first four elements can make a person with knowledge of the fifth (*on*), who understands how the knowledge of the empirical world always falls short, appear foolish whether in speech, in writing, or in the give and take of question and answer (343d5). This observation recalls the figure of the cave dweller who has freed himself, emerged into the light, and returned to the cave to try and converse with his former mates and convince them that reality is not what they see immediately before themselves. Such a person seems not enlightened but foolish. It also recalls the Athenian populace's inability to understand and value a figure like Socrates, an incomprehension that led to his death.

Philosophy, as Plato understands it, is an interactive process that takes place between a teacher and a student. Dionysius's book is nothing but the recording of bits of philosophical discourse heard or overheard and then repeated. In contrast, it is precisely through the deliberate and applied manipulation of the first three elements, and particularly of the slippages and resistances between them, that insight is sparked:

> It is necessary to learn these things, the true and the false, from the whole of being with all the work (*tribēs*) and time I spoke of at the beginning. But by rubbing (*tribomena*) each of these things against one another with exertion— names and arguments, observations and perceptions—by testing them in good faith and by using questions and answers without rancor or envy, reflection and intellect *shine forth*, extending to the limits of human potential.
> 344b, emphasis added

The recollection here of the earlier image of the spark of understanding blazing forth is not to be missed. "To be in the presence of philosophy is like when you are near a fire, up to the point when the lamp of the soul is lit, or the lamp lights itself as a soul, it's in this and according to this manner that philosophy is going to encounter reality" (Foucault 2008: 229).

Philosophy is in the first instance a desire for truth, but it is also a practice and a way of life that has at its core the interrogation of the accepted names and arguments for things in order to produce new knowledge, new relations to being, and hence a necessary resistance to claims of authority that are rooted in pretensions to epistemic absolutism. If philosophy cannot be learned and transmitted as a given set of observations, as what Plato terms *mathēmata*, then the philosopher himself can never be a lawgiver *per se*, can never be the person who transmits a set of unchanging norms that seek to govern others (Foucault 2008: 229–34). "It is when a soul of good quality has done the long, slow work of ascending and descending the forms of knowing, it is when it has practiced what Plato calls *tribē*—in the strict sense, a rubbing together—it is through this that the knowing of reality in its very being is going to be possible" (Foucault 2008: 232).

Without getting into the controversy over whether the *Seventh Letter* is by Plato or merely a product of those close to him, which is not relevant to Foucault's larger point, there is nothing in the philosophical digression foreign to the sweep of Platonic thought. It has long been recognized that in the *Symposium* the philosopher is not the possessor of wisdom but its lover, one who pursues wisdom through a set of rigorous practices, which bear upon lifestyle, dialogue, and education (Brown 1994: 169–70; Hunter 2004: 86–7). Knowledge, on this view, is not an object that can be exchanged, but something arrived at through testing and discussion that prepares students to approach knowledge on their own terms (Festugière 1950: 42–3, 19; Hadot 1995: 104–6). That pursuit is a form of self-fashioning. Philosophy is the creation of a certain type of subject, produced through a sustained dialogic engagement with others and the self (Koyré 1962: 20). That dialogue in Socratic practice takes place in the *elenchus*, a set of questions and answers designed to test the limits of the interlocutor's knowledge, as showcased in dialogues such as the *Apology* or the *Ion* and featured in Socrates' questioning of Agathon in the *Symposium*. The purpose of the *elenchus* is not to found an unassailable epistemological position or to produce knowledge that can be possessed and transmitted, but to convince the interlocutor of their soul's internal incoherence and of the consequent necessity to care for themselves as a propaedeutic to caring for others (Hadot 1995: 55, 102–5; Nehamas 1998: 75; Blondell 2002: 124). The goal of dialectical interchange is not to "teach," to fill the student with knowledge, but to provoke the interlocutor into an active understanding and break the hold of the immediate upon the soul (Brown 1994: 166–7; Blondell 2002: 100). It is less concerned with conformity and obedience than with transcending the limitations of the self as a knowing, erotic, social, and political being (Gadamer 1991: 4–5). This is the lesson of the *Seventh Letter*.

Foucault turns to Euripides and Plato to trace the genealogy of the philosophical subject as one who speaks truth to power (Gros 2008: 348–9, 357). The philosophical subject does so not by making pronouncements on specific policies, or as a professional philosopher giving lessons in a university, but by confronting power with the real of philosophy, with its labor, its experience (Foucault 2008: 210–11, 318; Gros 2008: 358–61). In doing so, Foucault is establishing "the ontology of the present": the way in which reality is defined and exists for us, not as a transcendental deduction, but as a thousand barely audible voices that inform, contradict, and determine one another and exist in a recursive relationship between present and past that constitutes the future as a determined set of possibilities (2008: 22).

*Parrhēsia*, in this context, is not just the fact of making a true statement. It is the self-conscious act of speaking the truth. It represents a decision and a way of being (Foucault 2008: 62, 64). It involves risk. Whether it is Socrates before the Athenian people, Plato before Dionysius the Younger, Seneca before Nero, Emma Goldman before the American bar, or Solzhenitsyn before the Soviet state, the parrhesiast puts themselves at risk to speak their truth. "Parrhesiasts are those who, at the limit, accept to die in order to have spoken the truth. Or more precisely, parrhesiasts are those who undertake to speak the truth at a price that has not been determined, which could include even their own death" (Foucault 2008: 56). For Foucault, the philosopher in antiquity, insofar as he leads a philosophical life, insofar as he dedicates himself to finding and speaking the truth and not simply to repeating philosophical truisms, is the parrhesiast par excellence. This is his political function:

> Philosophical discourse in its truth, inside the game it necessarily plays with politics in order to find there its truth, does not have to project what a political action ought to be. He does speak truth about the political action, he does not speak truth for the political action, he speaks truth in relation to political action, in relation to the exercise of politics, in relation to the political personage.
> 
> Foucault 2008: 265

As Plato and Dion were to Dionysius, the philosopher is to be a "truth speaker": a person who undertakes to speak the truth as a self-conscious act in relation to the exercise of power, an act that must always call that power into question, and that must freely risk the life of the speaker. The parrhesiast speaks not to advance a particular political position, which would instrumentalize and subordinate truth to power, but he or she speaks the truth as a risk to both life and power (Foucault 2008: 51–4, 64).

Thus, in his reading of the *Seventh Letter*, Foucault argues that Plato defines the role of the philosopher as one who must expose to the tyrant the *pragma* of philosophy, its true matter: the labor of interrogation and self-transformation that constitutes philosophy's relation to the real (2008: 220). That labor in turn is defined most clearly in the philosophical digression and the elements of knowledge discussed above. What Foucault wants to draw our attention to more than the elements is the labor (*tribē*) that goes into rubbing them against one another, the productive friction of insistent inquiry that leads to the spark of enlightenment. And it is precisely that *tribē* that Dionysius refuses in favor of writing his book, in favor of a philosophical performance that does not transform either his life or his rule (2008: 227). It is, however, the philosopher's role to put the tyrant to the test and to expose his lack of seriousness. In doing so, he speaks the truth to power, not to advance a prefabricated political agenda or to enact specific policy proposals, but to confront power with alternative truths to those on which it predicates its own existence. Thus, Foucault observes:

> For Plato, and in a general fashion it seems to me for all of Western philosophy, the true wager has never been to tell politicians what to do. Their wager has always been, before the politicians, before political practice, before politics, to exist as a philosophic discourse and philosophic truth-telling.
> 
> Foucault 2008: 266-7

The philosopher as parrhesiast is not the possessor of an absolute knowledge that entitles him to rule but one who speaks truth to power precisely insofar as he is a philosopher. That truth is not a set of information or a series of propositions but a form of life, a way of seeking the truth. It is not the deployment of instrumental knowledge consisting in the correlation of names (*onomata*) and appearances (*eidola*) through *logoi*, but it is the continuing and deliberate friction (*tribē*) between those elements of knowledge in a fashion that reveals the contingencies, interests, and limitations that govern those correlations. Philosophy practiced as *parrhēsia* emancipates the lover of wisdom from previous perceptions and opens up the possibility of acceding to a greater cohesion between the *on* and the *gnōston*, between being and the known, to enlightenment.

## IV

> This doubling or redoubling of the statement of the truth by the statement of the truth of the fact that I am thinking this truth and that, in thinking it, I say it, this is what is indispensable to the parrhēsiastic act.
> 
> Foucault 2008: 62

It is this philosophical *parrhēsia*, and this test of oneself and of others that is useful to the city, since by thus being the parrhēsiast in the middle of the city,

[Socrates] keeps it from sleeping. And, he says, if you condemn me to death, you know very well you will spend the rest of your life asleep.

Foucault 2008: 299

Truth as spoken by the parrhesiast is never neutral. It is never just the presentation of data. *Parrhēsia* is a deliberate and consequential act. This self-conscious choice to enunciate a particular truth in a particular context does not happen in a vacuum. It does not happen outside of history, outside of power, and because of that it is indissociably linked to freedom. Freedom in this sense is not the private ability to think something: it is a public act that engages the subject, a declaration of majority (Rajchman 1991: 118–20).

For many years prior to these lectures, the public enunciation of truth had been part of Foucault's political practice. In the early seventies, he had been a founder of the *Groupe d'information sur les prisons* (GIP), which was dedicated not only to exposing conditions within French prisons but also to letting prisoners and their families speak directly to the public. It was in the course of this work that Foucault first developed his analysis of power and began research on *Surveiller et Punir* (1975). It was also in the course of this work that he began to reflect more rigorously on the complex relations between truth and power and on the role the philosopher should play within them. His subsequent genealogy and theorization of *parrhēsia* and its relation to power is in part a response to what he perceived as the failure of the GIP to change conditions inside French prisons. It is also part of a larger effort to rethink what is and has been the role of truth-telling in governance (Lawlor 2016: 196–7).

*Parrhēsia* is a political act, but it does not advance a particular policy. Rather than being programmatic speech or a set of talking points, *parrhēsia* is an act of truth-telling that "creates a break and opens a risk: a possibility" (Foucault 2008: 61). It is an ethic of truth-telling: Socrates before the Athenian court, Plato before Dionysius, Diogenes in his tub before Alexander. *Parrhēsia* asks a fundamental question: what is the relationship between freedom and truth? Can there be truth-telling without freedom? Certainly the existence of true propositions does not necessarily presume either *parrhēsia* or a claim to freedom. It is not the words of the true statement itself that constitutes the parrhesiastic act; it is the affirmative choice to make that statement. The oracle of Apollo at Delphi speaks the truth, and the Pythia's utterance is not a parrhesiatic act, but Creusa's denunciation of Apollo is. The measurement of the polar ice caps is not *parrhēsia*. The statement that the polar ice is melting in the face of climate denial is. Every time a speaker stands up, assumes the risk inherent in the act, and speaks a deliberate truth is a moment of freedom, a moment that breaks open the world, if ever so slightly (Foucault 2008: 52, 55–6, 64–6; Lawlor 2016: 149, 170). It is rarer than we think.

On this level, *parrhēsia* is the opposite of the irony displayed in dialogues like the *Euthydemus* where Socrates feigns admiration for the learning of his interlocutors, while exposing their ignorance and bad faith. Although Socrates may be the archetypical ironist, his irony is not what renders him a parrhesiast. This is a distinction that Lawlor misses in his otherwise admirable account, proclaiming Socratic irony "the model of *parrhēsia*" (2016: 252). It is worth quoting Foucault on this point.

> In particular, nothing is further away ... than *parrhēsia* from the famous Socratic or Socratico-Platonic irony. In Socratic irony, what is happening? Well then, it is a game in which the master feigns not to know and leads the student to formulate what he does not know he knows. In *parrhēsia*, by contrast, as if it were a true anti-irony, the one who speaks the truth throws that truth in the face of the interlocutor, a truth so violent, so abrupt, said in such a decisive and definitive fashion that the other is no longer able to remain quiet, or to squelch their furor, or ... in the case of Dionysius with regard to Plato, attempted murder. Far from the interlocutor discovering in himself, through irony, the truth that he did not know he knew, in this case he is in the presence of a truth he cannot accept, that he cannot not reject, and that leads him to injustice, excess, madness, blindness.
>
> Foucault 2008: 54

When Socrates tells the Athenian court that in lieu of the death penalty for his crimes he proposes to be fed and lodged at public expense, like an Olympic victor, this is an act of *parrhēsia*. It will cost him his life. When he leads Phaedrus to recognize that Lysias's speech is less admirable than he thought, while initially professing admiration, it is not.

*Parrhēsia* refers not to the truth value of an enunciation, or to the tropes contained therein—there is more than a little irony in Socrates demanding to be treated like an Olympic victor—but to what Foucault terms a "dramatization" of speech. *Parrhēsia* refers to a context and a form of self-relation that characterizes an act of articulating a true statement. Rhetorical figures can and inevitably will be contained within any given parrhesiastic act, but *parrhēsia* cannot be defined within rhetoric because the veracity of a given statement is not a question for rhetorical analysis. Rhetoric, in the ancient world, seeks to sway deliberative or judicial bodies. That is its aim and measure. Philosophy is concerned with the truth. It is concerned with the individual lives of the people to whom it is addressed and with the need those individuals have to care for themselves, both as a matter of their own spiritual well being and as decision-makers in a legal or political context (Foucault 2008: 53, 80). It is on this level that Socrates' role as parrhesiast makes its impact felt:

> To philosophize is to occupy yourself with yourself, to exhort others to occupy themselves with themselves, and to do this by scrutinizing, testing, putting to proof what others know and what they do not know. That is what philosophical *parrhēsia* consists in. Philosophical *parrhēsia* identifies itself not simply with a mode of discourse, with a techniques of discourse, but with life itself. It is necessary for me, [Socrates says] "to live by philosophizing (*zēn philosophounta kai exetasonta emauton kai tous allous*)[7] and by examining, testing, and scrutinizing myself as well as others."
>
> Foucault 2008: 299, citing *Apology* 28e

It is not Socrates' irony that renders him a parrhesiast, but rather his dedication to living the philosophic life that allows him to deploy irony for parrhesiastic ends.

In this guise, *parrhēsia* is a virtue and a technique encountered throughout antiquity. It is deployed by those who seek to direct the consciences of others and who, like Horace's "free friend," assist them in establishing a critical self relation (Foucault 2008: 43). Over time, especially under Christianity, Foucault contends, there is a shift in meaning from the obligation of a master or teacher to be frank with a student, to a penitent's need to be truthful to his superior. *Parrhēsia* in late antiquity and the Middle Ages, he argues, ceases to be the domain of the philosopher and becomes that of the prelate, whether in his role as confessor or pastor leading his flock (Foucault 2008: 320). Modern philosophy can be seen from this perspective, at least in part, as the attempt to reappropriate this tradition of truth-telling from the church. Whether in the *Critique of Pure Reason*, the *Phenomenology of the Spirit*, or the *Genealogy of Morals*, philosophy's central concern is the determination of what is the truth, who gets to say it, and under what circumstances. In its most vital forms, it remains the critique of illusion, error, flattery, and mystification, both within the subject and in relation to others (Foucault 2008: 321, 326).

The philosophic life, Foucault contends, is a manifestation of truth. It is not simply a way to read or think about texts. It is not a technical solution to problems of logic or reasoning. It is a way of living that challenges others (Foucault 2008: 315–16). Like the dandy in Baudelaire or the subject in Kant's "What is Enlightenment," it entails a form of emancipation: shaping oneself in the present, assuming responsibility for one's life. It is a form of admonition. It is Plato before Dionysius telling him that to establish harmony in Sicily he must first establish it within himself: he must undertake the *tribē* that leads to a critical analysis of knowledge and truth. He must change his life. It is Diogenes the Cynic, naked in the *agora*, with his lamp searching for an honest man (Foucault 2008: 265, 270).

## V

What, then, is the philosophic life? And what for that matter is philosophy? If rhetoric is a way to exert power by telling an audience what it wants to hear—your country, your city, your way of life is the greatest the world has known—like Socrates' example of the chef who pleases his client by offering him cakes when he needs a strong purgative, philosophy is that medicine. Like any good physician, the philosophical doctor may rim the bitter cup with rhetorical honey, but philosophy makes its difference in the world of politics, in the real, not through a program, and not through appealing to the chauvinisms and vanities of its audience, be it prince or polis, but precisely through *parrhēsia*, through the act of speaking the truth. "Philosophy is the activity that consists in speaking the truth, in practicing veridiction in relation to power" (Foucault 2008: 211). By this formulation, Foucault does not mean that the philosopher should have the power to dictate the laws or to pronounce on the truth or falsity of a particular constitutional arrangement. Rather, the philosophical mode, like Plato's address to Dionysius, directly involves "the truth of Being and the practice of the soul, and what brings with it the transformation of the soul." Plato does not seek to convince Dionysius of a particular position in relation to Sicilian politics, to pronounce on the truth or falsity of his rule, rather he seeks to test Dionysius to see if he is ready and able to undertake the labor that is philosophy, the labor that makes the truth possible as something more than an expedient appeal (Foucault 2008: 308–9).

Truth, then, for philosophy, as Plato understood it, or at least as Foucault presents Plato's understanding, does not pre-exist discourse. This is a critical observation: for the discovery, creation, and articulation of truth is the essence of all our scientific, philosophical, and artistic work. If the truth existed before discourse, before the various human acts of discovering it through the *logos*, discourse would be nothing but rhetoric. There would be nothing but persuasion. Our universities could in fact be reduced to mere factories for the transfer of data to those willing to pay for its possession. Truth would exist as a set of unchanging contents or information of which we seek to convince others. There would be no rational act of discovery, no moment in which we transform ourselves and the world through our understanding and perception. The various forms of dialectic, the various forms of logical reasoning, our systems of verification and ratification, our histories and genealogies, our stories—all of which can only take place through the establishment of discursive communities—would be reduced to mere means to pre-established ends. There would be no meaningful distinction between the spokesperson and the philosopher, the scientist, or the artist. We do not know the truth and then find the words but, in constructing the words properly and coherently, in making the argument and engaging in conversation with others and with the world, we construct truths, whether in a journal article, a treatise, or a poem, truths which then must live and die in the world, must prove their worth in the world. Socrates cannot merely inform Alcibiades of the truth, and then let him go about his business. Dionysius the Younger cannot write a book filled with philosophical truisms and then be a philosopher. That is not the real of philosophy. That is not where its relation to Being resides. It requires a labor and a transformation of the self in which truth is never the mere instrument to another end. "For a discourse to be a discourse of truth, it does not need knowledge of the truth to be given in advance of the act of speaking, the truth needs to be a constant and permanent function of the discourse" (Foucault 2008: 303–4).

But this insistent labor of constructing the truth, if it is to have its effect in the real, if it is not to be mere verbiage, must find interlocutors willing and able to listen. Any discourse can be appropriated to ends radically different from its intended effect. Plato in the *Seventh Letter* says he will give counsel only to those willing to listen and act on his counsels. He then tells of the various ways he and Dion sought to convince the young Dionysius to undertake a regime of personal restraint and reform so as to show himself a faithful friend and dependable ally to others, but to no avail (*Seventh Letter* 330c–333c; Foucault 2008: 212–13). When Plato returns to Sicily the third and final time, after being convinced that Dionysius is finally ready to undertake the labor that is philosophy, he proposes a test. He will show to him the true matter of philosophy and how great the labor is:

> For having heard this, if he would be a proper philosopher and endowed with a divine aptitude worthy of the matter, he will think the road that he heard of is marvelous and that it is necessary to attempt it with all his strength and no other life is worth living. After this, having urged himself on to the utmost and the one leading him on the path, he does not let up before he has fully reached the end or he has taken up the power so that he is able to conduct himself without the one who has shown him the way.
>
> 340c2–8

But Dionysius showed himself just the opposite: "for he thought he knew many very great things and had exerted himself sufficiently on account of the things he had heard from others" (341b1–3). The real of philosophy is the mark it leaves on the soul of the interlocutor, the transformation it works, lest truth be just what we hear from others (Foucault 2008: 217–20).

The person who would govern then, as Plato argues both in the *Seventh Letter* and the *Republic*, must philosophize, but the person who would philosophize must bring themself to confront the reality, the *pragma* of philosophy, which is never a given set of truths that pre-exist the moment of inquiry (Foucault 2008: 236). The prince, like Marcus Aurelius, must govern his soul according to philosophy in order to govern others, otherwise he becomes indistinguishable from the tyrant, an all-desiring and hence all-fearing slave to his appetites. To be a philosopher for Plato and for Foucault, does not mean to hold certain views but to constitute yourself as a subject in a self-relation of emancipation, one in which you have the ability to think and philosophize on your own. It is only thus that one should exert power and speak truth to those who do (Foucault 2008: 271–2).

5

# The Courage of Truth: Philosophical Life in the Face of Death

> I was not able to start my course as usual at the beginning of January. I was sick, very sick. There were rumors going around saying I had messed up the dates to get rid of part of the audience. No, no, I was very sick. And so I ask you to forgive me.
>
> Foucault 2009: 3

> Socrates was not held back by the dangers ... He says it very clearly [in the *Apology*]: a man of any value does not have to "calculate his chances of life and death" ... Whatever the dangers of this *parrhēsia*, in this form, insofar as he is a man "of any value," he knows very well that he ought not to place in the balance the importance of this *parrhēsia* and his chances of life or death. "A man of any value ought only to consider, when he acts, if what he does is just or not, if he conducts himself as a man of courage or a coward."
>
> Foucault 2009: 78, citing *Apology* 28b

In late December of 1983, Foucault fell very ill. He was unable to begin his course until February. We have reason to believe that at this time he may have received a diagnosis of AIDS, but it is not sure and the antibodies test was not widely available. It may have simply been that he was falling ill more frequently with fevers and flu-like illnesses and that he and his doctors had surmised so. At any rate, in January of 1984 he wrote Maurice Pinguet, a friend from his student days at the École Normale, that he had been quite ill and had been treated with antibiotics. He wrote, "I thought I had AIDS, but a vigorous treatment put me back on my feet." The wording clearly allows for the possibility that since the antibiotics worked, he felt the diagnosis might not have been accurate. By March, he was once again ill with a flu-like illness and regularly in and out of the hospital. At this point, he no longer sought a diagnosis but only inquired how much time he had left (Gros 2009: 318).[1] As Gros observes, like Socrates, whom he references repeatedly in these lectures, Foucault was more concerned with failing to complete his mission than with death (Gros 2009: 319–20). At the beginning of his final lecture, he stood before his audience, gaunt, hands shaking and said, "I am going to try to give you two hours of lecture today, but I am not absolutely sure I will make it, I have a little bit of, actually quite a lot of, flu. I am going to do what I can. You will pardon me if we pause a bit" (Foucault 2009: 245). He gave the full lecture.

There remain many questions about the last year of his life. Did Foucault have reason to believe he might have the virus in the fall of 1983, when he went to San Francisco and gave a set of lectures? As much or as little as any gay man did. At this time, there was a tremendous amount of uncertainty in the gay community about the precise nature of the virus and how it was transmitted. No one claims he had a positive diagnosis in the fall, if he ever received one. Did he, as James Miller alleges, go to California to pursue "his own deliberately chosen apotheosis, his own singular experience of the 'The Passion'"? This is speculative at best and a phobia-fueled fantasy at worst. As Miller concedes, "What exactly Foucault did in the fall of 1983—and why—may never be known" (1993: 29). But the lurid speculations sparked by Miller's book continue. He ends his text saying the entire project began when a friend in 1987

> relayed a shocking piece of gossip: knowing that he was dying of AIDS, Michel Foucault in 1983 had gone to gay bathhouses in America, and deliberately tried to infect other people with the disease.
>
> At the time, I was no great admirer of so-called "post-structuralist" or "postmodernist" modes of thought.
>
> Miller 1993: 375

Although Miller in his book makes various qualifications and admissions about his data and the state of the evidence, the innuendo is clear. Foucault's thought, like that of his faddish French colleagues, is a dangerous virus. Their collective irresponsibility is shown by Foucault's reckless, if not homicidal, behavior. The entire book moves back and forth between texts by Foucault and scenes of excess. The exercise is more aimed at *damnatio memoriae* than a just appreciation of the work. One might think such sensationalism would have subsided, but Miller's caricature hangs on. In a recent lecture I gave on Foucault and the Cynics, an audience member, who is a recognized member of the North American Classics establishment, a feminist, and a liberal on sexual matters rose and asked me, how could I speak of Foucault and the truth when we know he infected all those innocent people and never told the truth. The reference was Miller's book.

None of this is to deny that in the early eighties Foucault saw the bathhouses of New York, San Francisco, and Toronto as laboratories of sexual experimentation and that he opposed measures to close them, although the interviews in which these statements are made date from 1982, well before the disease was widely understood (Foucault 1994l: 326, 331; 1994m: 337; 1994n: 740). Whether Foucault altered or did not alter his personal conduct later, we have no way of knowing. But his public comments became more circumspect as the threat was better understood.

Sexuality for Foucault is not a force to be liberated. It is something we create, not a fate to which we submit. The bathhouses were loci of self-creation, crucibles in which individuals could try on and shed identities, in the course of anonymous encounters: straight/gay, male/female, dominant/submissive (Foucault 1994l: 331; 1994n: 735–9, 743). The point for Foucault was not to liberate "homosexuals," and even less was it to lay down how gays should behave, but to produce a moment free from such identities in which new forms of pleasure, of friendship, of solidarity, and of subjectivity could be pursued (Foucault 1994g: 711; 1994n: 325, 334; Rajchman 1991: 10, 96–7; Macey 1993: 365). In his more utopian moments, he envisioned a truly "gay" culture that aspired to transcend the limits of the homosexual community to become what we might today term queer, naming a self-fashioned and preformed identity that was not limited to a given typology nor enforced by normative expectations of sexual roles, a culture that embraced relations of friendship and pleasure between men, between women, and between the genders and combinations undreamed of (Foucault 1994o: 295; 1994p: 308–11, 313; 2012a: 254–5; Rajchman 1991: 88). These transformative practices were not foreign to Foucault's philosophical concerns as expressed in figures like Socrates, Seneca, Kant, and Baudelaire, but they were also never simply their reflection, nor, as Miller would have us a believe, were the philosophical inquiries merely epiphenomenal to his own lurid vision of a sexual and material real. The last thing Foucault sought was to star in a "passion" play, whether as savior or brigand.

By April of 1984, Foucault was in and out of the hospital, rereading Kafka's journal and working on volume four of the *History of Sexuality*. His last lecture at the Collège was March 28. In May of 1984, he knew his time was short, and he withdrew from Paris, as was his wont when finishing books, to the family home in Vendeuvre-du-Poitou where he worked on revising the typescript of *Les aveux de la chair* in hopes of October publication. He had completely redrafted volumes two and three in August of 1983, splitting them into the form we know today. The essential research for these had been completed by 1981, and all the subsequent lectures were working toward his future projects on subjectivity and truth (Elden 2016: 151, 168, 188–9). Volumes two and three were published just days before his death.

In what follows, we will examine three major topics covered by Foucault in this final year of lectures. First, he offers an overview of the relation between truth-telling and power, returning to terms and themes broached in 1980. In this portion of the course, Foucault outlines several schemas for how we are to understand different forms of truth-telling and their relation to power and subjectivity. Second, he investigates Socrates as parrhesiast in the *Apology*, the *Alcibiades*, and the *Laches*. We close with a reading of his lectures on the Cynics, finishing with reflections on the philosophic *bios* as the life of truth.

I

Foucault's interest in parrhesia is doubtless founded on the fact the he recognizes himself in it.

Kelly 2014: 181

The word "game" (*jeu*) can lead you into error: when I say "game," I mean an ensemble of rules of production of truth. It is not a game in the sense of imitating or pretending ... it is an ensemble of procedures that lead to a certain result, which can be considered, as a function of its principles and its rules of procedures, as either valid or not.

Foucault 1994g: 725

In 1980's *Du gouvernement des vivants*, Foucault coined the term *alèthurgie* to name the "ensemble of possible procedures, verbal or not, through which one brings to light what is posited as true in opposition to the false, the hidden, the unsayable, the unforeseeable, the forgotten," making the argument that there is no exercise of power without "something like an *alèthurgie*" (Foucault 2012b: 8). Reflecting back on this form of analysis at the beginning of his 1984 course, Foucault argues that there are two fundamental ways of analyzing discourses in terms of truth. The first is epistemological, which analyzes what are the "structures proper to different discourses that present themselves and are received as true." The second, the "alethurgical," analyzes the type of act "through which the subject speaking the truth *manifests* itself, by which I mean to say, represents itself to itself and is recognized by others as speaking the truth." Whereas the first poses the question of the truth value of statements, the second examines acts and how they are performed. It asks "how the individual constitutes itself and is constituted by others as a subject performing a true discourse" (Foucault 2009: 4). He observes that for the first part of his career he was largely interested in the kinds of discourse that were spoken and the conditions under which one could speak the truth within them—psychiatry, medicine, economics, linguistics, penology, sexuality. In his later work, the axis switches from how one speaks the truth about different kinds of objects in the world to how the subject comes to speak the truth and how it constitutes itself as a speaker of truth (Foucault 2009: 5; Gros 2009: 314–15).

With this shift in emphasis, confession, as we have observed, becomes one of the lynchpins of Foucault's later thought. We might begin with *Surveiller et Punir* (1975), the first work in which Foucault featured an analytic of power. It is a text that emerged directly out of his political work in the *Groupe d'information sur les prisons* (*GIP*) to give voice to prisoners, their partners, and their families. In it, he seeks to chart how the logic of the penal reform movement in the late eighteenth and early nineteenth centuries produced the modern prison. Central to this movement was the importance of criminals recognizing their crimes, of criminals monitoring themselves and disciplining themselves, in short a logic of confession. Behind the conceptual apparatus of the penitentiary, of Bentham's dream of the panopticon, is the alethurgical discourse of a legal system that first pronounces you guilty, then seeks to constitute you as a subject that recognizes itself in that legal discourse, and finally asks you to perform your own *alèthurgie* in the form of a confession or an acceptance of responsibility. The next year sees the publication of volume one of the *History of Sexuality* (1976), in which the role of confession and various forms of discourse that demand the subject say who or what they are—therapeutic, scientific, penal, and religious discourses—become central to producing the truth of the normalized subject. In each of these cases, though, that truth is not articulated just to the self but always to a figure of authority through whose mediation the nature of the confessing subject is reflected back.

As shown in Foucault's reading of the *Alcibiades*, such practices well predate the therapist's couch or the priest's confessional, and even closely cognate practices operating in different contexts, with different founding assumptions, can produce very different effects (Foucault 2009: 6–7). One of Foucault's goals is to trace a genealogy of the practices through which we have created the modern disciplinary and confessing subject, so as to denaturalize this form of experience and open it up to examination and interrogation. Another, however, is to disentangle specific technologies of the self from individual configurations of truth and power so they can be repurposed for ends of our own choosing (Allen 2016: 132). The study of *parrhēsia* within the ancient culture of the self, thus, aims to produce a kind of prehistory through figures such as Socrates and Alcibiades or Seneca and Lucilius of a variety of later, equally famous couples: penitent and confessor, patient and psychiatrist, analysand and analyst (Foucault 2009: 9).

There are three basic elements to Foucault's history of truth: forms of knowledge, that are to be studied in terms of the specificity of how they articulate and validate truth; relations of power through which human beings and their institutions govern themselves and others; and the constitution of the subject of discourse through practices of the self. One of the common caricatures of Foucault, as we saw in Nussbaum's objections in Chapter 3, is that he reduces all knowledge to power (cf. Anderson 1993: 152). He specifically denies that charge at the beginning of this course, and his specification of these three elements is essential to understanding his response (Foucault 2009: 10; Kelly 2014: 88): for while there is no knowledge without power, and power cannot be exercised without both practical knowledge and a claim to truth, every form of knowledge is a complex combination of these three analytical elements that cannot exist in isolation from one another. Consider the Delphic oracle. Although the *testimonia* vary and the practices no doubt changed over its long history, the prophecies generally followed a specific format. A question was posed to the Pythia. She gave a response to the attendant priests. They transcribed it into Greek hexameters, which were given to the person posing the question. The prophecies themselves were often ambiguous and had to be interpreted by the postulants. Thus, there were specific forms of speech and validation inherent to the kind of truth produced. Those forms did not exist in a vacuum. There was an entire temple economy at Delphi, including the shrines and treasures provided by the various Greek and non-Greek states that consulted and accepted the authority of the oracle. These were forms of institutional power without which this production of truth could not exist. Finally, each person within this drama of truth had to undergo a specific preparation. The Pythia was a woman who served for life and remained sexually chaste throughout her service. The priests were trained and had to maintain standards of ritual purity. The postulant must bring a gift and should adhere to the two admonitions inscribed on the shrine, "know yourself" and "nothing to excess." Change these elements and the system collapses and must reform itself around different protocols. The knowledge produced by this system, then, is never simply an epiphenomenon or a ruse of power, but it is also never separate from it.

Consider an example from modern science, specifically behaviorist psychology. First, you have a set of theoretical and epistemological postulates about what counts as observable reality for the discipline of psychology and, thus, what counts as knowledge. Theories of what constitute positive and negative reinforcement and the various ways behaviors can be manipulated by them underlie this research. Propositions are then validated as true by demonstrating through simulations the effectiveness of these schedules of reinforcement, often through animal studies. Thus Professor Leonard Green at Washington University today continues a tradition of studying the effects of delaying and discounting rewards on human and animal behaviors through studying pigeons and claiming thereby to draw conclusions applicable to human economic behavior.[2] This form of truth would have appeared no more obvious to a fifth-century Athenian than the Delphic oracle would to Professor Green. His research, moreover, takes place within a highly complex set of institutional power relations involving the internal constitution of laboratories with their hierarchies and equipment, the universities in which they reside, the journals and professional societies that publish and validate the results of such experimental work, granting agencies that fund the work, and political institutions that fund the granting agencies. Lastly, there must be a rigorous process of individual formation that is required before one can assume the status of a person qualified to speak this sort of truth in an institutional setting. This requires a doctoral degree, acquiring and retaining a university position, exhibiting appropriate standards of professional decorum and collegiality, appropriate behavior, dress, sexual habits, and speech. The fact that none of this is natural can be shown by the reactions of others when one breeches these standards, which is not to say that they are arbitrary or capricious.

All of these elements have a complex history that can be studied. None of this means that there is no such thing as truth, that truth does not refer to things that are real, or that truth is merely a ruse for power. It does mean that truth is never simple, never self-evident, and always constructed within history and between people and their institutions (cf. Foucault 1971: 23, 37; 1975: 34–6; 2012a: 239).

Different modes of truth-telling exist simultaneously within cultures and sometimes within institutions. Anyone who has worked inside a large university is only too aware of this. The same is true of the ancient world. Foucault identifies four fundamental modes of truth-telling operative in the ancient Mediterranean: prophecy, wisdom, instruction, and *parrhēsia*. These correspond to: an enigmatic mode of revelation; a second mode that seeks to demonstrate what is being, nature, and the order of things; a mode that seeks to transmit established bodies of knowledge and know-how; and a polemical mode that asserts the truth concerning individuals and situations. We may argue whether this logical schema covers all possibilities, but it is coherent and examples of all four of these modes can be pointed to, sometimes within the same work. If we consider a text like the *Phaedrus*, it clearly combines demonstrations of the nature of love and rhetoric, practical instruction on speech writing, imaginative utterances in the prophetic mode, and arguably a polemical position in relation to Lysias and other professional speechwriters. Foucault argues that Greco-Roman culture tends to want to join the parrhesiatic mode with that of wisdom, so that if we consider the *Alcibiades*, Plato's *Seventh Letter*, or Seneca's *Letters to Lucilius*, all three combine philosophical demonstrations with modes of discourse in which the addressees are confronted with truths that range from the mildly discomfiting to the frankly dangerous. The philosophical master, unlike the prophet, must speak in his own name, and unlike the sophist, who merely passes along a technique, must believe what he teaches and directly address his charge.

There is nothing necessary about this ancient pairing of philosophy and *parrhēsia*, however. Within Medieval Christianity, the parrhesiastic mode is more commonly identified with the prophetic, as the great preachers of the time indicted their listeners for their sins while evoking the last judgment and the end of days. Wisdom, on the other hand, within the great Medieval universities became identified with teaching, with the transmission of knowledge and authority. In the modern world, Foucault remains more cautious, emphasizing that a fuller analysis needs to be undertaken, but he suggests that most often we see the prophetic mode joined with the discourse of politics and revolution, while philosophy has become the mode that attempts to speak the truth of Being, and science largely replaces that of instruction. As for *parrhēsia*, he suggest that in the modern world it ceases to have a clearly identified separate existence, but can be recognized in revolutionary indictments of the existing state of things, in philosophical reflections on ethics and our conception of the human, and in science when it assumes the form of the criticism of existing prejudices or dominant institutions (Foucault 2009: 27–30; Rajchman 1991: 129).

More specifically, Foucault argues, every act of truth-telling within philosophy, from ancient Greece to the present, is organized around three poles that govern the different modes of truth-telling: *aletheia*, or the truth of the enunciation itself; *politeia*, or the structures of power and governance in which the act of truth is formulated; and *ēthos*, the individual's self-constitution as the moral subject of his conduct and hence as a speaker of truth (Foucault 2009: 62). Philosophy as a form of life, from Greece to the present, he argues exists at the nexus of these three poles, so that one cannot pose the question of truth without simultaneously posing the question of governmentality and of the subject. Nonetheless, that does not mean there are no distinctions of genre within philosophical discourse as it has come down to us. Thus, philosophy as a form of instruction, specifically the way it is taught within the modern university, emphasizes the separation of these poles rather than their interdependence, cordoning them off into the disciplines of logic, political philosophy, and ethics (Foucault 2009: 63–4). Foucault, then, goes on to argue in a manner reminiscent of his more structural phase, in works such as *Les mots et les choses*, that each of the four modes of veridiction outlined above can be situated within these three poles and that together they define the different aspects of philosophical discourse. In the prophetic mode, thus, the discourse of philosophy envisions, not those poles' separation but their future coincidence, whether we are talking about Kalipolis in the *Republic*, the ideal realization of the Roman mixed constitution in Cicero's *De Republica*, or the end of class struggle in the *Communist Manifesto*. In the utopian future, there is no separation between truth, the form of our politics, and our ethical substance. In the mode of wisdom, however, philosophy would be the discourse that prescribes the truth of *ēthos* and *politeia*, endowing them with their "real" or "true" meaning, decreeing what constitutes justice, authenticity, and good faith. This is the philosopher as mandarin. Finally, the parrhesiastic mode in philosophy would inquire into the political and ethical conditions of truth (Foucault 2009: 64–5). "It is the discourse of the irreducibility of truth and at the same time the discourse of their necessary relation, of the impossibility from wherever one stands to think seriously about truth (*alētheia*), power (*politeia*), and *ēthos* without thinking about their fundamental, essential interrelation" (Foucault 2009: 65). *Parrhēsia* is thus always a challenge to existing power structures and not just those we would label authoritarian.

In the lecture leading up to this schema of the three poles of truth-telling within which the four different forms operate, Foucault observes in a reading of the *Athenian Constitution*, long erroneously attributed to Xenophon, that there is a fundamental incompatibility between democracy and *parrhēsia*'s critical discourse of truth. This topic had been touched upon in the previous year's reading of political *parrhēsia* in Euripides' *Ion* and the ensuing discussion of the problem of rhetoric in democracy. If the rhetorician is like the flatterer, the pastry chef in the *Gorgias* who tells the assembled citizens what they want to hear, offering them cakes when they require bitter gall, then a parrhesiast like Socrates has little chance to wake the city from its slumber. In the political thought of the Old Oligarch, as the author of the *Athenian Constitution* is often called today, but also in the work of many other ancient authors, there is a fundamental division between the many (*hoi polloi*) and the few (*hoi oligoi*), which is overlaid with a cognate distinction between the bad (*hoi kakoi*) and the good (*hoi agathoi*) or the best (*hoi aristoi*) (Foucault 2009: 43–4).³

On one level, this is a division based on class and on the resentments of a displaced aristocratic elite in relation to a rising democratic citizen body, much as Nietzsche narrates in the *The Genealogy of Morals* (1956). On another, while there is within this aristocratic literature of reaction a direct conflict between the way in which *ēthos* is understood (*kakos/agathos*) and the functioning of the democratic *politeia*, the territory on which this conflict takes place and on which it continues to be fought even today is that of truth, and the discourse of truth cannot but have both a certain tension with and requirement for democracy. For truth to function as *truth* rather than as propaganda or rhetorical manipulation, it can never be perfectly coincident with either political power or ethical substance. We do not vote on scientific truth. Our preferences about the reality of climate change or chemotherapy carry little weight in the determinations of truth in such matters (cf. Plato, *Laches* 184d5–e10). Nonetheless, there is a simultaneous necessity of democratic guarantees of *isonomia*, *isēgoria*, and *parrhēsia* for truth to retain its critical function, to exist *qua* truth. There can be no understanding of true discourse outside of *isēgoria*, except in the prophetic mode or in the form of a proclamation of a pure coincidence between power and truth (I am the king, the leader of the party, I speak the truth), neither of which offers a space from which the parrhesiast or the philosopher can speak. Nonetheless, the truth cannot be decided upon simply by the voices of the many without it again ceasing to be indistinguishable from power. Democratic truth, then, always depends on this contradiction that discourse must be open, everyone must have the right to speak, but only some discourses can be true, and they must present themselves first through the parrhesiastic act of direct personal engagement (I must believe what I say), and then through claims to validation whether that be through direct knowledge (like the shepherd in *Oedipus*), appeals to reason (like Socrates or Aristotle in the *Rhetoric*), or agreed upon protocols of verification: all forms of discourse that are themselves not democratic *per se* but either modes of wisdom, instruction, or *parrhēsia* (Foucault 2009: 45–6). It is this parrhesiastic intervention that Foucault hopes to reclaim for philosophy in the present as a critical discourse in relation to forms of governmentality, and Socrates is his primary model.

## II

> I would have done something terrible, men of Athens, if when the commanders had assigned me my place in the line—commanders whom you chose to lead me—at the battles of Potidaea, Amphipolis, and Delium, I had remained where those men assigned me, and just like any other I had run the risk of death, but when the god commanded me, as I thought and understood, to live by philosophizing and by testing myself and others, I should then leave the line, fearing death or anything else.
>
> *Apology* 28d10–29a1

> Perhaps someone may say, "Would you not be able to live (*zēn*), Socrates, once you have left us, being silent and keeping quiet?" This is the most difficult thing of all to persuade some of you. For if I say that this is to disobey the god and therefore it is impossible to keep quiet, you will not believe me and think I am being ironic. If I say it happens to be the greatest good for a human being to spend each day making arguments and testing others about virtue and the other things you hear me talking about, and that the unexamined life is not livable for a human being, you will believe me even less.
>
> *Apology* 37e3–38a6

During the last three years of Foucault's lectures at the Collège de France, Socrates served as the archetype of the philosopher as parrhesiast. He is omnipresent in these courses. The Platonic dialogues on which Foucault concentrated—the *Alcibiades*, the *Apology*, and in this final year, the *Crito*, the *Phaedo* and the *Laches*—were focused on Socrates. But he is present in other guises as well. His conduct was the explicit model for Plato in his confrontation with Dionysius in the *Seventh Letter*. Socrates was the key figure in Hadot's concept of ancient philosophy as spiritual practice. Even the Stoics considered themselves heirs to the Socratic tradition, as did the Cynics with whom Foucault closes this year's lectures. In 1984, however, when Foucault is sick and knows he is dying, he increasingly models himself on the Socrates of the *Apology*, unwilling to retreat from the post Apollo has assigned him, asking only how much time he has.

Socrates is an historically important figure, Foucault argues, because he combines and understands the traditional modes of truth-telling in a new way. Take the example of the Delphic oracle. As Foucault observes, normally one consults the oracle about a specific concern and then receives an answer, which must be interpreted. There follows a period between the postulant's interpretation and what happens in the real that either confirms or overturns that interpretation. Thus, Herodotus tells us in the *Histories* (1.85–9) that Croesus, king of Lydia, sent to the oracle to determine whether he should make war on Cyrus, king of the Persians. The answer came back that if Croesus fights this war a great empire will fall. Taking heart from this, he immediately prepared for war with the Persians, which led to the destruction of his empire. Only too late does he recognize his misunderstanding. Socrates' approach to the oracle is very different. His friend, Chaerephon, had gone to the oracle to ask if there was anyone wiser than Socrates, and the Pythia had responded "no one." Unlike Croesus, however, Socrates does not immediately offer an interpretation, let alone one which, like the Lydian king's, assumes the most favorable interpretation. Instead, Socrates tries to disprove its veracity. At the same time, he understands that testing the oracle borders on impiety, since it implies the god is a liar. He is in aporia:

> I was conscious of being wise (*sophos*) in nothing, either great or small. So what did he mean saying I am the wisest? For indeed he does not lie. That is not right. And for a long time I was at a loss (*ēporoun*) as to what he meant. And then, with great hesitancy, I turned to such an investigation (*zētēsin*) of the god. And I went to one of those who seemed to be wise in order to refute the prophecy and show the oracle that "this man is wiser, but you said I was."
> 
> 21b5–c2

Thus begins Socrates' investigation of the god and a new chapter as the gadfly of Athens, roaming the streets and interrogating whoever makes a claim to wisdom or knowledge. In each case, however, Socrates shows that while the politicians, the poets, and the artisans all seem wise, they, in fact, cannot give an account of themselves and their knowledge, and even when they truly do know a craft, like the artisans, they mistake this knowledge for a wisdom of general applicability. Socrates knows no more than these men except in one respect. He recognizes his ignorance. At length, Socrates concludes that in this alone, recognizing the limits of his own knowledge, he is wiser than the men he encounters, and therefore his mission is to keep questioning himself and others, so that each of us may come to know ourselves, care for ourselves, and seek wisdom. In this way, Socrates transforms the traditional enigmatic oracular pronouncement of a truth yet to be realized into a proposition to be tested over and over again within a set of discursive interactions whereby statements are shown to be either true or false by logical means and the mutual agreement of the interlocutors (Foucault 2009: 76). This process of question and answer, often leading to aporia and the recognition of ignorance, is commonly known as the *elenchus*, the Socratic process of examination and refutation (cf., *Theaetetus* 210a–d; *Sophist* 230a–d; Hadot 1995: 103; Szlezák 1999: 7; Nehamas 1998: 82–5; Blondell 2002: 124; Hunter 2004: 86–7).

If Socrates is not a practitioner of truth in the traditional oracular mode, he is also not a wise man (*sophos*). Unlike the Pythagoreans or the Pre-Socratics, he does not offer speculations on the nature of heaven and earth, even if he indicates that when younger he was interested in such matters. He has no esoteric doctrine that he passes on to adherents for a fee or after a set of initiation rites. His spiritual practice is the search for truth and the care of the self it entails. Lastly, he is not a teacher in the classic mode. Despite accusations to the contrary, he neither accepts money nor does he profess to pass on specific techniques of speaking, law-making, or other skills.

> I was never anyone's teacher. If someone should wish to listen to me speaking and practicing my way of life, whether young or old, I never begrudge it, nor do I only converse with those who pay, but all the same I offer myself for questioning to rich and poor and if anyone answering should wish to listen to what I might say.
>
> 33a5–b4

Socrates scrambles the traditional roles and places the philosopher in a fundamentally new position as a truth-teller, a truth that is not a skill, a form of traditional or scientific wisdom, or an oracular pronouncement. Rather, it is a truth that turns the gaze of the listener back upon the self and the work to be done. "Socrates says, I don't know anything, and if I pay attention to you it is not to transmit to you the knowledge you lack, it is so that once you understand you know nothing, you can learn from that and pay attention to yourself" (Foucault 2009: 82).

Foucault identifies three stages in Socratic practice: research (*zētēsis*), examination (*exetasis*), and care (*epimeleia*). There is the initial encounter, such as when Socrates sets out to understand the oracle; the testing, when he questions those who seem to be wise; and the care, both of himself and of those willing to listen and recognize their own ignorance (Foucault 2009: 80). The testing itself involves not only the *elenchus*, but also, and perhaps more profoundly as indicated by the *Alcibiades*, an encounter with the soul of Socrates. In the process of questioning and reaching aporia, the soul of the interlocutor comes to see itself reflected in the soul of Socrates, comes to realize that its knowledge, its awareness of itself and its place in the world is being tested by this encounter and this moment of reflection. Socrates functions both as a mirror, but also as a touchstone, a way of examining the self in terms of its own judgment (*phronēsis*), truth (*alētheia*), and soul (*psukhē*) (29e1–2; Foucault 2009: 77–9, 119).

Of course, as we know, this encounter with our reflection, this testing of ourselves in the presence of another can be discomfiting and often provokes resistance. Socrates was executed. People do not enjoy having their certainties disrupted (Foucault 2009: 131). One of the dialogues on which Foucault concentrates in these final lectures is the *Laches*. Its subject matter is generally considered to be courage (*andreia*), but this is not Foucault's primary interest. He is more concerned with questions of method. In the dialogue two gentlemen, Lysimachus and Melisias, want to know if their sons should be trained in the art of fighting in full armor. They run into two well-known generals, Nicias and Laches, and ask their opinion. The generals come down on opposite sides. Socrates, however, is with them and is asked to decide the question. He immediately points out the fallacy of Lysimachus and Melisias relying on a majority vote for answering such a question and pushes the discussion to another level: how does one decide on good teachers for young men and what should those teachers know? Everyone agrees that Nicias and Laches are in fact experts on the matter in question and in order to clarify how best the sons of Lysimachus and Melisias can be trained so as to exhibit excellence both for their households and the city, it is decided that the two generals will submit themselves to questioning by Socrates.

Laches, who is familiar with Socrates' methods, observes that the discussion will not limit itself to the question of how the youth may best be trained, let alone whether fighting in hoplite armor is the best method for doing so. Instead, Socrates, as is his wont, will soon turn the focus of conversation to the being of his interlocutor, requiring him to give an account of how he lives (*zēi*) his life (*bios*) and causing him to be tested by Socrates in the same way a coin is tested for its metallic content by a touchstone (*basanos*), a process that like the *tribē* of the *Seventh Letter* involves a salutary friction, which can prove unpleasant (Foucault 2009: 133–5).

> You do not seem to know that whoever may be closest to and enters into conversation with Socrates, must, even if he will have begun talking about something else, not stop being led along in the argument before he has fallen into giving an account (*logon*) of himself, of the manner in which he lives (*zēi*), and of the kind of life he has lived (*bion bebiōken*) to this point. Whenever that happens, Socrates will not release him before he has questioned/tested (*basanisē*)[4] him with respect to all these things well and truly. I am accustomed to this, and I know that it is necessary to suffer these things from this man, and I know well that I will still suffer them: for I rejoice, Lysimachus, in approaching him, and I think there is no harm in being reminded that we have not done or are not doing something properly, but looking forward then to the rest of your life (*bion*) it is necessary to avoid these things and wish according to Solon's saying, and judging it worthy, to learn as long as one lives (*zēi*) and not to think old age brings understanding. And so there is nothing unaccustomed or unpleasant to me to be tested (*basanizesthai*) by Socrates.
>
> *Laches* 187e6–188b5

Nicias replies that while he has not engaged in such conversations with Socrates, he enjoys listening to people offering arguments or accounts on how one can render one's life in tune with one's deeds (*ton bion sumphōnon*, 188d5) and that he is familiar with Socrates' deeds and finds him worthy of fine words and complete frankness (*logōn kalōn kai pasēs parrhēsias*, 189a1). Thus, the encounter with Socrates is a moment of testing, an examination of how one lives one's life within the game of truth, in which Socrates serves as the touchstone (*basanos*) that, through the use of *parrhēsia* or uncompromising honesty, causes the interlocutor to take themselves as an object of care. This, as Foucault observes, is not the political *parrhēsia* examined in the *Ion*, but an ethical *parrhēsia* whose primary object is our *bios* or "existence" (Foucault 2009: 84, 138–9).

The untested life is not livable for a human being. It is not indeed a life, but a realm of slumber and illusion, of false comforts, because we fail to examine what we have done or how things could be done better. The language in the

*Laches* anticipates Seneca's daily examination of conscience. This testing, as with *tribē* in the *Seventh Letter*, is the essence of the ancient philosophic life according to Foucault. He goes on to point out that Socrates argues to Crito in the dialogue of the same name, that the soul or "that part of us in which there is injustice and justice" is corrupted by the false. False opinions are those that will not withstand critical examination, opinions that are opposed therefore to "the truth." In this specific case, the false opinion is Crito's recommendation that Socrates follow the advice of the many (*hoi polloi*) and take advantage of Crito's resources to escape Athens and elude execution. Socrates rejects this suggestion and holds his place in the line, where the god has placed him, in the face of certain death (47d7–48b1; Foucault 2009: 95–6, 100–1).

False opinions, Plato has Socrates maintain elsewhere, are a kind of disease. They require the strong medicine of the *elenchus* and the frank friend, not the honeyed discourse of the flatterer or the pastry chef, even when it initially leaves a bitter taste. Foucault observes that in the *Phaedo* (89a5) Socrates is said to "cure" (*iasto*) his listeners through the elenchus (Foucault 2009: 98–9). Simmias and Cebes, two Pythagoreans, had just offered substantial arguments against Socrates' theory of the immortality of the soul. The interlocutors are deflated. Phaedo then recounts:

> Often I have wondered at and admired Socrates, but never more than then. The fact that he had a response was perhaps nothing strange. But I wondered first at how sweetly, good naturedly, and admirably he accepted these young men's arguments, and then at how sharply he perceived what we suffered from these arguments, and lastly how well he cured (*iasto*) us, and called us back who were defeated and in retreat, and turned us toward attending to and examining the argument.
>
> 88e4–89a7

It is thus no accident, Foucault argues, that Socrates says at the *Phaedo*'s end, moments before his death, that he and Crito owe (*opheilomen*) a cock to Asclepius for having been cured of their disease (118a7–8), which Foucault interprets as opinions that corrupt the soul (Foucault 2009: 103–4). Foucault with this interpretation marks a significant divergence from the standard reading of the passage and instead follows a suggestion made by Dumézil. Socrates, in fact, does not specify the malady or the precise cure. The general assumption has been that Socrates is speaking of his impending death as the cure for his disease, that his soul will be cured once it is free of the body, and there are passages in the first part of the dialogue that could support this interpretation, where the body is portrayed as a kind of prison and philosophy is termed a preparation for death (64a5–6). Moreover, as Foucault acknowledges, this is a reading shared by both Robin in his Budé and Burnet in his Oxford edition (Foucault 2009: 89–90; Burnet 1911: 147; Robin 1926: 102), and it has been supported more recently by Rowe (1993: 295–6). But for Foucault, the *locus classicus* of this traditional reading is the *Gay Science*, where Nietzsche exclaims in paragraph 340 of the fourth book, "this ridiculous and terrible last word means for those who have ears: 'O Crito, life is a disease!'" (Nietzsche 1974: 272). Such an interpretation was not a problem for the Catholic Robin, assured as he was of Christian immortality, and Burnet expresses no similar anxiety. But for Nietzsche, if the dying Socrates' last wish was to pronounce a malediction on life, if real life and health could be found only through death, it was an intolerable betrayal of the forces of vitality to the sickness that for Nietzsche was epitomized by the Christian embrace of death. It would represent an inversion of all that was affirmative in Greek culture and would situate philosophy at the origin of our civilization's obsession with asceticism and self-denial and so must be rejected. Yet for every passage in Nietzsche excoriating Socrates and Plato as the origins of our modern malaise, there are others expressing admiration. In the end, Nietzsche has a conflicted and deeply ambivalent relation to Socrates, Plato, and philosophy itself (Nietzsche 1956: 93–94; 2013: 94; Kofman 1986: 169, 234; 1989: 58, 293–318; Zuckert 1996: 25; Geuss 2017: 182–4).[5]

If Foucault, however, were to show there were another way to read the end of the *Phaedo*, then it would be possible to redeem both Socrates and Plato, which in many ways is the project Foucault has undertaken these last three years. This alternative interpretation, as we have seen, is to claim that Socrates is cured of false opinions—and, perhaps more importantly, Crito is said to be cured of the same, since he, unlike Socrates, is not about to die, though he too is said to owe the cock to Asclepius.[6] According to Foucault's interpretation, both Crito and Socrates, through the use of the *elenchus*, through Socrates' testing of himself and others, like a touchstone, have been cured of counterfeit or false opinions that corrupt the soul by leading it to despise argument, despair of knowledge, and to live in fear. Thus, shortly after the passage quoted above, when Socrates' arguments for the immortality of the soul seem to have run aground, he "cures" his interlocutors not by offering an incontrovertible proof of the soul's immortality, but by recommitting to the argument itself, by recommitting to a life, and when the time comes, to a death dedicated to making, examining, and testing arguments, to a life and a death that are examined and fully conscious (Foucault 2009: 98–9).

> Let us beware of this and not allow into our soul that no arguments are sound, but rather we do not yet possess them soundly, and we must be courageous and turn our attention to having them, for you and for the others, for the sake of your whole life, and for me, for the sake of my very death, since I risk presently in this very matter not acting like a lover of wisdom but like those poorly educated people who care only about winning an argument.
> 
> 90d4–91a3

It is for this life and this death that Crito and Socrates owe a debt of thanks to the healing god through whose intervention they have gained the ability to care for themselves and to take as the specific object of their care their *bios*, their life, and not just their death as Nietzsche lamented. Indeed, Socrates' life is described by Plato as anything but a malady. Rather, as Foucault himself observes, throughout the cycle of dialogues concerned with the death of Socrates, the *Apology*, the *Crito*, and the *Phaedo*, his is the perfect philosophic life. He spends each day in conversation on matters of virtue, testing himself and others. He is not troubled by greed, ambition, or the fear of death. "This unpolluted and pure life that is Socrates', how could you conceive it as being a sickness?" (Foucault 2009: 92).

It is this life, this *bios*, in turn that is the object of our care in dialogues such as the *Laches* (Gros 2012: 161–2). At the end of the *Laches*, after Socrates has demonstrated that neither Nicias nor Laches is able adequately to define courage (*andreia*) or its role in virtue (*aretē*), it is proposed that Lysimachus and Melesias turn their sons over to Socrates for training as the one who knows best how to care for the young (*tōn meirakiōn epimeleisthai*, 200c8). But Socrates, while eager to participate in the betterment of the youth, insists that he is the master of no *tekhnē* that will simply allow knowledge to be passed from him to the young men, as if it were a possession or a form of rote knowledge such as how to mend a broken pot or train a dog.

> If in our dialogue just now I had appeared to know, and these other two did not, then it would truly be just to invite me to this work, but now nonetheless we were all at a loss (*aporiai*) ... but since things are thus, examine what I think is best to advise you. For I say it is necessary—for there is no argument we can simply extract—that we all in common seek a teacher for especially ourselves concerning what is best—for we need one—and then for the young, sparing neither money nor anything else. I do not advise that we allow ourselves to be as we are now ... Let us in common act to take care (*epimeleian*) of ourselves and the young.
>
> 200e2–201b5

They agree to meet at Lysimachus's house at dawn to discuss how young and old may learn these things together in dialogue with Socrates, who will once again serve as the proof, the touchstone by which we test ourselves. He will not be lacking in the mission assigned to him by the god, "to spend each day making arguments and testing others about virtue" (Foucault 2009: 141–2).

At the end of his reading of the *Laches*, Foucault pulls back to make an explicit comparison with his earlier reading of the *Alcibiades*. If in the *Alcibiades* the self that is cared for is identified with the soul (*psukhē*), to distinguish the self from its possessions—as the cobbler is neither his tools nor the hands that wield them—the *Laches* does not make any such metaphysical claims. In it, the object of testing and care is the *bios* itself, which Foucault translates as "existence" (2009: 147–8). Whereas the *psukhē* assumes a substance or configuration that can be isolated, the *bios* merely names a mode of life or existence that can be shaped, given a form or style. To do so, one must take one's existence as an object of knowledge. One must imagine it as it exists for yourself and others, both in life and after death and as you would have it exist. Is this how you want to be received and to be remembered? Is this an existence you would find admirable. Or to return to Horace, that most Socratic of Roman poets:

> And may you forgive the modest vices by which I am held.
> Perhaps, long life, a frank friend, or my own counsel will free me from them
>   in large part.
> For when I lie on my couch or stroll in my portico, I am not absent from
>   myself.
> "This is more correct; doing that, I would live better; thus I would be welcome

To my friends; this is not pleasingly done; would I ever foolishly do anything
Like he did?" I turn these things over with myself, lips sealed.
*Satires* 1.4.130–6

Thus, while we generally associate a certain Platonic metaphysics of the soul with the Socratic care of the self, and Foucault readily admits that this strand of Socratico-Platonic thought would become dominant, nonetheless those metaphysical assumptions are not inherent to the gesture of caring for the self, any more than the concern with the shape of your existence renders you a bloodless aesthete or an apolitical dandy. Rather, Foucault would argue, there can be no ethics that does not care for the nature, form, and quality of the self (*ēthos*) it seeks to produce, and this concern finds it first theoretical expression in the Socratic dialogues of Plato. "This aesthetics of existence is an essential historic object that must not be forgotten to the advantage either of a metaphysics of the soul or an aesthetics of words and things" (Foucault 2009: 150).

Most importantly, though, it is an aesthetics of truth. Socrates never says do what you wish, follow your wildest caprice, be a hypocrite and coward—nor do Horace, Seneca, Plutarch, Kant, or Baudelaire. The aesthetics of existence is not a cry that all is permitted. It is an admonition to care for yourself and others, to submit your existence to the *logos*, to reasoned discourse and self-testing, to produce a life that is accountable, defensible, and admirable. It is perplexing that we would feel shame or have difficulty granting a substantial aesthetic dimension to our ethical and political pursuits. This difficulty says more about our conflicted relation to pleasure than about ancient philosophy's understanding of *to kalon* as an aspect of *to agathon* or about Foucault's Nietzschean "irresponsibility."

The admirable existence was always for Plato as for Foucault a true existence, and its fearless commitment to truth is what primarily accounts for the tension between Plato's advocacy of a Socratic form of *parrhēsia*, as portrayed in the *Apology*, and Athenian democracy (Foucault 2009: 205). The Socratic admonition to care for the self always involves a commitment to the courage of truth—the title of Foucault's final course—to *parrhēsia*, and to the combatting of false opinion, even unto death. What Foucault means by "truth" in this context, and what he argues Plato means as well, is something akin to Heidegger's notion of *alētheia* as the "unhidden" (see Chapter 1). The *logos alēthēs* is not one that hides its intentions. It is not alloyed with a foreign obscuring element (Foucault 2009: 201–2). It is not the speech of the *rhētor* who says what he believes his audience, whether prince or people, wants to hear, so as to sway that audience.

The *logos alēthēs* like the parrhesiast is self-identical, and thus in its fullest, ideal form, is incorruptible and a thing of beauty, an object of admiration. It would represent—again, in its fullest, most aspirational form—a transcendental signified, a form of meaning that is unchanging and capable of investing existence with significance. This is a notion not far removed from the Stoic idea of the identification of the sage with reason and nature itself, but it is equally cognate with Kant's categorical imperative, "Act only according to that maxim whereby you can, at the same time, will that it should become a universal law" (1993: 30). The *logos alēthēs* is incompatible with the citizen who demands to be told what he wants to hear or the politician who panders to those desires. It is equally incompatible with the sycophantic counselors and flatterers with whom princes and tyrants surround themselves (Foucault 2009: 203–4). And it is here that the full force of Socratic irony makes itself felt, not in the person of the parrhesiast confronting his audience—whether citizen, king, or student—with a truth it prefers not to hear, but in leading people through the *elenchus* to recognize that their words are neither consistent with themselves or their deeds. Socrates' irony reveals to his interlocutors that they cannot yet account for their lives, that their life possesses no *alēthēs logos* and thus they need, often in spite of themselves, to care for themselves and to strive to give themselves a *bios* livable for a human being, a form of life that is admirable and true (Foucault 2009: 215).

## III

In this West that has invented so many different truths and such multiple arts of existence, Cynicism does not stop reminding us that only a small amount of truth is necessary for whoever wishes to live truly and that only a small life is necessary when one truly grasps the truth.

Foucault 2009: 175

Nietzsche … inquired what possibilities Cynicism could offer beyond its historical uniqueness and past: possible modes of living; moral possibilities, particularly the problematization and critique of of morals; possibilities of shedding light on morals; possibilities of an enlightened personal style critical of morals; rhetorical-literary and polemical possibilities. Eventually he adopted all these possibilities of Cynicism, and finally he emphatically declared his allegiance to "Cynicism."

Niehues-Pröbsting 1996: 354

In Foucault's last three lectures, he turned to the Cynics. At a time when he was increasingly frail, he spoke of these ancient philosophers who, like the Platonists traced their lineage to Socrates, but who refused to accumulate a body of doctrine and who, according to tradition, lived their lives in the public square, who begged, ate scraps, and masturbated in public. The Cynics were the "dogs" of philosophy. They were the street corner preachers who confronted us with our conformity, our petty hypocrisies, our dishonesties (Goulet-Cazé 2017: 280–1, 359). Their bodies themselves were a locus of truth and a challenge to complacency (Branham 1996: 100–1). Foucault in his penultimate lecture says:

> Cynicism was not simply a crude, insolent, and rudimentary reminder of the problem of the philosophic life. It posed a very important question, or rather, it seems to me, it gave its position on the theme of the philosophic life by posing the following question: life, in order truly to be the life of truth, should it not be an other life, radically and paradoxically other?
>
> 2009: 226

This call for a radical otherness, as defined by the Platonic spark or the Cynic provocation, is at the center of the final Foucault, and it is this same call that retains its relevance to the present. In the end, what is most authentic is not the infinitely reproducible, a data set that is self-identical, but the moment of irreducible insight, of queer intelligibility, which makes possible a form of self-relation and of relation to others that is based on curiosity and care, one which opens new possibilities of self-invention and resistance, new forms of truth. Thus at the end of his lecture notes, Foucault writes, "But to finish what I want to insist on is this: there is no instilling of truth without an essential position of alterity: truth is never the same; there can only be truth in the form of another world, another life" (2009: 311). He did not have time to deliver these lines, however. Instead, the last words his audience heard were simply, "Well then, listen. I had some things to tell you concerning the general framework of these analyses. But, in the end, it's too late. So, thank you" (2009: 309). And it is perhaps to this final spirit of care, gratitude, and humility that we owe our greatest debt: his simple and moving commitment to the "courage of truth."

In this section, I want to focus on three areas: Cynic *parrhēsia*; Cynic *askēsis* or practice of the body; and the "true life," *alēthēs bios*, of Cynic philosophy as a transhistoric form of life and method of resistance. We should, however, start with a brief acknowledgment of the power of Foucault's reading. Marie-Odile Goulet-Cazé, one of the world's foremost scholars on Cynic philosophy, writes:

> Foucault has done more than offer an accurate reading of Cynic philosophy in its essence: he has given it a brilliant reception ... In effect, rather than envisage Cynicism as a philosophy of the past, whose message he must try to find by patiently reconstituting a puzzle of fragments, he has appropriated the Cynics for the present combat, because the life of struggle led by the "enthusiasts of virtue" ... joins up with the idea that was very dear to him of a philosophical militance.
>
> Goulet-Cazé 2017: 544

In short, Foucault not only offers us a convincing reading of the Cynics, in spite or maybe even because of the poor state of the evidence, but he also offers a reason why we should care, a reason why the Cynics should matter to us in their militance of truth (Goulet-Cazé 2017: 543; Gros 2009: 322).

In 1982's the *Hermeneutics of the Subject*, Foucault framed *parrhēsia*, "frank or open speech," as central to the relationship between the Stoic director of conscience and his disciple. It was a technique used by the master to engender a transformation of the disciple, making his self visible through the frank speech of the other. We might think of Persius's satires, which were designed to shock the reader out of their complacent sense of self-satisfaction (Foucault 2001a: 232, 362–3; Miller 2010; Gros 2012: 156–7). The following year Foucault focused primarily on the politics of *parrhēsia*. In 1984, however, his specific focus is on the philosopher as a speaker of truth, the philosopher as the person who had the courage to speak their truth to power, even in the face of scorn, ridicule, or death (Gros 2008: 352).

For Diogenes, the titular, if not actual, founder of the Cynic movement, *parrhēsia* is the most precious thing (*to kalliston*) a man possesses (Foucault 2009: 154; Goulet-Cazé 2017: 154). There are any number of anecdotes that illustrate this practice. Among the most famous is the following. One day

Diogenes was sunning himself. Alexander the Great approached him and admired his wisdom. He said, "ask me any favor you like." Diogenes replied, "Get out of my light" (D.L. 6.2.37). This refusal to recognize conventional authority was considered typical of Cynic speech. After the battle of Chaeronea, Diogenes was captured and presented to Philip of Macedon. When Philip asked him who he was, he replied, "a spy on your insatiable greed," for which he was rewarded with his freedom (D.L. 6.2.43). In each of these cases, Diogenes not only speaks fearlessly to the powerful but he speaks in a compressed and epigrammatic fashion an important truth: "You may hold great power, but you are just a man and you have no greater claim upon the things of this world than any other. Indeed, your belief that you do only demonstrates your delusion." Cynic *parrhēsia*, like its political cousin, not only speaks truth to power, it does so in a way that creates risk for the speaker. Unlike Plato before Dionysius or Alcibiades before the Assembly, Diogenes' goals are in no conventional sense political. Nonetheless, the Cynic parrhesiast is not just a speaker of truths but of unpalatable truths to which he binds his person. His speech is fundamentally different from the discourse of the impartial observer, who may speak the truth but incurs no necessary risk. The professional philosopher or classicist may fantasize that they are heroes of resistance, but we are much more mere technicians of discourse than Diogenes before Alexander or Plato before Dionysius (Goulet-Cazé 2017: 289–90, 295).

Diogenes' later heirs were well known for congregating on the street corners of Rome and other urban centers to harangue passersby. Their diatribes, which became the basis for much Roman satire (Bion was a Cynic), were frank often ridiculing speeches that provoked laughter in the surrounding crowd and forced the interlocutor to react (Branham and Goulet-Cazé 1996: 27; Branham 1996: 104; Griffin 1996: 200; Goulet-Cazé 2017: 346). The reaction was the point. Cynic *parrhēsia* as a philosophical practice was not designed to provide us with accurate information but to estrange ourselves from our own experience, and so to permit us to care for ourselves and thereby come to think differently (Branham 1996: 95). The Cynics' "courage of truth" invited condemnation and rejection even as they showed to their interlocutors that the principles by which they lived were not those they professed. "It is a question," Foucault writes, "of confronting their anger and of giving the image of what they both admit and valorize in their thought but reject and despise in their lives" (Foucault 2009: 215–26). Exposing us to our own cognitive dissonance is the Cynic's stock and trade.

Cynic philosophers, however, do not ply their trade only through their speech. Cynic philosophy is not merely a stand-up routine or a comic monologue, however biting it may be. The Cynics live this truth and profess it with their actions and their bodies. Cynic *parrhēsia* is inseparable from Cynic *askēsis*, which involves a complete transformation of the self by the self. The Cynic philosopher does not opine from the comfort of his country house on virtue, nature, or justice; he lives his truth in public. He makes his body an image of that truth. He eats in public, defecates in public, and has sex in public, not only to demonstrate the artificiality of the social conventions by which we veil the nature of our most basic acts but also to call each of us to account: in what ways are our modes of life a pretense, a sham, a lie? The very existence of the Cynic philosopher when he confronts us on the street is at once a confected provocation (there is really nothing more natural about defecating in the *agora* than behind a tree) and a challenge to our most deeply held but unexamined beliefs about the natural (*to kata phusin*) and the fine (*to kalon*) as well as the repulsive or abject (*to kakon*) (Goulet-Cazé 2017: 529, 530).

Thus for the Cynics, as Foucault notes, their mode of life and their commitment to *parrhēsia* are directly linked. The characteristics of that mode of life can be summed up simply. The Cynic carries his staff, upon which he can hang all his worldly possessions and bag in which he carries those possessions. He has no attachment to any place or any station, but wanders from place to place living off alms, a citizen of nowhere and of the entire universe (*kosmopolitēs*):

> In effect, if you want to keep watch over humanity and to tell it the truth, to tell it frankly and courageously all the dangers it runs the risk of encountering and where are its true enemies, for this, you have to be attached to nothing. To play the role of truth-teller and the one who rouses us from our slumbers, you have to be free of all attachments.
>
> Foucault 2009: 157–8

As Foucault underlines, this commitment to poverty and non-attachment is not just an abstract or spiritual commitment, as was the case for Seneca or the Epicureans, but involves actual material deprivation (Foucault 2009: 237). "The Cynic adopts a lifestyle that symbolizes his independence from the nonmoral values that enslave the majority of people" (Long 1996: 35). His job, as for any follower of Socrates, is to care for himself rather than his possessions and through his example teach others to do the same (Gros 2012: 164–5). Thus while we may analytically separate Cynic practices of life (*askēsis*) from the Cynic commitment to fearless speech (*parrhēsia*), in the way we might separate what a philosophy professor does with his life from what takes place in his classroom, for both the Cynics and Foucault, in the final analysis, no such distinction should be made, and both our lives and our speech will reflect each other for good or ill. As Diogenes writes in a passage cited from his *technē ēthikē*, "nothing succeeds in life without the practice [*askēsis*], and the practice is able to overcome all" (Goulet-Cazé 2017: 239 and 414, citing D.L. VI 71).

For the Cynic philosopher, then, the truth is visible on the surface of his or her body. It is not so much a question of making one's life conform to a pre-existing abstract rule as making "directly readable on the body the explosive and savage presence of a naked truth" (Gros 2012: 163). Thus, Foucault observes:

> To methodically develop in and through one's life the scandal of truth, this is what Cynicism practiced, beginning with its emergence in the fourth century, in the Hellenistic period, and continued to pursue to the end of the Roman empire and—as I would like to show—well beyond.
> 
> Foucault 2009: 160–1

For the Cynics and their heirs, truth is not merely a property of certain propositions, it is a *technē biou*, a particular form of life that of necessity not only includes veridiction but also makes the speaking of the truth possible (Gros 2012: 162–3).

The Cynic, then, for Foucault, is not the philosopher king, as we normally conceive him, but his parody: he is the carnival king who brings the high low and speaks the truth to power through contact with the body. The carnivalized king is the mad king, the beggar king, the king who is unrecognized by those in power. One of the figures Foucault uses to illustrate this point is Lear wondering in madness with his fool.

> King Lear after all begins with a story of *parrhēsia*, a test of frankness: who will speak the truth to the king? And King Lear is precisely the person who has not been able to recognize the truth where it is. And because of this

misrecognition of the truth, he in his turn is misrecognized ... In this in some ways political imagining of a misrecognized monarchy, I believe Cynicism played a great role.

Foucault 2009: 263; cf. Kinney 1996: 302

The Cynic, then, does not address himself to an elite group of cognoscenti or guardians but, like Lear, he wonders the desolate landscape in seeming madness speaking truths unwelcome and unrecognized by others, even as his initial failure to recognize the most basic truths in himself is what casts him into the darkness. The Cynic, with his staff, his pack, and simple cloak addresses all men and tells them that the life they think they lead is an illusion, that their pleasures are not real, their possessions are not theirs, and their desires deluded, and through this often unwelcome and misunderstood speech it becomes possible for another world to be imagined, and it is that new world that "ought," Foucault tells us, "to constitute the objective of Cynic practice" (Foucault 2009: 288).

The Cynic is engaged in a kind of spiritual combat. It is a combat with himself, as he seeks to wrest control of his appetites and his passions through the *askēsis*, and a combat against the customs, conventions, and institutions of daily life that cause delusion and hide the truth. The militancy of the Cynic and his claim to power—his claim to rule others, to be a kind of mad philosopher king—is predicated on both the truth that he fashions within himself through the *askēsis* and the license that truth gives him to speak it to others. The universalism of Cynic philosophy is not founded on a set of abstract truths or dogmas that are true in all times and all places, but on our endless capacity for self-deception (Foucault 2009: 257–8; Goulet-Cazé 2017: 529–30). There is a kind of virtuous circularity to the combat of the Cynic hero as his or her care for the self becomes a way of being occupied with others, and the care for others is reflected back into the care of the self (Foucault 2009: 286).

What Cynic *askēsis* claims to produce is a "true life," *alēthēs bios*, which in Cynic philosophy is one without artificiality, pretense, and often without the most basic characteristics of what other philosophers, including Plato and Seneca, considered civilized life.

> The true life becomes by the Cynic standard the life of the dog: shameless (the dog dares to meet his needs where it pleases him without hiding);

unperturbed (the dog is unperturbed by what may happen and is happy with what it has); discriminating, that is to say capable of discernment (the dog knows how to tell who are his friends and his enemies); and "phylactic," that is to say on guard, for the dog is able to consecrate himself to others and save his master's life.

Goulet-Cazé 2017: 531

The Cynics seek "to restamp or revalue the currency" (*parakharattein to nomisma*). This phrase was the original version of Nietzsche's "revaluation" or "transvaluation" of values (Goulet-Cazé 2017: 257–8). The dogs of philosophy sought to change the value of the symbolic tokens we exchange with one another, submitting them to the test of truth. They, like Socrates, seek to function as a touchstone (Gros 2012: 164).

Cynicism, thus, is a form of philosophy that does not stop posing the question, what sort of life enables one to practice truth-telling? What is the true life of the philosopher, the *bios philosophikos*? (Foucault 2009: 216). The person who lives the Cynic *bios*, in so far as he or she make the truth clear, is the person who casts a critical gaze upon reality. Like Socrates, they hail the person in the street and ask: "Do you conduct yourself well? Do things have to be as they are? Can we live differently?" The Cynic *bios*, as a form of provocation, "serves as an intermediary between this world and the principle of universal rationality, of order, and wisdom, of which it is the representative on earth" (Foucault 2014: 117).

In the end, while Cynicism begins life as a historically contingent formation of behaviors and modes of speech—it is hard to imagine Diogenes or Bion in the world of Homer and Hesiod, or even that of Archilochus and Thersites—in the end, for Foucault, Cynic life comes to function as a transhistoric category, informing both the image of the philosophic life and having a direct influence on Christian practices of asceticism (Foucault 2009: 161, 195–6; Hadot 2002: 64; Goulet-Cazé 2017: 528–9). It is but a short step from the philosopher with his staff and pack interpolating passersby and haranguing them on their lack of virtue, their material attachments, and the falsity of their lives to the barefoot Franciscan friars, the Dogs of Christ, with their carnivalesque humor, admonishing parishioners, begging for alms in the street, and turning the listener's gaze from their possessions to their souls (Foucault 2009: 152, 168, 172, 242, 293). In part, this is possible because Cynicism is less a body of doctrine than a manner of being, a way of forming the self in relation to truth and power (Foucault 2009: 164). As Frédéric Gros, the editor of the course, observes:

> The explosive coupling of truth-telling and a style of existence constitutes for Foucault a transhistoric constant of the Cynic attitude, of the sort he will also find in a certain ascetic Christian mysticism of privation and scandal, in certain revolutionary movements of the 19th century (anarchist currents, leftist militancy, etc.) and finally in modern art, since it no longer establishes a relation of imitation and ornamentation with the real, but is a reduction to the elementary, beginning with the aggressive refusal of social norms (Baudelaire, Flaubert, Manet).
> Gros 2012: 163; cf. Foucault 2009: 173–5

Yet this aggressive refusal is not a form of misanthropy but rather springs from the most profound solidarity with the whole of humankind. For Foucault, Cynic philosophy is not an antiquarian interest, but a way of thinking differently, a method of fundamentally reorienting our relation to the world, and thus of changing the world and its truth (Foucault 2009: 228).

In March of 1984, Foucault went to see his doctor. He asked how long he had to live. He still had lectures scheduled. He did not want to be absent. He had the mission of truth, a mission that his body itself revealed, a mission to which his presence at the lectern gave testimony (Foucault 2009: 78; Gros 2009: 318–19). He begins his final lecture by noting: "I am going to try to do two hours of lecturing today, but I am not absolutely sure I will make it to the end, because I have a touch, even a true case, of the flu. So, I am going to do what I can. You will pardon me if we need to stop for a certain time" (Foucault 2009: 245). More gravely ill than he let on to his audience, the philosopher did not leave his post till the two hours were done, and with his body, as he lectured on the Cynics, through his practice, he spoke frankly to us. He exhibited the "courage of truth": a truth that like the torso of the archaic Apollo Rilke saw in the Louvre addresses each of us and says with love, solidarity, and implacable rigor, "you must change your life." Or, in the words of the final Foucault himself, "Philosophic heroism, philosophic ethics, will no longer find its place in the practice of philosophy, once it has become a mere profession of instruction, but in this other form of the philosophic life, displaced and transformed, in the political field: the revolutionary life," a life that is revolutionary in both the way it lives and in its devotion to truth, a life of thinking, and therefore being, differently (Foucault 2009: 196).

## IV

What is in the eyes of the Cynic true pleasure? It's a pleasure that results from the contempt of pleasure and has nothing to do with what civilized life has us commonly call pleasure. Cynicism is a hedonism, since it aims at pleasure, but there too we find a revaluation, since this pleasure is the consequence of a contempt for traditional pleasure.

Goulet-Cazé 2017: 414

> And so each dinner guest drains different goblets,
> Each according to his pleasure, free of ridiculous rules,
> whether boldly he clasps passionate cups or more joyously drinks
> from modest vessels. Then, the conversation picks up,
> not about others' houses and villas, nor whether Lepos dances
> well or ill, but we debate what strikes closer to home
> and what it is wrong for us not to know; whether men are happy
> from riches or virtue; does right or custom lead us to friendship;
> and what is the nature of the good, and what its highest form?

Horace, *Satires* 2.67–76

Socrates tells the jurors who have convicted him and who are about to sentence him to death that he cannot cease from the behavior that has caused them so much irritation and still have a life that is livable for a human being, because what "happens to be the greatest good (*to megiston agathon*) for a human being is to spend each day making arguments and testing others about virtue and the other things you hear me talking about" (*Apology*, 38a2–3). This is what makes life worth living; this is his duty to the god; this is his highest pleasure. As the subsequent philosophical tradition makes clear, this examination of life, this becoming conscious of our existence and how it can be shaped and re-formed has many styles and deploys many techniques. For the Cynics, it takes one form, for Horace another, but each in their own way is engaged in the four functions of ancient philosophy Foucault outlined in the *Hermeneutics of the Subject*: care of the self; spiritual practice; *parrhēsia* or *libertas*; and self-knowledge. In each case, this pursuit is not opposed to pleasure. It does not depend on the renunciation of pleasure but on an understanding of true pleasure as coterminous with the good. *To kalliston*, that which is "the finest, the most beautiful," can never be opposed to or in opposition with *to megiston agathon*, "the greatest good," even if the nature of that good, and what it means to form one's life according to that good—and so to experience the greatest, most dependable, least alloyed pleasure—is what is under debate. And that debate, and the process of the truth-telling that is its foundation, a truth-telling that can never be merely a matter of rhetoric and one that is opposed to flattery, is precisely the process of examining ourselves and others about what constitutes the nature of that good and how we can approach it in our lives, whether that examination is to be imagined in the form of Plutarch's dialogue on *erōs*, the Socratic *elenchus*, Horace's after-dinner conversation, Seneca's correspondence with Lucilius, or the Cynic philosopher's street-corner harangue.

I suspect some readers will say, "Wait! Who is this moral philosopher you are describing here? This cannot be the Foucault of 'bodies and pleasures,' the Foucault of the bathhouses imagined by James Miller, the Foucault who wrote a history of sexuality that left out so many people, so many kinds of sex. You have confected a Foucault who reminds us more of Mortimer J. Adler, than the transgressive philosopher of madness, prisons, and sexuality." I have two responses. First, if I have argued anything in this book from beginning to end it is that we neglect the traditional philosophical questions underlying Foucault's work at our peril. The *History of Sexuality* was never an attempt to write a chronology of sex or the forms of its expression, let alone of gender and its complex relations to sex and sexuality. Sex, as Foucault famously argues, was created by sexuality, and sexuality is a discourse. There is no simple given in the world that corresponds to "sex," although the term unifies and refers to a complex of organs, sensations, acts, and norms that are real. The *History of Sexuality* is an attempt to trace that genealogy, to historicize the discourse that says that each of us has "a" sex and that this sex inscribes something meaningful about our being, that it tells us who we are and that we must learn to speak its truth and thereby come to know our truth: that we are men or women, straight or gay, cis or trans, fetishists or voyeurs. Sexuality's bestiary is all but infinite in its power to categorize and anatomize. Sexuality is a discourse of truth, and

Foucault's genealogy aims to denaturalize the forms of subjectivity, self-knowledge, and veridiction that this discourse demands and produces.

Second, I would argue that we should also take care not to underestimate the radicality of Foucault's reading of moral philosophy, of his seeing truth, pleasure, and the good as inextricably tied with one another. The opposition of truth and pleasure, of pleasure and the good, and the suspicion of pleasure that underlies many of these critiques make Foucault's point. Moreover, the demonstration of the contingency of the opposition of truth and pleasure, of its substantial artificiality, through his reading of the ancient philosophical tradition, not only forces us to rethink our understanding of these topics, but also underlines the limitations of our understanding of his project. The challenge to rethink sexuality from the standpoint of bodies and pleasures is not a call for the "liberation" of certain kinds of pleasure, it is not a demand for enjoyment, but a challenge to rethink what pleasure might mean and how it relates to differently constituted bodies.

> And we ought to dream that one day, perhaps, in a different economy of bodies and pleasures, we will no longer understand how the ruses of sexuality and of the power that sustains its apparatus came to submit us to the monarchy of sex to the point of devoting ourselves to forcing its secret and extorting from its shadows the truest of confessions.
> Foucault 1976: 211

His utopian dream is not Freudian polymorphic perversity. It does not mandate the multiplication of pleasures or their necessary connection with specific bodies, let alone specific activities or postures. What it does recognize is that a different economy of bodies and pleasures, a different way of understanding and relating the fact of our embodiment to the kinds and qualities of pleasures we experience, is intimately linked, not to some natural sex or human nature as a given that must express itself through our existence, but to structures of truth and power. In changing those structures, we not only create new ways of being, but new truths, and, necessarily, new pleasures, new ways of creating conscious and examined lives that are livable for a human being. We find an emancipation from the tutelage of received authority that Kant defines as the essence of our enlightenment.

The philosophic life poses these questions in an unyielding fashion. It is not opposed to pleasure but demands that we give an account of our pleasures, that we test our pleasures and test ourselves through them, not so that we, like the tyrant, may become a slave to our desires, but precisely so we shall not. The philosophic life in antiquity took two primary forms, according to Foucault, a Platonizing aesthetics of purity in which one tries to separate the soul from all that could disturb or enslave it; and a stylistics of self-sufficiency and independence, cultivated by the Stoics and Cynics and, in their own way, the Epicureans. But these separate forms are provisional. In each case, the goal is a form of life where the self becomes its own master and finds pleasure in itself or in circumstances that it can control and so will not lead to grief, disorder, and suffering. The philosopher is a doctor of the soul (Foucault 2009: 235, 249).

Whether as a Cynic, a Stoic, or a Platonist, the *bios alēthēs* of the philosopher calls for a form of rupture with the surrounding world that is transgressive. It can appear to be an assault on normal life (Gros 2009: 327–8). This, Foucault claims, is in fact the nature of truth. It always possesses a form of alterity. It always says, "not x, but y." "You may think you live a virtuous life, but in fact you cannot even define virtue." "You may think your system of government is just, but have you tested it, have you defined justice and looked inside your prisons?" "You may think phlogiston is the element that permits things to burn, but actually it is the oxygen that surrounds them." As Foucault wrote, but did not live to say, "Truth is never the same; there can only be truth in the form of another world, another life" (Foucault 2009: 311). In this light, Platonism's, Cynicism's, and early Christianity's insistence on the *bios alēthēs* amidst our pervasive lies, compromises, and injustices makes the envisioning of another world an urgent political task. The dandy, the sexual nonconformist, the revolutionary, and the philosopher are not opposed figures but different figurations of what a life committed to truth, in all its beauty and all its strangeness, could be and why it must be fought for.

# Notes

## Introduction

1 There are many examples of this; see among others Foucault (1988a: 145–6; 1988b: 17–18; 2011: 6; 2012a: 243); Brion and Harcourt (2012: 266); Rajchman (1991: 122); Macey (1993: 404); Veyne (1997); Attières (2012: 31). Compare Geuss (2017: 157).
2 Certainly, people were executed before for saying annoying or inconvenient things, but Socrates' commitment was not to any one proposition or confessional statement but to the practice of truth in general.
3 The bibliography on these questions is vast. Highlights include Foucault (1994h); Wallace (1991: xv); Alliez (1992: 221); Wolff (1992: 234–42); Annas (1993: 19); Hadot (1995: 57); Vlastos (1996: 1, 38–9, 58–9, 91–2); Nehamas (1998: 71, 87, 96); Blondell (2002: 10–19, 111); Castel-Bouchouchi (2003: 176).
4 These stories are recounted by Plato at the beginning of the *Seventh Letter*, a text which will attract Foucault's attention in his later years and to which we shall return.
5 All translations are my own unless otherwise specified.
6 See Diogenes Laertius (6.20–81); Dio Chrysostom (Or. 6.17, 7.188, 8.14, 8.36, 10.29–30); Julian (Or. 6202c); and other scattered references, gathered in the secondary material. See Branham and Goulet-Cazé (1996: 14); Long (1996: 29); Goulet-Cazé (1996: 67); Branham (1996: 88, 100); Griffin (1996: 200–1); Krueger (1996: 223–7, 235); Goulet-Cazé (2017: 241, 280–1, 407, 531–2).
7 The bibliography is vast. See among others, Heidegger (1982: 115, 129–31; 1998); Foucault (1988b: 12–13; 2011: 86–7, 94–5n.10); Defert (2011: 257, 272, 275); Mortensen (1994: 81–2); Zuckert (1996: 37, 49–50, 56); Jones (2011: 189); Brion and Harcourt (2012: 271); Miller (2020b). Plato, however, was a complex figure, and it would be wrong to see his legacy simply as being the first metaphysician. His texts are profoundly overdetermined. Platonism, the metaphysical tradition derived from those texts, represents an abstraction that fails to do them full justice. See Miller (2015b) and Frank (2018).
8 A posthumous version was published by Nietzsche's sister based on notes and drafts.
9 As Defert notes, it is no accident that Pierre Klossowski's translation of Heidegger's book on Nietzsche had been published that same year.

10 Again, the bibliography is very large; see among other things, Foucault (1984a: 35; 1994b: 214; 1994c: 415); Kremer-Marietti (1985: 278–9); Martin, Gutman, and Hutton (1988: 4); Rajchman (1991: 4–7); Zizek (1992: 180–1); Davidson (1994); Halperin (1995: 67–86); Veyne (1997); Larmour, Miller, and Platter (1998: 32–3); Black (1998); Foxhall (1998: 122–3); Taylor (2009: 8–9, 77).

11 Foucault and Derrida had a long and complex personal history that was marked by both polemic and personal regard. For a treatment of their relationship in the context of the DeMan affair, see Miller (2016).

12 The bibliography here is voluminous and filled with controversy and polemic. For some of the most important points, see Zonana (1988); Macey (1993: 470–8); J. Miller (1993: 21–5, 348–55); Eribon (1994: 52–4); Halperin (1995: 32–3, 171); duBois (1998: 100–2); White (2004).

13 Full disclosure, I am currently a member of the *AJP* editorial board.

14 The controversy received front page coverage in *The New York Times*. For a good summary of the origins, effects, and lore surrounding Luck's statement, see Adler (2014).

15 See, for example, Edmunds (1988); Dean-Jones (1992: 73); Edwards (1993: 56–7); Goldhill (1995: xii, 44–5).

16 For a contemporary continuation and refinement of this work, see Blondell and Ormand (2015).

17 In 1992, three un-tenured assistant professors with a very small budget, two from Texas Tech and one from the University of Georgia, organized what they believed to be the first conference on volumes two and three of the *History of Sexuality* in Lubbock, Texas. Somewhat naively, they invited most of the major scholars and to their surprise both Halperin and Richlin accepted, along with Page duBois. The upshot was a memorable if harrowing conference that included Halperin refusing to take questions from Richlin and departing early after chastising the hosts for not having invited the right people, plus a student performance of the *Lysistrata* and a trip to a western wear store. The final result was Larmour, Miller, and Platter's 1998, *Rethinking Sexuality: Foucault and Classical Antiquity*.

18 In fact, Richlin's "Not Before Homosexuality" (1993) demonstrates the politics were more complicated than this simple picture would lead one to believe, and much depended on philological discussions of words like *cinaedus*. See also Parker (2015) and Boehringer (2015).

19 On Foucault's conception of specific intellectuals and their role in society, see Martin (1988: 9); Rajchman (1991: 102); Flynn (1994: 43–4); Foucault (1994d: 612; 1994e: 747; 2012a: 259); Attières (2012: 12, 17); Adorno (2012: 38–9). On the complexities of Foucault's relation with feminism, see Macey (1993: 221–2, 319,

358, 374–5, 450); Edwards (1993: 75); Foucault (1994d: 612; 1994f: 288–9; 2012: 256); Halperin (1995: 90); Elden (2016: 64–5).

# Chapter 1

1. A neologism coined by Foucault, meaning "an act of truth," emphasizing that truth is not a quality of things or propositions but something done by people.
2. While Foucault is sometimes considered an anti-Marxist thinker, this is an oversimplification. He certainly polemicizes against the dogmatic Marxism of the French Communist Party, but we know that in the sixties he engaged with Luxembourg, Che Guevara, and the Black Panthers. In his later years, he remarked on the similarity between his interests and those of the Frankfurt School (Kelly 2014: 27, 67, 182).
3. Compare Jameson's discussion of similar arguments going on within French Marxism at the time (1981: 23–58).
4. Charles Stocking reminds me *per litteras* that Foucault may well have derived this notion in part from his reading of Dumézil. See Foucault (2012a: 17).
5. When I state, "the sky is blue," pragmatically I ask you to believe the sky is blue, but the proposition itself does not logically entail a demand for its acceptance.
6. The implicit message of truth, no matter how complex the mechanisms of its production, is that it is reality and we need only open our eyes to see it. But, in fact, the truth is never simply out there or it would not need to be discovered. There are no facts, even scientific ones, without observers and interpreters. Facts are segmented bits of the real that are rendered intelligible and communicable and hence subject to verification. There are no facts in a world without humans. There is only the silence of the real.
7. On the various versions of Foucault's reading in circulation, see Defert (2011: 277); Foucault (2012a: 73n1; 2012b: 42n2).
8. See Miller (2007: 204–13; 2015a). See also Foucault's statements in *L'herméneutique du sujet* (2001a: 31–2, 180–2). For more on this complex and often oversimplified "antagonism, which is not one," see Eribon (1994: 234–8, 248–59); Halperin (1995: 121); Lane (2000: 312–19, 324, 344); Rabaté (2003: 7–8); Shepherdson (2003: 150n15); Castel-Bouchouchi (2003: 188–9); Dean (2003: 241–2); Armstrong (2005: 131, 269); Whitebook (2005); and Sissa (2008).
9. *Pace* Vernant and Vidal-Naquet (1990).
10. He qualifies it as "aggressively and flatly positivist" (Foucault 2012b: 47).

11 One of the areas in which Foucault's reading is not completely satisfactory is his failure to recognize this irony and address its relation to truth. To be fair, it is not Foucault's purpose to offer a complete reading of the play but to examine it to make his larger genealogical and philosophical point (Foucault 2012a: 70). That said, it is in passages such as this, where the speaker's discourse seems to signify beyond his conscious control, that the possibility of a psychoanalytic reading of the text continues to make its force felt.
12 And it is should be stressed that myth is an act of imagination that is not theorizeable within the terms of the myth itself.
13 On the limits of Oedipus's powers of deliberation and his "paranoia," see Hall (2012). On the *OT* as a tragedy on the limits of knowledge, which serves as a model for Plato's *Apology of Socrates*, see Beer (2012: 108) and Fagan (2009).
14 The Sphinx.
15 As the editor of the course, Senellart, observes, derivatives of the word *tekmērion* only appear twice in the *OT*, although the word occurs several times in Sophocles' *Electra*. It is a puzzle why Foucault insists on it. As Senellart points out, it may well be that he is considering *tekmērion* and *sēmeion* largely indistinguishable, as before Aristotle they were used interchangeably (Foucault 2012b: 56–7, 69nn31–2). Certainly, there is a consistent image of Oedipus as someone who combines one piece of evidence with another, moving from clue to clue or sign to sign until he arrives at the "truth."
16 For their descent from Cadmus and membership in the ruling house of Thebes, see Hogan (1991: 25).
17 On the development of tyranny as an alternative to traditional aristocratic rule and its implication in new forms of knowledge and value, see Foucault (2011: 111–25).
18 Cf. Nagy (1979); Nagy (1990: 122–7).
19 For other examples, see pregnant line endings such as 76, *egō kakos*, or 81, *lampros hōsper ommati*. Or note that when the chorus says Laius died at the hands of "travelers" (*odoiporōn*), they come very close to saying *Oidipodōn* ("Oedipuses") (292). See also the chorus's reference to Jocasta when first addressing the messenger from Corinth as *gunē de mētēr th'hēde tōn keinou teknōn* (928), "that wife and mother of the children of that man." The Greek, with the immediate juxtaposition of the first two nouns at the beginning of the line, allows the suggestion that she is "the wife and mother" before clarifying at the line's end. In other instances, the expression is more overt, as when Jocasta says that many men sleep with their mothers in their dreams (980–2). See Telò's brilliant close reading of the play's diction from a post-Freudian psychoanalytic perspective (2020: 250–65).

20 At one point, he advances the intriguing but clearly speculative thesis that theater in Indo-European societies from classical to early modern takes as its central problem, how can a sovereign exercise power legitimately? (Foucault 2012a: 48).
21 An early form of Christian confession examined in the next section.

# Chapter 2

1 I would argue that although Freud in his more deterministic moments borders on this view, he frequently complicates it in interesting and useful ways. His followers are often more schematizing and less inclined to nuance, particularly those who would see psychoanalysis as a science compatible with modern medical treatment protocols. Others like Lacan and those who follow in his wake generally avoid this kind of model.
2 See *Critique of Pure Reason* (xvi–xviii).
3 Although to be fair, what Hegel actually means is more like: the world is only real to us to the extent that it can appear in discourse and therefore be subject to reason, the *logos*.
4 For reasons of space, I am forced to be schematic. On sexuality as a hidden internal identity, see Foucault (2012a: 255); Rajchman (1991: 87–9). On the *History of Sexuality* as a historicization but not a repudiation of psychoanalysis, particularly in the case of Freud and Lacan, see Eribon (1994: 234, 257); Lane (2000: 320–1); Dean (2003: 241–2); Castel-Bouchouchi (2003: 188–9); Armstrong (2005: 130–1, 184, 269); Ayouch (2016).
5 The principle of isomorphism is sometimes crudely reduced to the notion of penetrator and penetrated, and certainly in places it functions like that (cf. Catullus 16). But while Foucault on occasion is guilty of this schematization and so is Dover, upon whom he draws, isomorphism, like any social principle, is much more adaptable and flexible than a simple reduction to sexual positions. What it does argue and what the texts show is that sexual relations are conceptualized in terms of a social model based on the dominance of the masculine head of household and his position within the citizen body. See Renaut's excellent discussion (2016).
6 Literally, "keep them with their hand."
7 See Miller (1998), as well as Foucault (1966: 64–5); Dreyfus and Rabinow (1982: 27, 52, 59); Kremer-Marietti (1985: 9–10, 22–8, 102–10); Frow (1986: 79); Sedgwick (1990: 46–7); Macey (1993: 176); Flynn (1994: 30, 43); Rouse (1994: 94).

8  In *Subjecting Verses* (2004), I argued that the collapse of the republic and the emergence of the principate provided the historical conditions of possibility for the flowering of Latin erotic elegy as one symbolic system collapsed and another began to take hold.
9  The notion of technologies of the self will be an important one for Foucault in these years; we will define it more precisely in Chapter 3.
10 Heraclides attributes this distinction to Pythagoras. See Iamblichus (*On the Pythagorean Life* 58). The three-lives division is known to Plato (*R.* 581c) and Isocrates (*Antid.* 217). Many thanks to Philip Horky for giving me a look at his forthcoming commentary on Aristotle's ethics.

## Chapter 3

1  Foucault marks out Aristotle as an exeption to this rule (2001a: 18–19).
2  A version can be found in the work of A.J. Festugière, who in his 1935 *Contemplation et vie contemplative selon Platon* wrote, "philosophy is the care of the soul" (1950: 130).
3  See *inter alia*, Brown (1994: 165); Hadot (1995: 55, 102–5); Nehamas (1998: 72, 82–5); Blondell (2002: 10–13, 43, 100, 124); Hunter (2004: 86–7).
4  See Laurand on Foucault's neglect of *pothos* in Musonius Rufus's account of marriage (2003: 97–9); and Jaffro on Foucault's undervaluing rhetoric in Stoic practice and the radical nature of the rupture with the self entailed in philosophical conversion in Epictetus (2003: 64–8).
5  For an excellent account of the Stoic conception of nature, see Holmes (2019).
6  Pradeau also limits his critique to the *History of Sexuality*, though by this time he had access to the *Hermeneutics of the Subject*.

## Chapter 4

1  As Gros (2008: 358) and Elden (2016: 200) note, abbreviated versions of these lectures were presented in the fall of 1983 at Berkeley and later published in *Fearless Speech* (2001b). The versions presented at the Collège de France are fuller and should be considered authoritative.
2  In 1961, Foucault submitted as his minor thesis an introduction to and translation of Kant's *Anthropology*, which took "freedom" as one of its major themes (Fimiani 2012: 93–94n2).

3  There are minor differences between the text of the extract and the Gros edition (2008).
4  *Isonomia* was a fundamental concept of Athenian democracy, as exemplified in *skolia* sung at Athenian symposia. See Page *PMG* 893–6.
5  Referring to the necessity of Plato leaving Sicily, amidst death threats from Dionysius the Younger's soldiers (*Seventh Letter* 350a)
6  What follows is an abbreviated and altered treatment of Miller (forthcoming).
7  Foucault's transcription of the Greek is slightly off. The original reads, "philosophounta me zēn dein exetazonta emauton kai tous allous."

# Chapter 5

1  For a fuller bibliography on these questions, see the "Introduction."
2  See Rachlin and Green (1972); Kagel, Battalio, and Green (1995); and Hand (2007) *inter alia*.
3  For a more comprehensive account of these vocabularies, with special reference to their use in comedy, see Neil (1901: 202–9). These schemata, however, are not universal. See Pericles' more democratic formulations in Thucydides 2.40.
4  See des Places (1964), who lists *elenkhos* as a synonym of *basanos*.
5  See the new edition of Nietzsche's lectures on Plato (2019).
6  Foucault offers no actual evidence that Crito is "cured," beyond the claim that both he and Socrates owe a cock to Asclepius owing to the use of the first person plural.

# References

Adler, Eric. 2014. "The '*AJP Today*' Controversy Revisited." *Classical World* 108: 67–95.

Adorno, Francesco Paolo. 2012. "La tâche de l'intellectuel: Le modèle socratique." *Foucault: Le courage de la vérité*. Ed. Frédéric Gros. Paris: Presses Universitaires de France. 35–59.

Agamben, Giorgio. 1998. *Homo Sacer: Sovereign Power and Bare Life*. Trans. Daniel Heller-Roazen. Stanford: Stanford University Press.

Allen, Amy. 2016. "The History of Historicity: The Critique of Reason in Foucault (and Derrida)." *Between Foucault and Derrida*. Eds. Yubraj Ayral, Vernon W. Cisney, Nicolae Morar, and Christopher Penfield. Edinburgh: Edinburgh University Press. 125–37.

Alliez, Eric. 1992. "Ontologie et logographie: La pharmacie, Platon et le simulacre." *Nos Grecs et leurs modernes: Les Stratégies contemporaines d'appropriation de l'antiquité*. Ed. Barbara Cassin. Paris: Seuil. 211–31.

Anderson, Perry. 1993. *A Zone of Engagement*. New York: Verso.

Annas, Julia. 1992. *Hellenistic Philosophy of Mind*. Berkeley: University of California Press.

Annas, Julia. 1993. *The Morality of Happiness*. New York: Oxford University Press.

Armstrong, Richard. 2005. *A Compulsion for Antiquity: Freud and the Ancient World*. Ithaca: Cornell University Press.

Armstrong, Richard. 2012. "Freud and the Drama of Oedipal Truth." *A Companion to Sophocles*. Ed. Kirk Ormand. Malden: Wiley-Blackwell. 477–91.

Attières, Philippe. 2012. "Dire l'actualité. Le travail de diagnostic chez Michel Foucault." *Foucault: Le courage de la vérité*. Ed. Frédéric Gros. Paris: Presses Universitaires de France. 11–34.

Ayouch, Thamy. 2016. "De l'herméneutique au stratégique: Sexuations, sexualités, normes et psychanalyse." *Foucault, la sexualité, l'antiquité*. Eds. Sandra Boehringer and Daniele Lorenzini. Paris: Kimé. 167–86.

Bannet, Eve Tavor. 1989. *Structuralism and the Logic of Dissent: Barthes, Derrida, Foucault, Lacan*. Urbana: University of Illinois Press.

Baudelaire, Charles. 1968. "Le peintre de la vie moderne." *Baudelaire: Oeuvres complètes*. Ed. Marcel A. Ruff. Paris: Seuil. 546–65.

Beer, Josh. 2004. *Sophocles and the Tragedy of Athenian Democracy*. Westport: Praeger.

Beer, Josh. 2012. "*Oedipus Tyrannus*." *Brill's Companion to Sophocles*. Ed. Andreas Markantonatos. Leiden: Brill. 93–110.

Benatouïl, Thomas. 2003. "Deux usages du stoicisme: Deleuze, Foucault." *Foucault et la philosophie antique*. Eds. Frédéric Gros and Carlos Lévy. Paris: Kimé. 17–49.

Bertani, Mauro and Alessandro Fontana. 1997. "Situation du cours." In Michel Foucault, *Il faut défendre la société. Cours au Collège de France, 1976*. Eds. Mauro Bertani and Alessandro Fontana. Paris: Gallimard/Seuil. 245–63.

Black, Joel. 1998. "Taking the Sex Out of Sexuality: Foucault's Failed History." *Rethinking Sexuality: Foucault and Classical Antiquity*. Eds. David H.J. Larmour, Paul Allen Miller, and Charles Platter. Princeton: Princeton University Press. 42–60.

Blondell, Ruby. 2002. *The Play of Character in Plato's Dialogues*. Cambridge: Cambridge University Press.

Blondell, Ruby, and Kirk Ormand, eds. 2015. *Ancient Sex: New Essays*. Columbus: Ohio State University Press.

Bloom, Alan. 1987. *The Closing of the American Mind: How Higher Education Has Failed Democracy and Impoverished the Souls of Today's Students*. New York: Simon & Schuster.

Boehringer, Sandra. 2015. "The Illusion of Sexual Identity in Lucian's *Dialogues of the Courtesans* 5." *Ancient Sex: New Essays*. Eds. Ruby Blondell and Kirk Ormand. Columbus: Ohio State University Press. 253–84.

Boehringer, Sandra. 2016. "Refuser les universaux: Une histoire Foucaldienne de la sexualité antique, une histoire au present." *Foucault, la sexualité, l'antiquité*. Eds. Sandra Boehringer and Daniele Lorenzini. Paris: Kimé. 33–61.

Boyne, Roy. 1990. *Foucault and Derrida: The Other Side of Reason*. London: Unwin Hyman.

Branham, R. Bracht. 1996. "Defacing the Currency: Diogenes' Rhetoric and the *Invention* of Cynicism." *The Cynics: The Cynic Movement in Antiquity and Its Legacy*. Eds. R. Bracht Branham and Marie-Odile Goulet-Cazé. Berkeley: University of California Press. 81–104.

Branham, R. Bracht, and Marie-Odile Goulet-Cazé. 1996. "Introduction." *The Cynics: The Cynic Movement in Antiquity and Its Legacy*. Eds. R. Bracht Branham and Marie-Odile Goulet-Cazé. Berkeley: University of California Press. 1–27.

Brion, Fabienne, and Bernard E. Harcourt. 2012. "Situation du Cours." Michel Foucault, *Mal faire, dire vrai: Fonction de l'aveu en justice*. Eds. Fabienne Brion and Bernard E. Harcourt. Chicago: University of Chicago Press/Louvain: UCL Presses Universitaires de Louvain. 263–326.

Brouwer, René. 2014. *The Stoic Sage: The Early Stoics on Wisdom, Sagehood, and Socrates*. Cambridge: Cambridge University Press.

Brown, Wendy. 1994. "'Supposing Truth Were a Woman . . .': Plato's Subversion of Masculine Discourse." *Feminist Interpretations of Plato*. Ed. Nancy Tuana. University Park: Penn State University Press. 157–80.

Burnet, John. 1911. *Plato's Phaedo*. Oxford: Clarendon Press.

Calame, Claude. 2016. "Sujet du désir et sujet du discours Foucaldiens: La sexaulité face aux relations érotiques de Grecques et Grecs." *Foucault, la sexualité, l'antiquité*. Eds. Sandra Boehringer and Daniele Lorenzini. Paris: Kimé. 99–118.

Castel-Bouchouchi, Anissa. 2003. "Foucault et le paradoxe du platonisme." *Foucault et la philosophie antique*. Eds. Frédéric Gros and Carlos Lévy. Paris: Kimé. 175–93.

Culham, Phyllis, and Lowell Edmunds, eds. 1989. *Classics: A Discipline and Profession in Crisis?* Technical ed. Alden Smith. Lanham: University Press of America.

Davidson, Arnold I. 1994. "Ethics as Ascetics: Foucault, the History of Ethics, and Ancient Thought." *The Cambridge Companion to Foucault*. Ed. Gary Gutting. Cambridge: Cambridge University Press. 115–40.

Davidson, Arnold I. 2002. "Préface" to Hadot Pierre, *Exercices Spirituels et philosophie antique*. Revised edition. Paris: Albin Michel. 7–14.

Davila, Jorge. 2003. "Ethique de la parole et jeu de la vérité." *Foucault et la philosophie antique*. Eds. Frédéric Gros and Carlos Lévy. Paris: Kimé. 195–208.

Dawe, R.D. 2006. *Sophocles: Oedipus Rex*. Revised edition. Cambridge: Cambridge University Press.

Dean, Tim. 2003. "Lacan and Queer Theory." *The Cambridge Companion to Lacan*. Ed. Jean-Michel Rabaté. Cambridge: Cambridge University Press. 238–52.

Dean-Jones, Lesley. 1992. "The Politics of Pleasure: Female Sexual Appetite in the Hippocratic Corpus." *Helios* 19: 72–91.

Defert, Daniel. 2011. "Situation du cours." In Michel Foucault, *Leçons sur la volonté de savoir. Cours au Collège de France, 1970–71. Suivi de "Le Savoir d'Oedipe."* Ed. Daniel Defert. Paris: Hautes Études/Gallimard/Seuil. 257–79.

Deleuze, Gilles, and Félix Guattari. 1972. *Anti-Oedipus*. Paris: Minuit.

Denyer, Nicholas, ed. 2001. *Plato: Alcibiades*. Cambridge: Cambridge University Press.

Derrida, Jacques. 1967. "Cogito et Histoire de la Folie." *L'écriture et la différence*. Paris: Seuil. 51–97.

des Places, Édouard. 1964. *Platon: Lexique*. Paris: Les Belles Lettres.

Detienne, Marcel. 1996. *The Masters of Truth in Archaic Greece*. Trans. Janet Lloyd. New York: Zone Books.

Dover, Kenneth. 1978. *Greek Homosexuality*. Cambridge, MA: Harvard University Press.

Dreyfus, Hubert L., and Paul Rabinow. 1982. *Michel Foucault: Beyond Structuralism and Hermeneutics*. Chicago: University of Chicago Press.

duBois, Page. 1998. "The Subject in Antiquity after Foucault." *Rethinking Sexuality: Foucault and Classical Antiquity*. Eds. David H.J. Larmour, Paul Allen Miller, and Charles Platter. Princeton: Princeton University Press. 85–103.

Editorial Board. 1987. "*AJP* Today." *American Journal of Philology* 108.3: vii–x.

Edmunds, Lowell. 1988. "Foucault and Theognis." *Classical and Modern Literature* 8: 79–91.

Edwards, Catherine. 1993. *The Politics of Immorality in Ancient Rome*. Cambridge: Cambridge University Press.

Elden, Stuart. 2016. *Foucault's Last Decade*. Malden: Polity Press.

Eribon, Didier. 1994. *Michel Foucault et ses contemporains*. Paris: Fayard.

Euripides. 1959. "Ion." Trans. Ronald Frederick Willetts. *The Complete Greek Tragedies*. Eds. David Grene and Richmond Lattimore. Chicago: The University of Chicago Press. 9–81.

Evans, Fred. 2016. "'Murmurs' and 'Calls': The Significance of Voice in the Political Reason of Foucault and Derrida." *Between Foucault and Derrida*. Eds. Yubraj Aryal, Vernon W. Cisney, Nicolae Morar, and Christopher Penfield. Edinburgh: Edinburgh University Press. 153–68.

Fagan, P. 2009. "Plato's Oedipus: Myth and Philosophy in the *Apology*." *Re-examining Socrates in the* Apology. Eds. P. Fagan and J. Russon. Evanston: Northwestern University Press. 85–101.

Fejes, Andreas, and Magnus Dahlstedt. 2013. *The Confessing Society: Foucault, Confession, and Practices of Lifelong Learning*. London: Routledge.

Festugière, A.J. 1950. *Contemplation et vie contemplative selon Platon*. Second edition. Paris: Vrin. Original, 1935.

Fimiani, Mariapaola. 2012. "Le Véritable amour ou le souci commun du monde." *Foucault: Le Courage de la verité*. Ed. Frédéric Gros. Paris: Presses Universitaires de France. 87–127.

Fineberg, Brenda. 1991. Configurations of Desire in the Elegies of Tibullus. Dissertation. University of Chicago.

Flynn, Thomas. 1994. "Foucault's Mapping of History." *The Cambridge Companion to Foucault*. Ed. Gary Gutting. Cambridge: Cambridge University Press. 28–46.

Foucault, Michel. 1961. *Folie et déraison, Histoire de la folie à l'âge classique*. Paris: Plon.

Foucault, Michel. 1966. *Les mots et les choses*. Paris: Gallimard.

Foucault, Michel. 1971. *L'ordre du discours*. Paris: Gallimard.

Foucault, Michel. 1972. "Mon corps, ce papier, ce feu." *Histoire de la folie à l'âge classique suivi de Mon corps, ce papier, ce feu et La folie, l'absence de l'oeuvre*. Paris: Gallimard. 583–603.

Foucault, Michel. 1975. *Surveiller et punir: Naissance de la prison*. Paris: Gallimard.

Foucault, Michel. 1976. *La volonté de savoir. L'Histoire de la Sexualité*. Vol. 1. Paris: Gallimard.

Foucault, Michel. 1983. "Preface." In Gilles Deleuze and Félix Guattari, *Anti-Oedipus: Capitalism and Schizophrenia*. Trans. Robert Hurley, Mark Seem, and Helen R. Lane. Minneapolis: University of Minnesota Press. xi–xiv.

Foucault, Michel. 1984a. *L'Usage de plaisirs. L'Histoire de la sexualité*. Vol. 2. Paris: Gallimard.

Foucault, Michel. 1984b. *Le souci de soi. L'Histoire de la sexualité*. Vol. 3. Paris: Gallimard.

Foucault, Michel. 1984c. "What is Enlightenment?" Trans. Catherine Porter. *The Foucault Reader*. Ed. Paul Rabinow. New York: Pantheon. 32–50.

Foucault, Michel. 1986. *La pensée du dehors*. Paris: Fata Morgana.

Foucault, Michel. 1988a. "The Political Technology of Individuals." *Technologies of the Self: A Seminar with Michel Foucault*. Eds. Luther H. Martin, Huck Gutman, and Patrick H. Hutton. Amherst: University of Massachusetts Press. 145–62.

Foucault, Michel. 1988b. "Technologies of the Self." *Technologies of the Self: A Seminar with Michel Foucault*. Eds. Luther H. Martin, Huck Gutman, and Patrick H. Hutton. Amherst: University of Massachusetts Press. 16–49.

Foucault, Michel. 1994a "La Fonction politique de l'intellectuel." *Dits et écrits: 1954–1988*. Vol. 3. Eds. Daniel Defert and Fran.ois Ewalt. Paris: Gallimard. 109–14.

Foucault, Michel. 1994b. "Subjectivité et vérité." *Dits et écrits: 1954–1988*. Vol. 4. Eds. Daniel Defert and François Ewalt. Paris: Gallimard. 213–18.

Foucault, Michel. 1994c. "L'écriture de soi." *Dits et écrits: 1954–1988*. Vol. 4. Eds. Daniel Defert and François Ewalt. Paris: Gallimard. 415–30.

Foucault, Michel. 1994d. "À propos de la généalogie de l'éthique: un aperçu du travail en cours." *Dits et écrits: 1954–1988*. Vol. 4. Eds. Daniel Defert and François Ewalt. Paris: Gallimard. 609–31.

Foucault, Michel. 1994e. "L'intellectuel et les pouvoirs." *Dits et écrits: 1954–1988*. Vol. 4. Eds. Daniel Defert and François Ewalt. Paris: Gallimard. 747–52.

Foucault, Michel. 1994f. "Entretien avec M. Foucault." *Dits et écrits: 1954–1988*. Vol. 4. Eds. Daniel Defert and François Ewalt. Paris: Gallimard. 286–95.

Foucault, Michel. 1994g. "L'éthique du souci de soi comme pratique de la liberté." *Dits et écrits: 1954–1988*. Vol. 4. Eds. Daniel Defert and François Ewalt. Paris: Gallimard. 708–29.

Foucault, Michel. 1994h. "Theatrum Philosophicum." *Dits et écrits: 1954–1988*. Vol. 2. Eds. Daniel Defert and François Ewalt. Paris: Gallimard. 75–99.

Foucault, Michel. 1994i. "Les technologies de soi." *Dits et écrits: 1954–1988*. Vol. 4. Eds. Daniel Defert and François Ewalt. Paris: Gallimard. 783–813.

Foucault, Michel. 1994j. "Qu'est-ce que les Lumières?" *Dits et écrits: 1954–1988*. Vol. 4. Eds. Daniel Defert and François Ewalt. Paris: Gallimard. 563–78.

Foucault, Michel. 1994k. "Qu'est-ce que les Lumières?" *Dits et écrits: 1954–1988*. Vol. 4. Eds. Daniel Defert and François Ewalt. Paris: Gallimard. 679–88.

Foucault, Michel. 1994l. "Choix sexuel, acte sexuel." *Dits et écrits: 1954–1988*. Vol. 4. Eds. Daniel Defert and François Ewalt. Paris: Gallimard. 320–35.

Foucault, Michel. 1994m. "Foucault: Non aux compromis." *Dits et écrits: 1954–1988*. Vol. 4. Eds. Daniel Defert and François Ewalt. Paris: Gallimard. 336–7.

Foucault, Michel. 1994n. "Michel Foucault, une interview: sexe, pouvoir et la politique de l'identité." *Dits et écrits: 1954–1988*. Vol. 4. Eds. Daniel Defert and François Ewalt. Paris: Gallimard. 735–46.

Foucault, Michel. 1994o. "Entretien avec M. Foucault." *Dits et écrits: 1954–1988*. Vol. 4. Eds. Daniel Defert and François Ewalt. Paris: Gallimard. 86–95.

Foucault, Michel. 1994p. "Le triomphe social du plaisir sexuel: une conversation avec Michel Foucault." *Dits et écrits: 1954–1988*. Vol. 4. Eds. Daniel Defert and François Ewalt. Paris: Gallimard. 308–14.

Foucault, Michel. 1997. *Il faut défendre la société. Cours au Collège de France, 1976*. Eds. Mauro Bertani and Alessandro Fontana. Paris: Gallimard/Seuil.

Foucault, Michel. 2001a. *L'herméneutique du sujet. Cours au Collège de France, 1981–82*. Ed. Frédéric Gros. Paris: Hautes Études/Gallimard/Seuil.

Foucault, Michel. 2001b. *Fearless Speech*. Ed. Joseph Pearson. New York: Semiotext(e).

Foucault, Michel. 2008. *Le gouvernement de soi et des autres. Cours au Collège de France, 1982–83*. Ed. Frédéric Gros. Paris: Hautes Études/Gallimard/Seuil.

Foucault, Michel. 2009. *Le courage de la vérité: Le gouvernement de soi et des autres II. Cours au Collège de France, 1984*. Ed. Frédéric Gros. Paris: Hautes Études/Gallimard/Seuil.

Foucault, Michel. 2011. *Leçons sur la volonté de savoir. Cours au Collège de France, 1970–71. Suivi de "Le Savoir d'Oedipe."* Ed. Daniel Defert. Paris: Hautes Études/Gallimard/Seuil.

Foucault, Michel. 2012a. *Mal faire, dire vrai: Fonction de l'aveu en justice*. Eds. Fabienne Brion and Bernard E. Harcourt. Chicago: University of Chicago Press/Louvain: UCL Presses Universitaires de Louvain.

Foucault, Michel. 2012b. *Du gouvernement des vivants. Cours au Collège de France, 1979–80*. Ed. Michel Senellart. Paris: EHESS/Gallimard/Seuil.

Foucault, Michel. 2014. *Subjectivité et vérité. Cours au Collège de France, 1979–80*. Ed. Frédéric Gros. Paris: EHESS/Gallimard/Seuil.

Foucault, Michel. 2017. *Subjectivity and Truth. Lectures at the College de France 1980–1981*. Ed. Frédéric Gros. Trans Graham Burchell. London: Palgrave Macmillan.

Foucault, Michel. 2018. *Les aveux de la chair. Histoire de la sexualité*. Vol. 4. Ed. Frédéric Gros. Paris: Gallimard.

Foxhall, Lynn. 1998. "Pandora Unbound: A Feminist Critique of Foucault's History of Sexuality." *Rethinking Sexuality: Foucault and Classical Antiquity*. Eds. David H.J. Larmour, Paul Allen Miller, and Charles Platter. Princeton: Princeton University Press. 122–37.

Frank, Jill. 2018. *Poetic Justice: Rereading Plato's Republic*. Chicago: University of Chicago Press.

Frede, Michael. 1994. "The Stoic Notion of a *Lekton*." *Language: Companions to Ancient Thought*. Ed. Stephen Everson. Cambridge: Cambridge University Press. 109–28.

Freud, Sigmund. 1965. *The Interpretation of Dreams*. Trans. James Strachey. New York: Avon Books.

Frow, John. 1986. *Marxism and Literary History*. Cambridge, MA: Harvard University Press.

Gadamer, Hans-Georg. 1991. *Plato's Dialectical Ethics: Phenomenological Interpretations Relating to the Philebus*. Trans. Robert M. Wallace. New Haven: Yale University Press.

Geuss, Raymond. 2017. *Changing the Subject: Philosophy from Socrates to Adorno*. Cambridge, MA: Harvard University Press.

Goldhill, Simon. 1995. *Foucault's Virginity: Ancient Erotic Fiction and the History of Sexuality*. Cambridge: Cambridge University Press.

Goulet-Cazé, Marie-Odile. 1996. "Religion and the Early Cynics." *The Cynics: The Cynic Movement in Antiquity and Its Legacy*. Eds. R. Bracht Branham and Marie-Odile Goulet-Cazé. Berkeley: University of California Press. 47–80.

Goulet-Cazé, Marie-Odile. 2017. *Le Cynisme, une philosophie antique*. Paris: Librairie Philosophique J. Vrin.

Gratton, Peter. 2016. "Philosophy on Trial: The Crisis of Deciding Between Foucault and Derrida." *Between Foucault and Derrida*. Eds. Yubraj Aryal, Vernon W. Cisney, Nicolae Morar, and Christopher Penfield. Edinburgh: Edinburgh University Press. 251–62.

Griffin, Miriam. 1996. "Cynicism and the Romans: Attraction and Repulsion." *The Cynics: The Cynic Movement in Antiquity and Its Legacy*. Eds. R. Bracht Branham and Marie-Odile Goulet-Cazé. Berkeley: University of California Press. 190–204.

Gros, Frédéric. 2001. "Situation du Cours." In Michel Foucault, *L'herméneutique du sujet. Cours au Collège de France, 1981–82*. Ed. Frédéric Gros. Paris: Hautes Études/Gallimard/Seuil. 487–526.

Gros, Frédéric. 2008. "Situation du Cours." In Michel Foucault, *Le gouvernement de soi et des autres. Cours au Collège de France, 1982–83*. Ed. Frédéric Gros. Paris: Hautes Études/Gallimard/Seuil. 348–61.

Gros, Frédéric. 2009. "Situation du Cours." In Michel Foucault, *Le courage de la vérité: Le gouvernement de soi et des autres II. Cours au Collège de France, 1984*. Ed. Frédéric Gros. Paris: Hautes Études/Gallimard/Seuil. 314–28.

Gros, Frédéric. 2012. "La *parrêsia* chez Foucault (1982–1984)." *Foucault: Le courage de la vérité*. Ed. Frédéric Gros. Paris: Presses Universitaires de France. 155–66.

Gros, Frédéric. 2014. "Situation du Cours." In Michel Foucault, *Subjectivité et vérité. Cours au Collège de France, 1979–80*. Ed. Frédéric Gros. Paris: EHESS/Gallimard/Seuil. 303–21.

Gros, Frédéric. 2016. "*L'Usage des plaisirs* et *Le Souci de soi*: Généalogie d'un texte." *Foucault, la sexualité, l'antiquité*. Eds. Sandra Boehringer and Daniele Lorenzini. Paris: Kimé. 19–30.

Hadot, Pierre. 1977. "Exercices Spirituels." *Annuaire de l'École pratique des hautes études: Section des sciences religieuses*, 84: 25–70.

Hadot, Pierre. 1992. *La citadelle intérieure. Introduction aux Pensées de Marc Aurèle*. Paris: Fayard.

Hadot, Pierre. 1995. *Qu'est-ce que la philosophie antique?* Paris: Gallimard.

Hadot, Pierre. 2002. *Exercices spirituels et philosophie antique*. Revised edition. Paris: Albin Michel.

Hall, Edith. 2012. "The Necessity and Limits of Deliberation in Sophocles' Theban Plays." *A Companion to Sophocles*. Ed. Kirk Ormand. Malden: Wiley-Blackwell. 300–15.

Halperin, David M. 1990. *One Hundred Years of Homosexuality and Other Essays on Greek Love*. New York: Routledge.

Halperin, David M. 1995. *Saint Foucault: Towards a Gay Hagiography*. New York: Oxford University Press.

Halperin, David M., John J. Winkler, and Froma Zeitlin. 1990. *Before Sexuality: The Construction of Erotic Experience in the Ancient Greek World*. Princeton: Princeton University Press.

Hand, Eric. 2007. "Impulse Keeps Us Living in Present." *Baltimore Sun*. February 9. https://www.baltimoresun.com/news/bs-xpm-2007-02-09-0702090235-story.html

Hankinson, R.J. 2003. "Stoic Epistemology." *The Cambridge Companion to the Stoics*. Ed. Brad Inwood. Cambridge: Cambridge University Press. 59–84.

Harward, J. 2014. *The Platonic Epistles: Translated with Introduction and Notes*. Cambridge: Cambridge University Press. Original, 1932.

Heidegger, Martin. 1982. "The Age of the World Picture." *The Question Concerning Technology and Other Essays*. Trans. William Lovitt. New York: Harper Torchbooks. 115–54.

Heidegger, Martin. 1998. "Plato's Doctrine of Truth." Trans. Thomas Sheehan. *Pathmarks*. Ed. William McNeill. Cambridge: Cambridge University Press. 155–82.

Henderson, John. 1993. "Persius' Didactic Satire: The Pupil as Teacher." *Ramus* 20: 123–48.
Hirsch, E.D. 1987. *Cultural Literacy: What Every American Needs to Know*. Boston: Houghton Mifflin.
Hogan, James C. 1991. *A Commentary on the Plays of Sophocles*. Carbondale: Southern Illinois University Press.
Holmes, Brooke. 2019. "On Stoic Sympathy: Cosmobiology and the Life of Nature." *Antiquities Beyond Humanism*. Eds. Emanuel Bianchi, Sara Brill, and Brooke Holmes. Oxford: Oxford University Press. 239–70.
Hunter, Richard. 2004. *Plato's Symposium*. Oxford: Oxford University Press.
Jaffro, Laurent. 2003. "Foucault et le stoïcisme: Sur l'historiographie de L'herméneutique du sujet." *Foucault et la philosophie antique*. Eds. Frédéric Gros and Carlos Lévy. Paris: Kimé. 51–83.
Jameson, Fredric. 1981. *The Political Unconscious: Narrative as a Socially Symbolic Act*. Ithaca: Cornell University Press.
Janan, Micaela. 1994. *"When the Lamp is Shattered": Desire and Narrative in Catullus*. Carbondale: Southern Illinois University Press.
Jones, Rachel. 2011. *Irigaray: Towards a Sexuate Philosophy*. Cambridge: Polity.
Kagel, John H., Raymond C. Battalio, and Leonard Green. 1995. *Economic Choice Theory: An Experimental Analysis of Animal Behavior*. Cambridge: Cambridge University Press.
Kamerbeek, J.C. 1967. *The Plays of Sophocles. Part IV, The Oedipus Tyrannus*. Leiden: Brill.
Kant, Immanuel. 1991. "An Answer to the Question: 'What is Enlightenment?'" *Political Writings*. Ed. Hans Reiss. Trans. H.B. Nisbet. Second edition. Cambridge: Cambridge University Press. 54–60.
Kant, Immanuel. 1993. *Groundwork of the Metaphysics of Morals*. Third edition. Trans. James W. Ellington. Indianapolis: Hackett.
Kelly, Mark G.E. 2014. *Foucault and Politics: An Introduction*. Edinburgh: Edinburgh University Press.
Kinney, Daniel. 1996. "Heirs of the Dog: Cynic Selfhood in Medieval and Renaissance Culture." *The Cynics: The Cynic Movement in Antiquity and Its Legacy*. Eds. R. Bracht Branham and Marie-Odile Goulet-Cazé. Berkeley: University of California Press. 294–329.
Knox, Bernard. 1979. "Why is Oedipus Called *Tyrannos*?" *Words and Actions: Essays on the Ancient Theater*. Baltimore: Johns Hopkins University Press. 87–96.
Kofman, Sarah. 1986. *Nietzsche et la scène philosophique*. Paris: Galilée.
Kofman, Sarah. 1989. *Socrate(s)*. Paris: Galilée.
Koyré, Alexandre. 1962. *Introduction à la lecture de Platon, suivi de Entretiens sur Descartes*. Paris: Gallimard.

Kremer-Marietti, Angèle. 1985. *Michel Foucault: Archéologie et généalogie*. Second edition. Paris: Livre de Poche.

Krueger, Derek. 1996. "The Bawdy and Society: The Shamelessness of Diogenes in Roman Imperial Culture." *The Cynics: The Cynic Movement in Antiquity and Its Legacy*. Eds. R. Bracht Branham and Marie-Odile Goulet-Cazé. Berkeley: University of California Press. 222–39.

Lane, Christopher. 2000. "The Experience of the Outside: Foucault and Psychoanalysis." *Lacan in America*. Ed. Jean-Michel Rabaté. New York: The Other Press. 309–47.

Larmour, David H.J., Paul Allen Miller, and Charles Platter, eds. 1998. "Introduction: Situating the History of Sexuality." *Rethinking Sexuality: Foucault and Classical Antiquity*. Princeton: Princeton University Press. 3–41.

Laurand, Valéry. 2003. "Souci de soi et marriage chez Musonius Rufus: Perspectives politiques de la krâsis stoïcienne." *Foucault et la philosophie antique*. Eds Frédéric Gros and Carlos Lévy. Paris: Kimé. 85–116.

Lawlor, Leonard. 2016. *From Violence to Speaking Out: Apocalypse and Expression in Foucault, Derrida, and Deleuze*. Edinburgh: Edinburgh University Press.

Leonard, Miriam. 2005. *Athens in Paris: Ancient Greece and the Political in Post-War French Thought*. Oxford: Oxford University Press.

Liapis, Vayos. 2012. "Oedipus Tyrannus." *A Companion to Sophocles*. Ed. Kirk Ormand. Malden: Wiley-Blackwell. 84–97.

Long, A.A. 1968. *Language and Thought in Sophocles: A Study in Abstract Nouns and Poetic Technique*. London: Athlone Press.

Long, A.A. 1996. "The Socratic Tradition: Diogenes, Crates, and Hellenistic Ethics." *The Cynics: The Cynic Movement in Antiquity and Its Legacy*. Eds. R. Bracht Branham and Marie-Odile Goulet-Cazé. Berkeley: University of California Press. 28–46.

Lorenzini, Daniele. 2016. "Le désir comme 'transcendental historique' de l'histoire de la sexualité." *Foucault, la sexualité, l'antiquité*. Eds. Sandra Boehringer and Daniele Lorenzini. Paris: Kimé. 137–49.

Macey, David. 1993. *The Lives of Michel Foucault*. New York: Pantheon.

Macintosh, Fiona. 2009. *Sophocles: Oedipus Tyrannus*. Cambridge: Cambridge University Press.

Martin, Luther H., Huck Gutman, and Patrick H. Hutton, eds. 1988. "Introduction." *Technologies of the Self: A Seminar with Michel Foucault*. Amherst: University of Massachusetts Press. 1–8.

Martin, Rux. 1988. "Truth, Power, Self: An Interview with Michel Foucault October 25, 1982." *Technologies of the Self: A Seminar with Michel Foucault*. Eds. Luther H. Martin, Huck Gutman, and Patrick H. Hutton. Amherst: University of Massachusetts Press. 9–15.

McGushin, Edward. 2016. "Deconstruction, Care of the Self, Spirituality: Putting Foucault and Derrida to the Test." *Between Foucault and Derrida*. Eds. Yubraj Aryal, Vernon W. Cisney, Nicolae Morar, and Christopher Penfield. Edinburgh: Edinburgh University Press. 104–22.

Miller, James. 1993. *The Passion of Michel Foucault*. Cambridge, MA: Harvard University Press.

Miller, Paul Allen. 1998. "Catullan Consciousness, the 'Care of the Self,' and the Force of the Negative in History." *Rethinking Sexuality: Foucault and Classical Antiquity*. Eds. David H.J. Larmour, Paul Allen Miller, and Charles Platter. Princeton: Princeton University Press. 171–203.

Miller, Paul Allen. 2004. *Subjecting Verses: Latin Love Elegy and the Emergence of the Real*. Princeton: Princeton University Press.

Miller, Paul Allen. 2005. *Latin Verse Satire: An Anthology and Critical Reader*. London: Routledge.

Miller, Paul Allen. 2007. *Postmodern Spiritual Practices: The Construction of the Subject and the Reception of Plato in Lacan, Derrida, and Foucault*. Columbus: Ohio State University Press.

Miller, Paul Allen. 2010. "Persius, Irony, and Truth." *American Journal of Philology* 131: 233–58.

Miller, Paul Allen. 2015a. "Enjoyment Beyond the Pleasure Principle: Antigone, Julian of Norwich, and the Use of Pleasures." *The Comparatist* 39: 47–63.

Miller, Paul Allen. 2015b. "Dreams and Other Fictions: The Representation of Representation in *Republic* 5 and 6." *American Journal of Philology* 136: 37–62.

Miller, Paul Allen. 2016. "Ghosts in the Politics of Friendship." *Dead Theory: Derrida, Death, and the Afterlife of Theory*. Ed. Jeffrey Di Leo. London: Bloomsbury. 111–32.

Miller, Paul Allen. 2019. *Horace*. London: Bloomsbury.

Miller, Paul Allen. 2020a. "Against Agamben: or Living your Life, *Zōē* versus *Bios* in the late Foucault." *Biotheory: Life and Death after Capitalism*. Eds. Jeffrey DiLeo and Peter Hitchcock. London: Routledge. 23–41.

Miller, Paul Allen. 2020b. "Plato as World Literature." *Philosophy as World Literature*. Ed. Jeffrey DiLeo. New York: Bloomsbury. 47–58.

Miller, Paul Allen. Forthcoming. "Plato's Seventh Letter or How to Fashion a Subject of Resistance." *The Politics of Form*. Ed. Phiroze Vasunia. London: Bloomsbury.

Mortensen, Ellen. 1994. *The Feminine and Nihilism: Luce Irigaray with Nietzsche and Heidegger*. Oslo: Scandinavian University Press.

Nagy, Gregory. 1979. *The Best of the Achaeans: Concepts of the Hero in Archaic Greek Poetry*. Baltimore: Johns Hopkins University Press.

Nagy, Gregory. 1990. *Pindar's Homer: The Lyric Possession of the Epic Past*. Baltimore: Johns Hopkins University Press.

Nealon, Jeffrey T. 2016. "Living and Dying with Foucault and Derrida: The Question of Biopower." *Between Foucault and Derrida*. Eds. Yubraj Aryal, Vernon W. Cisney, Nicolae Morar, and Christopher Penfield. Edinburgh: Edinburgh University Press. 237–50.

Nehamas, Alexander. 1998. *The Art of Living: Socratic Reflections from Plato to Foucault*. Berkeley: University of California Press.

Neil, R.A. 1901. *Aristophanes: The Knights*. Cambridge: Cambridge University Press.

Newman, Robert J. 1989. "*Cotidie Meditare*: Theory and Practice of *Meditatio* in Imperial Stoicism." *Aufstieg un Welt Niedergang der römischen*. Vol. 36.3. Eds. Wolfgang Haase and Hildegard Temporini. Berlin: Walter de Gruyter. 1473–1517.

Niehues-Pröbsting, Heinrich. 1996. "The Modern Reception of Cynicism: Diogenes in the Enlightenment." *The Cynics: The Cynic Movement in Antiquity and Its Legacy*. Eds. R. Bracht Branham and Marie-Odile Goulet-Cazé. Berkeley: University of California Press. 329–65.

Nietzsche, Friedrich. 1956. *The Birth of Tragedy*. In *The Birth of Tragedy and the Genealogy of Morals*. Trans. Francis Golffing. New York: Doubleday. 1–146.

Nietzsche, Friedrich. 1972. *The Antichrist*. No trans. New York: Arno Press.

Nietzsche, Friedrich. 1974. *The Gay Science*. Trans. Walter Kaufmann. New York: Vintage Books.

Nietzsche, Friedrich. 2013. *On the Genealogy of Morals*. Trans. Michael A. Scarpitti. London: Penguin.

Nietzsche, Friedrich. 2019. *Platon*. Ed. Anne Merker. Paris: Les Belles Lettres.

Nightingale, Andrea Wilson. 1995. *Genres in Dialogue: Plato and the Construct of Philosophy*. Cambridge: Cambridge University Press.

Nussbaum, Martha. 1994. *The Therapy of Desire*. Princeton: Princeton University Press.

Ormand, Kirk. 2016. "Peut-on parler de perversion dans l'antiquité? Foucault et l'invention du raisonnement psychiatrique?" Trans. Sandra Boehringer and Isabelle Chatelêt. *Foucault, la sexualité, l'antiquité*. Eds. Sandra Boehringer and Daniele Lorenzini. Paris: Kimé. 63–86.

Orrells, Daniel. 2015. "Freud's Phallic Symbol." *Classical Myth and Psychoanalysis: Ancient and Modern Stories of the Self*. Eds. Vanda Zajko and Ellen O'Gorman. Oxford: Oxford University Press. 39–58.

Parker, Holt N. 1997. "The Teratogenic Grid." *Roman Sexualities*. Eds. Judith P. Hallett and Marilyn B. Skinner. Princeton: Princeton University Press. 49–65.

Parker, Holt N. 2015. "Vaseworld: Depiction and Description of Sex at Athens." *Ancient Sex: New Essays*. Eds. Ruby Blondell and Kirk Ormand. Columbus: Ohio State University Press. 23–142.

Penfield, Christopher. 2016. "Introduction." *Between Foucault and Derrida*. Eds. Yubraj Aryal, Vernon W. Cisney, Nicolae Morar, and Christopher Penfield. Edinburgh: Edinburgh University Press. 1–26.

Pradeau, Jean-Francois. 2009. *Platon, l'imitation de la philosophie*. Paris: Aubier.

Pradeau, Jean-Francois. 2012. "Le sujet ancien d'une éthique modern." *Foucault: Le courage de la vérité*. Ed. Frédéric Gros. Paris: Presses Universitaires de France.

Rabaté, Jean-Michel. 2003. "Lacan's Turn to Freud." *Cambridge Companion to Lacan*. Ed. Jean-Michel Rabaté. Cambridge: Cambridge University Press. 1–24.

Rachlin, Howard, and Leonard Green. 1972. "Commitment, Choice and Self Control." *Journal of Experimental Analysis of Behavior* 17.1: 15–22.

Ragland-Sullivan, Ellie. 1986. *Jacques Lacan and the Philosophy of Psychoanalysis*. Urbana: University of Illinois Press.

Rajchman, John. 1991. *Truth and Eros: Foucault, Lacan, and the Question of Ethics*. London: Routledge.

Rekret, Paul. 2016. "The Aporia and the Problem." *Between Foucault and Derrida*. Eds. Yubraj Aryal, Vernon W. Cisney, Nicolae Morar, and Christopher Penfield. Edinburgh: Edinburgh University Press. 189–206.

Renaut, Olivier. 2016. "Sexualité antique et principe d'activité: Les paradoxes Foucaldiens sur la pédérastie." *Foucault, la sexualité, l'antiquité*. Eds. Sandra Boehringer and Daniele Lorenzini. Paris: Kimé. 121–35.

Richlin, Amy. 1991. "Zeus and Metis: Foucault, Feminism, Classics." *Helios* 18: 160–80.

Richlin, Amy. 1993. "Not Before Homosexuality: The Materiality of the *Cinaedus* and the Roman Law Against the Love Between Men." *Journal of the History of Sexuality* 3: 523–73.

Richlin, Amy. 1998. "Foucault's *History of Sexuality*: A Theory Useful for Women?" *Rethinking Sexuality: Foucault and Classical Antiquity*. Eds. David H.J. Larmour, Paul Allen Miller, and Charles Platter. Princeton: Princeton University Press. 138–70.

Robin, Léon, ed. 1926. *Platon: Phédon*. Paris: Les Belles Lettres.

Rouse, Joseph. 1994. "Power/Knowledge." *The Cambridge Companion to Foucault*. Ed. Gary Gutting. Cambridge: Cambridge University Press. 92–114.

Rowe, C.J. 1993. *Plato: Phaedo*. Cambridge: Cambridge University Press.

Rusten, Jeffrey. 1990. *Sophocles: Oidipous Tyrannos. Commentary*. Bryn Mawr: Thomas Library, Bryn Mawr College.

Said, Edward. 1984. "Michel Foucault, 1926–84." *Raritan* 4: 1–11.

Sedgwick, Eve Kosofsky. 1990. *Epistemology of the Closet*. Berkeley: University of California Press.

Senellart, Michel. 2012. "Situation du cours." In Michel Foucault, *Du gouvernement des vivants. Cours au Collège de France, 1979–80*. Ed. Michel Senellart. Paris: EHESS/Gallimard/Seuil. 321–50.

Sforzini, Arianna. 2016. "Corps de Plaisir, corps de désir: La théorie augustinienne du mariage relue par Michel Foucault." *Foucault, la sexualité, l'antiquité*. Eds. Sandra Boehringer and Daniele Lorenzini. Paris: Kimé. 153–65.

Shepherdson, Charles. 2003. "Lacan and Philosophy." *The Cambridge Companion to Lacan*. Ed. Jean-Michel Rabaté. Cambridge: Cambridge University Press. 116–52.

Sissa, Giulia. 2008. *Sex and Sensuality in the Ancient World*. Trans. George Staunton. New Haven: Yale University Press.

Suzuki, Shunryū. 2006. *Zen Mind, Beginner's Mind: Informal Talks on Zen Meditation and Practice*. Boston: Weatherhill.

Szlezák, Thomas A. 1999. *Reading Plato*. Trans. Graham Zanker. London: Routledge.

Taylor, Chloë. 2009. *The Culture of Confession from Augustine to Foucault: A Genealogy of the "Confessing Animal."* New York: Routledge.

Telò, Mario. 2020. *Archive Feelings: A Theory of Greek Tragedy*. Columbus: Ohio State University Press.

Tredennick, Hugh, ed. and trans. 1969. *Plato: The Last Days of Socrates*. London: Penguin.

Vernant, Jean-Pierre, and Pierre Vidal-Naquet. 1990. "Oedipus Without Complex." *Myth and Tragedy in Ancient Greece*. Trans. Janet Lloyd. New York: Zone Books. 85–112.

Veyne, Paul. 1997. "The Final Foucault and His Ethics." Trans. Catherine Porter and Arnold I. Davidson. *Foucault and Interlocutors*. Ed. Arnold I. Davidson. Chicago: University of Chicago Press. 225–33.

Veyne, Paul. 2001. *La société romaine*. Paris: Seuil.

Veyne, Paul. 2003. *Seneca: The Life of a Stoic*. Trans. David Sullivan. London Routledge.

Vlastos, Gregory. 1996. *Socrates, Ironist and Moral Philosopher*. Ithaca: Cornell University Press.

Wallace, Robert M. 1991. "Introduction." In Hans-Georg Gadamer, *Plato's Dialectical Ethics: Phenomenological Interpretations Relating to the Philebus*. Trans. Robert M. Wallace. New Haven: Yale University Press. ix–xxiii.

White, Allen. 2004. "Reagan's AIDS Legacy: Silence Equals Death." *SF Gate*. http://www.sfgate.com/opinion/openforum/article/Reagan-s-AIDS-Legacy-Silence-equals-death-2751030.php

Whitebook, Joel. 2005. "Against Interiority: Foucault's Struggle with Psychoanalysis." *The Cambridge Companion to Foucault*. Second edition. Ed. Gary Gutting. Cambridge: Cambridge University Press. 312–47.

Wilson, Emily. 2012. "Sophocles and Philosophy." *Brill's Companion to Sophocles*. Ed. Andreas Markantonatos. Leiden: Brill. 537–62.

Winkler, John J. 1990. *The Constraints of Desire: The. Anthropology of Sex and Gender in Ancient Greece*. New York: Routledge.

Wohl, Victoria. 2015. *Euripides and the Politics of Form*. Princeton: Princeton University Press.
Wolff, Francis. 1992. "Trios: Deleuze, Derrida, Foucault, historiens du platonisme." *Nos Grecs et leurs modernes: Les Stratégies contemporaines d'appropriation de l'antiquité*. Ed. Barbara Cassin. Paris: Seuil. 232–48.
Žižek, Slavoj. 1992. *Enjoy Your Symptom: Jacques Lacan in Hollywood and Out*. New York: Routledge.
Zonana, Victor F. 1988. "Cuba's AIDS Quarantine Center Called 'Frightening.'" *Los Angeles Times*. November 4. http://articles.latimes.com/1988-11-04/news/mn-1196_1_aids-quarantine-center
Zuckert, Catherine H. 1996. *Postmodern Platos: Nietzsche, Heidegger, Gadamer, Strauss, Derrida*. Chicago: University of Chicago Press.

# Index

Adler, Mortimer J. 186
Aelian 58
aesthetics 2, 85–6, 113–14, 117–19, 127, 140, 175, 188
Agamben, Giorgio 18, 58, 79–80
Agathon 106, 145
*agathon, to* 114, 118, 175, 186
AIDS 11, 155–6
Alcibiades 86–7, 92–3, 95, 97, 99–105, 120, 135, 138, 152, 158, 160, 179
Alcmeon of Croton 32
*alētheia* 5, 30, 32, 163, 164, 169, 175–6, 178, 182, 188
   *see also* truth
*alèthurgie* 15, 18, 26, 36, 38, 40, 134, 158–9
Alexander, The Great 148, 179
Anacreon 74
analytic philosophy 127
*andreia* 169, 173
Antipatros 72
*aphrodisia* 59–60, 63–4, 71–2, 76, 78–9, 83
Apollo 29, 31, 34–5, 37, 39, 48, 93, 132–4, 136, 148–9, 166, 184
aporia 3, 98, 167–9, 174
archeology 1, 7, 91
Archilochus 183
*aretē* 74, 92, 173
Aristophanes 63
Aristotle xiv, 5–7, 10, 59, 79–80, 135, 165, 192 n.15, 194 n.1, 194 n.10
Artaud, Antonin 1
Artemidorus 57, 61–6, 68, 70
Asclepius 171–2, 195 n.6
*askēsis* 25, 77, 88, 106, 178, 180–2
Athens 2–4, 7, 30, 33, 48, 69, 87, 95, 101, 104, 106, 126, 130–7, 143, 146, 148–9, 161, 166–7, 171, 175, 195 n.4
Augustine 24
Augustus 75
Aurelius, Marcus 105, 115–16, 153

Bakhtin, Mikhail 10
*basanos* 170, 195 n.4
Bataille, Georges 1
bathhouses 156–7, 186
Baudelaire, Charles 112, 118–19, 127, 129–30, 140, 151, 157, 175, 184
Bennet, William 9–10
Bentham, Jeremy 159
Bion 179, 183
biopolitics 18, 49, 79–80, 90
biopower 17, 80
*bios* 58, 76–81, 86, 93, 95, 104, 113, 119, 121, 141, 158, 170, 173, 174, 176, 178, 181–3, 188
Black Panthers 191 n.2
Bloom, Allan 9–10

Caesar, Julius 72
Callimachus 72
care of the self 7, 49, 52, 79–80, 84, 85–9, 92, 94–5, 97–106, 108, 113–14, 118–20, 123, 127–9, 131, 138, 145, 150, 167–70, 173–9, 181–2, 185, 194 n.2
Cassian, John 40
Cato, the Elder 111
Cato, the Younger 111
Catullus 63, 70, 72, 193 n.5
Chaerophon 167
Cheney, Lynne 9
Christianity 21, 25, 39–40, 42–7, 49, 51, 58, 60–1, 64, 77, 80–1, 84, 89, 93, 112, 150, 163, 172, 183–4, 188, 193 n.21
Cicero xiv, 85, 164
*cinaedus* 55, 190 n.18
Clement of Alexandria 40
confession 7, 18–21, 23–5, 29, 39–45, 47, 49, 51–2, 58, 64, 80, 84–5, 107, 130, 133, 136–7, 159–60, 193 n.21
*connaissance* 5

Creon 31, 33, 37
Creusa 131–4, 136–7
Crito 171–3, 195 n.6
Croesus 167
Cynics xiv, 4, 7, 25, 55, 88, 95, 108, 151, 157, 158, 166, 176–6, 188
Cyrus 167

dandy 112–13, 118–19, 127, 130, 151, 175, 188
Davidson, Arnold 110
Davila, Jorge 94
de Man, Paul 10–11
deconstruction 10–12
Defert, Daniel 11
Deleuze, Gilles 2, 85, 105
Delian League 131–2
Delphic oracle 24, 48, 91, 93, 132–3, 148, 160–1, 166
Demetrius (the Cynic) 108
democracy 106, 126, 134–9, 164–5, 175, 195 n.4, 195 n.3
Derrida, Jacques 11, 58, 61–2, 66–8, 91, 190 n.11
des Places 195 n.4
Descartes, Edouard René 48, 58, 61, 65–6, 91, 94
Detienne, Marcel 5
Dio Cassius xiv, 8
Diogenes (the Cynic) 4, 148, 151, 178–9, 181, 183
Diogenes Laertius 32
Dion 139–41, 146, 153
Dionysius, the Elder 138
Dionysius, the Younger 137–40, 144, 146, 148–9, 151–3, 166, 179, 195 n.5
*discretio* 45
Dover, Kenneth 14, 193 n.5
duBois, Page x, 190 n.17
Dumézil, Georges 171, 191 n.4

*egkrateia* 78–9
Elden, Stewart 19–20, 194 n.1
elegists 70, 194 n.8
*elenchus* 98, 102, 145, 168–9, 171–2, 176, 186, 195 n.4
elephant 58–60, 67
Epictetus 45, 57, 87, 108, 111, 115, 194 n.4
Epicureans 77, 88, 90, 112, 120, 180, 188

*epimeleia* 74, 86–7, 92, 97, 102, 168, 173–4
  see also "care of the self"
*epistēmē* 141–2
epistemology 2, 25, 42, 54, 65, 127, 145, 159, 161
*erōs* 88, 92, 105, 186
Eros 70, 169
ethics 2, 8, 45, 75, 80, 84–5, 89, 92, 94, 104–5, 107, 112–14, 119, 121, 127, 139–49, 163–5, 170, 175, 184, 194 n.10
*ēthos* 89, 126–7, 129–30, 163–5, 175
ethos 88, 120–2
Euripides, *Ion* 126, 130–45, 164, 170
*exomologesis* 39, 43, 45, 47

feminism 9–10, 12–13, 157, 190 n.19
Festugière, A. J. 194 n.2
flattery 96, 100, 136, 151, 164, 171, 176, 186
flesh 8, 42, 51, 59–60, 72, 80–1, 86
Foucault, Michel
  *Aveux de la chair* (*History of Sexuality*, vol 4) 8, 40, 42, 51, 158
  *Le courage de la vérité* 155–88
  *Du gouvernement des vivants* 8, 17–49, 84, 158
  *Le gouvernement de soi et des autres* (*Government of the Self and Others*) 123–53
  *L'herméneutique du sujet* (*Hermeneutics of the Subject*) 66, 77, 83–122, 123, 185, 191 n.8
  *Histoire de la folie* (*History of Madness*) 8, 54, 58, 66
  *Leçons sur la volonté de savoir* 4–8, 24, 29, 47
  *Mal faire, dire vrai* (*Wrongdoing, Truth-Telling*) 8, 36, 89
  *Les mots et les choses* (*The Order of Things*) 54, 67, 164
  *Le souci de soi* (*History of Sexuality*, vol. 3) 8–14, 16, 42, 51–2, 57, 61, 84, 104, 110, 113–14, 158, 186, 190 n.17
  *Subjectivité et vérité* 51–81
  *Surveiller et Punir* (*Discipline and Punish*) 159
  *L'usage de Plaisir* (*History of Sexuality*, vol. 2) 8–14, 16, 42, 51–2, 69, 114, 158, 186, 190 n.17

*La volonté de savoir* (*History of Sexuality*, vol 1) 5, 8–9, 12, 14–15, 18–20, 79, 159, 186–7
Foxhall, Lynn 12
Francis of Sales, Saint 58
Franciscans 183
Frankfurt School 10, 127, 191 n.2
freedom 1, 41–2, 45, 48, 53, 63, 79, 81, 85, 87, 90, 91, 96, 104, 108–11, 116, 118, 120–1, 123, 127, 129, 135, 148–9, 157, 179–80, 194 n.2
Freud, Sigmund 7, 24, 27–8, 58, 61–4, 66, 187, 192 n.19, 193 n.1, 193 n.4

Gadamer, Hans Georg 10
Galen xiv, 124
gay 11, 13, 156–7, 186
gender 14, 42, 60, 64, 69, 121, 157, 186
  studies 9
Gildersleeve, Basil 11–13
Goldman, Emma 146
Goulet-Cazé, Marie-Odile 178, 183, 185
government 17–20, 22–4, 26, 46, 54, 56, 87–8, 95, 98, 101, 103, 105–6, 119–21, 123, 125, 144, 147–8, 153, 160, 163, 188
governmentality 17–20, 41, 49, 51, 53, 56, 58, 70, 76, 86, 119–20, 125–7, 163, 165
Green, Leonard 161
Gros, Frédéric 56, 66, 72, 79, 156, 181, 184, 194 n.1, 195 n.3
Guattari, Félix 85
Guevara, Che 191 n.2

Hadot, Pierre 83, 86, 89, 92, 110, 113–18
Halperin, David x, 13, 190 n.17
Hegel, G.W.F. 55–6, 127–8, 150, 193 n.3
Heidegger, Martin 5, 25, 30, 91, 117, 175, 189 n.9
Herodotus 31, 59, 167
Hesiod 32–3, 48, 183
heteronormativity 11, 14
heterosexuality 13–15, 60
Hierocles 72
Hirsch, E. D. 9–10
Holmes, Brooke 194 n.5
Homer 5, 24, 32–5, 48, 183
  *Iliad* 30, 48

homosexuality 11, 13–15, 60, 157, 190 n.18
Horace 72, 107, 109, 150, 174–5, 185–6
Husserl, Edmund 94

Ion 130, 132–8
Iran 1
irony 28, 32–4, 36, 96, 132, 138, 149–50, 166, 176, 192 n.11
*isēgoria* 123, 135–6, 165
isomorphism 63, 69–70, 72–4, 77, 106, 193 n.5
*isonomia* 123, 135, 165, 195 n.4

Jaffro, Laurent 194 n.4
Jameson, Fredric 10, 191 n.3
Jocasta 29, 31–3, 35–7, 39, 48, 192 n.19
Juvenal 63

*kalliston, to* 178, 186
*kalon, to* 114, 118, 175, 180
*kalos* 113
Kant, Immanuel 6, 42, 53–5, 65, 126–30, 141, 150–1, 157, 175–6, 187, 194 n.2
Kelly, Mark G.E. 158
knowledge 2, 5–7, 17–18, 20–5, 27–30, 32–3, 35, 38–40, 42, 44–8, 52–7, 60, 65–6, 78, 86–90, 92–4, 98, 107, 114, 123–4, 126–7, 133, 135, 138, 141–7, 151–2, 160–3, 165, 167–9, 172–4, 186, 192 n.13, 192 n.17
  *see also* self-knowledge

Lacan, Jacques 193 n.1, 193 n.4
Laurand, Valéry 194 n.4
Lawlor, Leonard 1, 42, 85, 137, 149
Lear, King 181–2
*libertas* 96, 107, 185
Locke, John 10
*logos* 1, 31, 45, 67–8, 100, 116, 129–30, 141, 143, 152, 175–6, 193 n.3
Lubbock, Texas 190 n.17
Lucilius (friend of Seneca) 46, 104, 107–8, 111, 120, 160, 186
Luck, Georg 11–13, 190 n.14
Luxembourg, Rosa 22, 191 n.2

McGushin, Edward 88
Malthus 80

marriage 26, 29, 33, 47, 52, 54–8, 60, 69–78, 106, 132, 194 n.4
Marx, Karl 55, 164
Marxism 10, 22, 76, 191 nn.2–3
*mathēsis* 77
*meletē* 77
metaphysics 2, 5–6, 30, 41, 65, 105, 112, 174–5, 189 n.7
Miller, James 156–7, 186
monogamy 55–6, 58–9
Mucius Scaevola 111
Musonius Rufus 52, 55, 57, 72, 194 n.4

neo-Kantianism 127
neo-Platonism 112
Nero 146
New Criticism 10
Niehues-Pröbsting, Heinrich 177
Nietzsche, Friedrich 1, 5–7, 10, 22, 47, 57, 65, 76, 81, 91, 104–5, 110, 127–8, 165, 172–3, 175–6, 183, 189 nn.8–9, 195 n.5
Nussbaum, Martha 110, 113, 160

Oedipus 7, 23–4, 27–9, 31–9, 43–5, 47–8, 52, 65, 95, 133–4, 192 n.13, 192 n.15, 192 n.19
   *see also* Sophocles
ontology xiii–iv, 1, 53, 75–6, 85, 105, 115, 122, 125–8, 145

paganism 39, 58, 81
*parrhēsia* xiv, 15, 45, 80, 83, 85–6, 94–6, 100, 107, 120, 124–6, 130–1, 133–8, 146–51, 155, 158, 160, 162–5, 170, 175–6, 178–81, 185
pederasty 10, 55, 64, 70, 72–5, 92, 101–2, 106, 120
Pericles 87, 134, 195 n.3
Persius 178
Philip of Macedon 179
philosopher, the 55, 57, 66, 71–2, 75, 78–9, 86, 89–90, 95–6, 100, 103, 105–6, 108–9, 116, 119, 126, 137–8, 140–1, 144–8, 150–3, 164–6, 168, 177–84, 186, 188
philosophy 12, 4–6, 8–9, 12, 15–16, 22, 30–31, 41–2, 45–6, 48, 52–8, 61, 64–5, 67, 71, 74, 76–8, 80, 85–91, 93–6, 98, 100–1, 104–5, 107, 109–14, 116–18, 120, 123–4, 126–7, 131, 137–47, 150–3, 157–8, 162–6, 171–3, 177–88, 192 n.11, 194 n.2, 194 n.4
*phronēsis* 169
*phusis* 72, 74, 116, 118, 180
Physiologus 58
Pinguet, Maurice 155
Plato x, xiv, 4–6, 9–10, 30, 35, 46, 48, 52–3, 55, 59, 61–2, 65, 69–72, 75, 78–9, 85–7, 90, 94, 98, 101, 105, 114, 119, 124, 126, 128, 131, 135, 137–49, 151–3, 162, 165–6, 171–3, 175, 179, 182, 189 n.4, 189 n.7, 192 n.13, 194 n.10, 195 n.5, 195 nn.5–6
   *Alcibiades* 85–7, 92–3, 97–105, 107, 116–19, 124, 158, 160, 162, 166, 169, 174
   *Apology* 3, 79, 86, 99, 113, 123, 140, 145, 150, 155, 158, 166, 173, 175, 185, 192 n.13
   *Crito* 166, 173
   *Euthydemus* 149
   *Euthyphro* 2–3
   *Gorgias* 136, 164
   *Ion* 145
   *Laches* 158, 165–6, 169–71, 173–4
   Myth of the Cave 5, 30, 35, 48, 52, 65, 90, 119, 128, 143; *see also* Republic
   *Phaedo* 166, 171–3
   *Phaedrus* 55, 73, 92, 106, 140, 149, 162
   *Philebus* 98, 100
   *Republic* 25, 30, 61–2, 65, 87, 98, 103, 140, 153, 164; *see also* Myth of the Cave
   *Seventh Letter* 46, 78, 90, 126, 131, 137–47, 153, 162, 166, 170–1, 189 n.4, 195 n.5
   *Sophist* 168
   *Symposium* 35, 70, 73, 92, 106, 145
   *Theaetetus* 98, 168
Platonism 2, 25, 177, 188, 189 n.7
pleasure 1, 14, 52, 60–1, 63–4, 69 71–5, 78–9, 113–15, 118, 121, 127, 157, 175, 182, 185–8
Pliny, the Elder 58
Pliny, the Younger 77
Plutarch 4, 52, 55, 57, 69–71, 73–5, 77, 88, 106, 120, 175, 186

polis 7, 18, 69–70, 79, 103, 120, 134, 151
*politeia* 163–5
politics xiii, 2, 5, 12–13, 18, 22–3, 27, 33, 42, 46, 56–7, 59–60, 62–3, 70–1, 75, 77–80, 85, 91, 94, 98, 105–6, 110, 119–22, 125–8, 131, 135–40, 145–8, 150–1, 159, 162–5, 170, 175, 178–9, 184, 188, 190 n.18
Polybius 135
poststructuralism 9–10, 12, 156
power xiii–xiv, 1, 4, 6–9, 16–18, 20–9, 31–5, 38–41, 45, 47, 56, 59–60, 63, 66, 68, 70, 73–4, 76, 80, 85, 87, 90, 95, 100, 103–6, 110, 114, 117, 119–22, 125, 127, 131, 134–5, 137–9, 145–8, 151, 153, 158–65, 178–9, 181–2, 184, 186–7, 193 n.20
Pradeau, Jean-François 116, 119, 194 n.6
prisons 1, 4, 49, 95, 148, 159, 186, 188
*psukhē* 93, 99, 100, 103–4, 118, 169, 174
psychoanalysis 10, 27, 52, 63–4, 124, 192 n.11, 192 n.19, 193 n.1, 193 n.4
Pythagoras 79, 194 n.10
Pythagoreanism 32, 92, 107, 168, 171

queer theory 9, 13, 15, 157

Reagan, Ronald 9, 11
repression 51–3, 64, 81
repressive hypothesis 61, 81
resistance xv, 1, 20, 26, 38, 41, 60, 110, 144, 169, 177–9
revolution 1, 42, 54, 86, 121, 125, 127, 163, 184, 188
rhetoric 31, 62, 95–6, 124, 150–2, 162, 164–5, 176–7, 186, 194 n.4
Richlin, Amy x, 12–13, 190 nn.17–18
Rilke, Rainer Maria 184
Rome 12, 17, 55, 61–2, 70–1, 75, 83–5, 87, 89–90, 94, 96, 103, 106, 111, 118–19, 123, 164, 174, 179, 181
    Roman Empire 12, 17, 55, 70, 78, 85, 89, 103, 106, 118, 123, 181
    Roman Republic 71, 75, 164

Sappho 12
Sartre, Jean-Paul 53
science 1–2, 5, 7, 22–5, 40, 54, 57, 77, 90–1, 93, 117, 128, 136, 152, 160–1, 163, 165, 191 n.6, 193 n.1
self-knowledge 24–6, 28, 45, 48–9, 52–3, 84–8, 91–5, 120, 140–1, 187
Seneca 45, 84, 93, 96, 103–12, 114–16, 118, 146, 157, 160, 175, 180, 182
Septimius Severus 8, 17, 20, 23, 25, 38, 51, 95
sex 12, 14, 19, 74, 186–7
sexual acts/practices 13–15, 42, 55, 58, 60, 62, 72, 75, 83, 85, 121, 157, 162, 193 n.5
sexual identity 60
sexuality 1–2, 4, 7, 9, 12–15, 19, 26, 42, 49, 51, 53, 59–61, 63, 65, 80–1, 95, 157, 159, 186–7, 193 n.4
Socrates xiii–xv, 2–4, 6–9, 25, 31, 45–6, 48, 65, 68, 73, 79, 85–8, 91–2, 97–102, 104–6, 109, 113, 120, 123, 135–6, 138, 139, 144–6, 148–52, 155–8, 160, 164–77, 181, 183, 185–6, 189 n.2, 195 n.5
Solzhenitsyn, Alexander 146
sophism 6
sophists 6, 31, 163
Sophocles xiv, 7, 26–39, 62, 70, 192 n.15
    *Oedipus Tyrannos* 26–40, 44–5, 47–8, 51–2, 55, 62, 65, 67, 77, 133–4, 165, 192 n.13, 192 n.15
speech act theory 125
spiritual practices xiv, 15, 25, 46, 49, 66, 77, 80, 83, 89, 91–4, 96, 100, 104, 106, 108, 113, 115, 118, 120, 138, 166, 168, 185
spirituality 26, 85, 88–91, 112–13, 119
Statius //
Stocking, Charles 191 n.4
Stoicism 44–6, 55, 71, 77, 85, 90–1, 96, 101, 104–5, 108–13, 115–16, 118–19, 127, 176, 178, 194 nn.4–5
Stoics xiv, 4, 9, 25, 46, 72, 75, 77, 85, 88, 93, 95, 104–5, 110–13, 116–18, 124, 140, 166, 188
structuralism 10, 164
subject, the xiv, 4–6, 9, 14–15, 18, 20–1, 24–6, 29–30, 32–4, 37, 39–48, 52–4, 57, 60–1, 64, 66–8, 75, 77–8, 80, 83–5, 87–8, 91–6, 99, 106–9, 111, 115, 118–19, 123–8, 130–1, 134, 139, 141, 145, 148, 151, 153, 159–60, 163

subjectivation 26, 38, 47, 49, 105, 119
subjectivity 8, 17, 20–1, 25, 40–1, 52–3, 60–2, 68, 72, 76–8, 81, 83, 88, 90–1, 101, 103, 106–7, 125, 157–8, 187

technologies of the self xiv, 15, 44, 51–2, 58, 63, 72, 105, 107, 110, 113, 121–2, 124–5, 160, 194 n.9
*tekhnē* 32, 35, 58, 76–8, 80, 85–6, 93, 95, 113, 119, 121, 173
Tertullian 40, 44–5
Thersites 48, 183
Thucydides 195 n.3
*tribē* 144, 146–7, 151, 170–1
truth xiii–iv, 1–9, 14–49, 51–8, 60–8, 74, 76–80, 83–6, 88–97, 101, 106–7, 114, 117–18, 120, 122–7, 129–31, 133–8, 143–53, 157–65, 168–71, 175–88, 189 n.2, 191 n.1, 191 n.6, 192 n.11, 192 n.15
  regimes of 22–3, 25, 27–31, 34–5, 42, 54, 91
  scientific 24, 90–1, 161–3, 165, 191 n.6
  of the self xiv, 14–15, 19–21, 24, 40, 42–4, 46–8, 54, 60, 64–6, 71, 85, 90, 93, 130
  *see also alētheia*

unconscious 27, 48

veridiction 5, 18, 20, 24, 31, 34, 36, 38–40, 42, 48, 56–7, 93, 95, 125–6, 151, 164, 181, 187
verification 2, 5, 20, 23, 31, 35, 37–8, 54, 56–7, 152, 165, 191 n.6
Veyne, Paul 104, 112, 118

Winkler, Jack 13
women 12–14, 52, 60, 64, 68–9, 71, 73–4, 157, 161, 186
Women's Classical Caucus 12–13

Xenophon 55, 60, 68–75, 105–6, 164
Xuthus 132–4, 136

Zeitlin Froma 13
Zen 93
*zōē/zēn* 58, 79–80, 92, 169–70

www.ingramcontent.com/pod-product-compliance
Lightning Source LLC
Chambersburg PA
CBHW062219300426
44115CB00012BA/2128